STOP AND FRISK

Stop and Frisk

The Use and Abuse of a
Controversial Policing Tactic

Michael D. White and Henry F. Fradella

NEW YORK UNIVERSITY PRESS

New York

NEW YORK UNIVERSITY PRESS
New York
www.nyupress.org

References to Internet websites (URLs) were accurate at the time of writing. Neither the author nor New York University Press is responsible for URLs that may have expired or changed since the manuscript was prepared.

Library of Congress Cataloging-in-Publication Data
Names: White, Michael D. (Michael Douglas), 1951– author. | Fradella, Henry F., author.
Title: Stop and frisk : the use and abuse of a controversial policing tactic / Michael D. White and Henry F. Fradella.
Description: New York : New York University Press, [2016] | Includes bibliographical references and index. | Also available as an e-book.
Identifiers: LCCN 2016015952| ISBN 9781479835881 (hbk ; alk. paper) | Subjects: LCSH: Stop and frisk—United States. | Stop and frisk—United States—History. | Stop and frisk—Law and legislation—United States. | Stop and frisk—New York (State)—New York. | Police discretion—United States. | Racial profiling in law enforcement—United States.
Classification: LCC HV8080.P2 W45 2016 | DDC 363.2/3—dc 3
LC record available at https://lccn.loc.gov/2016015952

New York University Press books are printed on acid-free paper, and their binding materials are chosen for strength and durability. We strive to use environmentally responsible suppliers and materials to the greatest extent possible in publishing our books.

Manufactured in the United States of America

10 9 8 7 6 5 4 3 2 1

Also available as an ebook

CONTENTS

ACKNOWLEDGMENTS

We would like to extend our thanks to Dr. Weston Morrow for his collaboration with us on the chapter on the impact and consequences of stop and frisk in New York and elsewhere. Weston's dissertation has significantly improved our understanding of the dynamics of SQF in New York City, particularly with regard to use of force, and we are proud to have him as a co-author of chapter 4. We are also grateful for the editorial contributions of Natalie Todak and Megan Parry. And we sincerely appreciate the guidance and support of Ilene Kalish and the staff at New York University Press.
—MDW and HFF

I would like to offer my sincere gratitude to Hank Fradella, co-author of *Stop and Frisk*. Hank is a wonderful colleague and friend, and his insights, contributions, and legal knowledge have improved the book immensely. *Stop and Frisk* is my fourth book. When I wrote the first book, my kids (Devon, Gabi, and Logan) were eight, five, and three. Now they are eighteen, fifteen, and thirteen. The last decade seems to have gone by in the blink of an eye. So much has happened, and I would not trade away a single memory. And to my wife, Alyssa: you and I are like an expensive bottle of fine wine that continues to improve with age (even though our preference leans toward the $8 bottle). This book, like everything I do, is dedicated to my family.
—MDW

First and foremost, I want to thank my colleague and friend Mike White, for inviting me to be a part of this book. Many researchers in our field pigeonhole each other as falling into a particular "camp"—theoretical criminology or applied criminal justice, with the latter including areas such as policing, corrections, and particular subfields, such as homicide studies, sex crimes, terrorism, and so on. Some of our colleagues view legal scholarship as being completely foreign to criminology. Worse yet, they embrace a disciplinary distinction in ways that are dismissive to both traditional legal scholarship and social-scientific legal studies. Mike White is a rare breed of scholar who does not look at such superficial differences. Rather, he seeks out commonalities and actively builds bridges in ways I appreciate deeply. Collectively, he and I both believe that our collaboration—one between a policing scholar and a legal scholar—allowed us to produce a book that is stronger than it would have been without the insights and contributions of the other. We hope our efforts improve our collective understanding of a complex and vexing social issue.

Second, this is my ninth book. It was, by far, the easiest collaboration with a co-author in which I have ever had the pleasure of engaging, thanks to Mike and Weston.

Finally, I thank my family—especially my husband, Kyle—for putting up with the long hours I spend at my computer. I dedicate this book to our life together, with my undying appreciation for your support and patience, Kyle.

—HFF

1

Two Tales of Stop and Frisk

[T]here must be a narrowly drawn authority to permit a reasonable search for weapons for the protection of the police officer, where he has reason to believe that he is dealing with an armed and dangerous individual, regardless of whether he has probable cause to arrest the individual for a crime. The officer need not be absolutely certain that the individual is armed; the issue is whether a reasonably prudent man, in the circumstances, would be warranted in the belief that his safety or that of others was in danger.
—Chief Justice Earl Warren, *Terry v. Ohio*, 1968[1]

In conclusion, I find that the City is liable for violating plaintiffs' Fourth and Fourteenth Amendment rights. The City acted with deliberate indifference toward the NYPD's practice of making unconstitutional stops and conducting unconstitutional frisks. Even if the City had not been deliberately indifferent, the NYPD's unconstitutional practices were sufficiently widespread as to have the force of law.
—Judge Shira Scheindlin, *Floyd v. City of New York*, 2013[2]

The two quotes above represent fifty-year bookends to the stop and frisk—or *Terry* stop—story.[3] The first quote is from the U.S. Supreme Court majority opinion in the *Terry v. Ohio* case, written by Chief Justice Earl Warren. The facts of the *Terry* case highlight the core principles of stop, question, and frisk (SQF). In October 1963, a Cleveland detective witnessed two men standing near a jewelry store. The detective observed the suspects as they continued to move up and down the street and look into the windows of the jewelry store. When they were joined by a third man, the detective suspected that they were either about to rob the store or were casing it for a later robbery. The detective approached the suspects, identified himself as a police officer, and because he thought that they might be armed, he conducted a "pat-down" search over the clothes of the suspects. Two of the three men were armed with revolvers and were subsequently arrested and prosecuted for carrying concealed weapons. Both were convicted and appealed their case to the U.S. Supreme Court. In 1968 the Court upheld the convictions and acknowledged the constitutionality of "stop and frisk" searches—as indicated by the quote from Chief Justice Warren. Though the basic principles underlying SQF can actually be traced back to English common law, the Court's ruling in the *Terry* case formalized the authority of the police to stop citizens on the street based on a standard of proof lesser than probable cause, and it also gave them the right to conduct superficial "pat-down" searches of those citizens whom they stop (under certain conditions).

The second quote is from the federal district court ruling in the case of *Floyd v. City of New York* (2013).[4] This ruling was the culmination of more than a decade of litigation against the New York Police Department (NYPD) for its use of SQF. The genesis of the NYPD's reliance on SQF can be traced back to the dramatic increases in crime, violence, and disorder that occurred during the late 1980s, much of it associated with the drug trade.[5] The explosion of violence during the late 1980s and early 1990s is evidenced by the number of homicides in New York, which jumped from 1,392 in 1985 to 2,262 in 1990 and remained above 2,000 through 1992. The level of social and physical disorder that emerged in conjunction with the violence was similarly destructive.[6]

In 1994 William Bratton was hired as the police commissioner of the NYPD. Bratton had just achieved considerable success cleaning up the New York City subway system as the Transit Police chief, and he was hired by Mayor Rudolph Giuliani to bring that success to the streets of New York. Bratton revamped and restructured the NYPD in a number of ways, including a focus on both disorder and low-level crime as well as illegal gun carrying. SQF became the primary tactic employed by all NYPD officers to combat disorder, low-level crime, and illegal gun possession. Indeed, seizure of illegal firearms through SQF became a major performance indicator for officers. Physician Garen Wintemute noted that in just three years, the NYPD made over 40,000 gun arrests and confiscated more than 50,000 guns.[7] Bratton's philosophical, structural, and operational changes to the NYPD coincided with historic drops in crime, perhaps best illustrated by homicides, which fell precipitously through the rest of the decade and into the twenty-first century. From 2003 through 2009, the city averaged 540 homicides annually, down from more than 2,000 in 1992. The causes of the New York City crime decline, and the role of the NYPD (and SQF) in that decline, have been hotly contested.[8]

The Controversy

Over the next two decades, the NYPD's use of stop and frisk continued to increase, peaking at over 685,000 stops in 2011. During this time, however, serious questions had begun to emerge in New York regarding the practice, especially with regard to the disproportionate impact on minority citizens. In 1999 the Office of the New York State Attorney General released a report that examined 175,000 stops and raised serious questions about their constitutionality (15 percent did not meet the reasonable suspicion threshold), as well as racial disparities in those who were subjected to SQF.[9] Criminologist Jeffrey Fagan and colleagues noted that "by the end of the decade, stops and frisks of persons suspected of crimes had become a flashpoint for grievances by the City's minority communities."[10] Allegations of racial discrimination in stops conducted by the NYPD led to two lawsuits. The first, *Daniels v. City of New York*,[11] was filed in 1999 by the Center for Constitutional Rights (CCR) and settled in 2003. As part of the settlement, the NYPD agreed to maintain a written anti–racial profiling policy; to audit officers' stops to ensure their adherence to both department policy and the law; and to provide the results of those audits (as well as data on all stops) to the CCR on a quarterly basis.[12] Despite this settlement, the CCR filed a second suit in 2008, *Floyd v. City of New York*,[13] alleging that the NYPD had violated the earlier settlement and was continuing to "engage in racial profiling and suspicion-less stops of law-abiding New York City residents."[14] The controversy came to a head in August 2013, when Judge Shira Scheindlin of the federal district court in Manhattan ruled that the NYPD's stop and frisk program was unconstitutional; the second quote at the start of this chapter is from the judge's ruling in the *Floyd* case.

The ruling in *Floyd* demonstrated how the use of stop and frisk as a widespread crime-control strategy could go terribly wrong, leading to the violation of the constitutional rights of thousands of mostly minority New York City residents for a period of nearly twenty years. Importantly, Judge Scheindlin's ruling in *Floyd* was one of several cases pending before her at the time that involved NYPD's SQF practices. *Ligon v. City of New York*[15] involved stops outside private residences, and *Davis v. City of New York*[16] involved stops in public housing. All three cases alleged Fourth and Fourteenth Amendment violations.

A number of studies have documented the disproportionate focus of stop and frisk on minority citizens in New York's low-income, high-crime neighborhoods, as well as the severe and varied impact caused by those stops. For example, the Vera Institute of Justice surveyed more than five hundred young, mostly minority New Yorkers (aged thirteen to twenty-five) and found that 44 percent reported being stopped by the NYPD nine or more times; nearly half reported that the officer threatened or used physical force during the stop.[17] The Center for Constitutional Rights interviewed fifty-four individuals who had been stopped by police and concluded,

> These interviews provide evidence of how deeply this practice impacts individuals and they document the widespread civil and human rights abuses, including illegal profiling, improper arrests, inappropriate touch-

ing, sexual harassment, humiliation and violence at the hands of police officers. The effects of these abuses can be devastating and often leave behind emotional, psychological, social and economic harm.[18]

Scholars have also demonstrated the low return on the hundreds of thousands of *Terry* stops. Criminologist Delores Jones-Brown and colleagues found that, of the 540,320 stops in 2008, just 6 percent resulted in an arrest (and an additional 6.4 percent resulted in a summons).[19] Jones-Brown and colleagues also noted that, as the percentage of "innocent stops"—those not resulting in summons or arrest—has consistently remained between 86 and 90 percent, the percentage of stops resulting in the recovery of a gun has dropped by 60 percent (from 0.39 percent in 2003 to 0.15 percent in 2008).[20] These findings are especially troubling given that there are indications that large numbers of stops occurred without formal documentation (e.g., one police commander estimated that only one in ten stops was documented by officers on the department's formal SQF form, the UF-250).[21]

Though the SQF issue is often viewed as solely a New York problem, the strategy has generated similar controversies in other jurisdictions throughout the United States. The Philadelphia Police Department stopped more than 250,000 citizens in 2009, and in November 2010 the American Civil Liberties Union (ACLU) of Pennsylvania filed a lawsuit in federal court alleging that the Philadelphia Police Department was engaged in widespread racial profiling. In June 2011 the U.S. District Court for the Eastern District of Pennsylvania approved a settlement agreement (i.e., consent decree) between the plaintiffs and the Philadelphia Police Department, which included quarterly analysis of stop data by the ACLU, appointment of an independent monitor, retraining of officers, and new protocols governing SQF practices.[22] A report by the ACLU of New Jersey examined SQF activities of the Newark Police Department during the last half of 2013 and concluded, "Newark police officers use stop-and-frisk with troubling frequency; Black Newarkers bear the disproportionate brunt of stop-and-frisks; [and] the majority of people stopped [75 percent] are innocent."[23] An investigation into SQF activity by the Miami Gardens Police Department found that, from 2008 to 2013, officers had stopped 65,328 individuals, and nearly 1,000 citizens had been stopped ten or more times. Moreover, only 13 percent of those stopped were arrested.[24] Similar controversies have arisen in Baltimore, Chicago, and Detroit.[25] Clearly, police overuse and misuse of stop and frisk is not just a New York problem. It can occur anywhere.

The Disconnect between Principle and Practice

The discussion over the last several pages highlights the disconnect between stop and frisk in principle and in practice. On the one hand, *Terry* stops are constitutionally permissible and are grounded in a historical and legal tradition dating back hundreds of years. The basis of a police officer's authority to stop and question a suspicious person can be traced back to English common law, and has been affirmed by a host of court cases and federal law both before and after the ruling in *Terry v. Ohio* in 1968. For example, under English common law, watchmen and private citizens had the authority to "arrest any suspicious night-walker, and detain him till he give a good account of himself."[26] In 1939 in the United States, the Interstate Commission on Crime drafted the Uniform Arrest Act, which outlined nine different types of police-citizen contact, including "questioning and detaining suspects" and "searching suspects for weapons."[27] The SQF practice was, of course, formally established in the 1968 ruling in *Terry v. Ohio*, but since then, the Court has both consistently reaffirmed the constitutionality of SQF and expanded officers' authority during such stops.[28] For example, in *Alabama v. White* (1990), the Court extended police officers' authority to conduct vehicle stops based on anonymous tips alleging criminal activity.[29] In *Whren v. United States* (1996), the Court held that pretextual stops were constitutional, allowing officers to stop citizens for minor violations in order to investigate for other, more serious criminal activity.[30] Last, police leaders have consistently asserted that SQF is a critically important tool for police to effectively combat crime. In 2014 (after the federal court ruling in the *Floyd* case), Police Commissioner William Bratton said of SQF, "you cannot police without it."[31]

On the other hand, the events in New York, Philadelphia, Miami Gardens, and other jurisdictions tell a very different story. It is a tale of gross overuse and misuse of the strategy, violations of citizens' Fourth and Fourteenth Amendment rights, strained police-community relationships, low or no police legitimacy, and significant emotional, psychological, and physical consequences experienced by citizens. This is also a story of abused police discretion. The decision by a police officer to initiate a *Terry* stop is an exercise in discretion. There is a long history of police problems with discretion, ranging from use of deadly force and automobile pursuits to arrest decisions in domestic violence calls. The stories from New York and elsewhere illustrate that unjust, unconstitutional stop and frisk represents another in a long line of failures by police departments to properly guide and control their officers' use of discretion.

As a consequence, the term "stop and frisk" has in many places become synonymous with racial profiling. The line between a sound, constitutionally approved police practice and racial profiling has become so blurred that some city and police leaders have faced media scrutiny and backlash from citizens when they consider adopting a stop and frisk program.[32] Recent events in Detroit illustrate the now intimate connection between racial profiling and the practice. In late 2013 the Detroit Police Department partnered with the Manhattan Institute to develop an SQF program in Detroit. The announcement of the program drew significant criticism from local civil rights advocates and local media. Referring to the *Floyd* ruling in New York, an op-ed by the editor of a local newspaper concluded, "Because of this recent ruling and long-documented history of racial tension within the city, bringing the program to Detroit would likely create a complicated judicial process before results could even be seen on the streets, ultimately doing more harm than good."[33]

The central focus of this book is the disconnect between current perceptions of SQF as a form of racial discrimination by police and the strategy's historical, legal, and discretionary foundations. The majority of our focus is on what has transpired during the five decades between *Terry v. Ohio* and *Floyd v. City of New York*, though considerable attention is given to the history of the strategy (chapters 2 and 3) and its future (chapters 5 and 6). We will take the reader on a long journey in an effort to reduce the confusion surrounding stop and frisk; this is accomplished by viewing the practice through a wider lens grounded in the historical, legal, and discretionary traditions of the practice. The primary thesis of the book rests on the premise that SQF has a proper place in twenty-first-century policing, with several critically important stipulations. First, SQF must be used justly, meaning that all stops meet constitutional standards regarding reasonable suspicion. Second, there is a large body of research examining police discretion, abuses of discretion, and how best to properly control that discretion. This body of research serves as an anchor for the examination of stop and frisk, and provides a road map for ensuring fair, constitutional, and appropriate use of the practice. This framework is centered on effective hiring practices, proper training, clear administrative guidance, and sufficient supervisory oversight.[34] Police departments must follow this road map.

Third, stop and frisk should be employed with sensitivity to citizens' concerns, and assessment of the strategy should occur through a procedural justice lens. Procedural justice is defined as fair treatment of individuals by police in a manner characterized by citizen participation (being given the opportunity to state one's case), fairness and neutrality, dignity and respect, and demonstration of trustworthy motives.[35] During a stop and frisk, was a citizen treated with dignity and respect? Was the citizen given a voice? Was the officer transparent and neutral? Did the officer convey trustworthy motives? Procedurally just treatment of citizens is perhaps the most viable mechanism for generating police legitimacy,[36] and the framework represents a barometer by which to measure the impact and consequences of SQF practices. If these stipulations are met, stop and frisk can serve as a valuable tool in a police department's repertoire of crime-control strategies, and it can be integrated with the prevailing strategies employed in twenty-first-century policing: problem-oriented policing, community-oriented policing, hot spots policing, and pulling levers/focused deterrence. If police fall short of these stipulations, the consequences can be severe and long-standing. In New York, the result was a two-decade-long failure in race relations that compromised the NYPD's ability to engage with minority residents and, more than likely, impaired its ability to effectively respond to crime.

The Historical Undercurrent of Racial Injustice in Policing

The historical, legal, and discretionary foundations of SQF provide an anchor for this book, but there are also persistent social forces that shape our discussion—specifically, the undercurrent of racial injustice and discrimination that has served as a backdrop to professional policing in the United States for the last 175 years. The larger race relations problems that have defined American policing must be considered by readers of this book, especially as we move toward consideration of the future of SQF and how it can be coupled with evidence-based practices in twenty-first-century policing. As an illustration, the authors use a historical framework developed by police scholars Kelling and Moore[37] to contextualize police history into three eras (political, reform, community problem-solving), and to make the case that American policing has entered a new era, which we call twenty-first-century policing. Though the Kelling and Moore framework is widely cited by many, it has been criticized for overlooking the role of racism in professional policing. Public policy experts Williams and Murphy, for example, argue that the origins of American policing are rooted in slave patrols in the South, and that the advances that have occurred through the "reform" and "community problem-solving" eras excluded minority citizens.[38]

More recently, racial injustice has emerged in disparities in police use of force, including deadly force,[39] use of K-9s,[40] and of course, SQF.

Though each of these areas has the potential to generate harm, the deleterious effects of SQF are perhaps much greater given the frequency with which it is used (daily; see chapter 4) compared to the use of force and other critical incidents.[41] The recent, highly publicized deaths of Eric Garner, Michael Brown, and Freddie Gray illustrate the tragic circumstances that can unfold during a stop. On July 17, 2014, NYPD officers approached Eric Garner on a street corner in Staten Island because they suspected that he was selling unlicensed cigarettes. The incident was captured on a bystander's cell phone. After brief questioning, officers attempted to take Garner, a 400-pound man, into custody. During the struggle, Officer Daniel Pantaleo applied a chokehold. Garner can be heard stating nearly a dozen times that he cannot breathe. Garner lost consciousness after the struggle and was pronounced dead an hour later. Five months later, a grand jury returned a decision to not indict Officer Pantaleo.

On August 9, 2014, Ferguson Police Officer Darren Wilson observed Michael Brown and Dorian Johnson walking in the middle of the street. There is no video of the incident and the facts are disputed, but what is clear is that the initial stop of Brown and Johnson led to a struggle between Wilson, who was still seated in his patrol car, and Brown, who was next to the car. Physical evidence supports Officer Wilson's assertion that there was a struggle over Wilson's gun and that one shot was fired while he was still in his car. Wilson got out of the patrol car and fired several more shots, which killed Michael Brown. Officer Wilson claimed that Brown had turned and was charging at him. Other testimony indicated that Brown had his hands up and was posing no threat to Wilson. Protests and civil disorder began shortly after Brown's death and continued for several days. On August 16, Missouri governor Jay Nixon declared a state of emergency in Ferguson. On November 24, a grand jury declined to indict Officer Wilson for Michael Brown's death.

On April 12, 2015, Baltimore police officers attempted to stop and question Freddie Gray. Gray fled from the officers but was quickly taken into custody and arrested for possessing an illegal switchblade. During his transport in a police van, Gray slipped into a coma; he died several days later, on April 19. Autopsy findings indicate that Gray died from injuries to his spinal cord. Though there are questions about whether force was used during the arrest, Baltimore Police Commissioner Anthony Batts acknowledged that Freddie Gray was not properly secured during the van transport. Protests and civil disorder erupted after Gray's death. On May 1, six officers were charged with Freddie Gray's death by the State Attorney's Office, and on May 21, a grand jury indicted the six officers.

The deaths of Eric Garner, Michael Brown, and Freddie Gray highlight the racial injustice backdrop for this book. As we consider the new era of twenty-first-century policing, and the role that SQF can play as we go forward, the undercurrent of racial injustice in policing is still unmistakable, and Williams and Murphy's claim that police reform has ignored minority communities remains true. The minority view of twenty-first-century policing is not defined by advances in policing, such as evidence-based strategies and data-driven decision making, but rather by persistent evidence of racial discrimination. The evidence supports this minority view. As we stated previously, SQF programs in several cities have been challenged and (in some cases) established as racially discriminatory. The Civil Rights Division of the U.S. Department of Justice has investigated racially discriminatory police practices in nearly thirty law enforcement agencies over the last two decades, resulting in numerous court-imposed consent decrees.[42] And since the summer of 2014, there has been a continuing cascade of racially charged police killings of citizens that have grabbed national headlines, produced widespread public protest and civil disorder, and led to a White House–driven initiative for police reform. The minority view of twenty-first-century policing is defined by the names of those who have died at the hands of police: Eric Garner, Michael Brown, Freddie Gray, and others whose deaths raise similar questions of racial injustice.

In sum, this book tells a story that is grounded in historical, legal, and discretionary foundations. But we also recognize the larger backdrop of racial injustice that must shape any discussion of police history and police future. Recognition of the backdrop of racial injustice is perhaps more acute now than any time in recent memory, as Michael Brown, Eric Garner, and Freddie Gray have become household names. We urge readers of this book to bear in mind this important historical backdrop as it provides critically important context for our thoughts on stop and frisk.

An Overview of *Stop and Frisk*

A brief overview of the organization of this book is warranted. Chapters 2 and 3 review the historical and legal traditions. Chapter 2 begins with an examination of the Fourth Amendment and the core legal principles involved, including search, seizure (of persons and property), expectations of privacy, the Reasonableness and Warrants Clauses, and the burdens of persuasion (from reasonable suspicion and probable cause to beyond a reasonable doubt). The chapter also traces the historical foundations of SQF, from its English common-law traditions to the Uniform Arrest Act in the United States in 1939. The historical and legal review in chapter 2 sets the stage for an investigation of the contemporary legal context of SQF in chapter 3. The authors describe in detail the facts, holding, and rationale of the foundational court cases for SQF in the 1960s, including *Terry v. Ohio, Sibron v. New York* (1968),[43] and *Peters v. New York* (1968).[44] Chapter 3 also covers the notable cases post-1968 that have served to increase the authority granted to police to stop, question, and frisk citizens. The expansion of reasonable suspicion and frisk authority—from nonparticularized suspicion in *Michigan Department of State Police v. Sitz* (1990)[45] to pretextual suspicion in *Whren v. United States* (1996)—opened the door to potential abuses of police authority during *Terry* stops by conflating a low burden of proof with a highly discretionary police activity.

Chapter 4 devotes considerable attention to the emergence of the practice in New York City in the 1990s, and tells "the New York story" through 2014—from the debate over its role in the New York City crime decline to the litigation alleging racial profiling. This book offers a full discussion of the evidence examining the role of the NYPD (and SQF) as a contributing factor in the New York City crime decline—from the work of criminologists like Zimring, Kelling, and Smith and Purtell, on the one hand, to Rosenfeld, Baumer, Xie, and Harcourt, on the other. The authors draw heavily from a special issue of *Justice Quarterly* in 2014, which was devoted to the New York City crime decline.[46] The authors also review available evidence on the diminishing returns from SQF activities over time, as well qualitative information describing the "human impact" of SQF in New York, captured in stories of emotional, psychological, physical, and economic harm suffered by mostly poor, minority New Yorkers. Importantly, chapter 4 also examines use of the strategy elsewhere, highlighting cases where the experience has been very similar to New York, such as Philadelphia, Chicago, Detroit, Newark, and Miami Gardens. Unfortunately, the available research on SQF practices in other cities, including prevalence, impact, and consequences, is much more scant, and the authors are forced to draw on media sources, litigation (court cases and expert reports), and publicly available reports from advocacy groups. The primary takeaway from chapter 4 is that the available evidence on the role of SQF in the crime decline in New York and elsewhere is mixed at best, while the evidence on the negative and collateral consequences of unjust, abusive SQF practices is clear and persuasive.

The final two chapters transition from the past to the future of the strategy. In chapters 5 and 6, we build on the practice's strong legal and historical traditions to make a case for continued use of *Terry* stops, albeit under very specific conditions. In chapter 5 we assert that, at its core, stop and frisk is an exercise in discretion. Over the last four decades researchers have devoted significant scholarly attention to identifying the principles of effective control of police discretionary decision making in the field. This research offers numerous lessons on strategies that police departments can employ to reduce discretion control problems, most notably, proven internal mechanisms such as careful recruit selection, proper training and supervision, strong commitment from the top of the organization, and administrative policy that is clear and enforced. The authors also highlight the critical role of external oversight. In sum, the discretionary framework allows us to draw on what we already know about controlling police officer behavior, and it provides direction to police departments in their efforts to eliminate racial bias and other problem behavior during *Terry* stops.

In chapter 6 the authors draw on criminologists Kelling and Moore's historical review of policing[47] to demonstrate that the profession has entered a new era, which we call *twenty-first-century policing*. Using Kelling and Moore's seven criteria, the authors delineate the key features of twenty-first-century policing. The twenty-first-century police department is proactive and data-driven, collaborative with a wide range of stakeholders, and engages in strategic planning, research, and evaluation. Considerable attention is devoted to police legitimacy as a critically important outcome for the twenty-first-century police department, and procedural justice is highlighted as the primary pathway for police to achieve legitimacy. The events of the summer of 2014 and the spring of 2015 provide direct evidence of the continuing undercurrent of racial injustice in policing,[48] despite the significant advances made in twenty-first-century policing. The chapter addresses this racial dichotomy and then turns to charting a course for stop and frisk in twenty-first-century policing, with sensitivity to racial injustice as a guiding theme. More specifically, the authors describe the primary strategies employed by police departments in this new era—problem-oriented policing, community-oriented policing, hot spots and targeted offenders strategies, order-maintenance policing—and the proper role for stop and frisk is articulated for each given strategy. Specific attention is also given to police officer body-worn cameras and external oversight as mechanisms to both enhance police legitimacy and serve as accountability controls that can prevent racially discriminatory practices. Chapter 6 concludes with an overview of the key takeaways from each of the previous chapters, from the strong historical, legal, and discretionary traditions of SQF and the persistent race-relations problems that continue to define American policing, to the current body of research on the impact and consequences of SQF, to its role in the future of policing. The authors end by arguing that, in twenty-first-century policing, SQF should be assessed in terms of both legal (i.e., articulable reasonable suspicion) and procedural justice standards. Police departments that apply these standards will not only avoid unjust and unreasonable *Terry* stops, they will also achieve legitimacy in the eyes of their citizens.

2

The Historical Context

The stop and frisk story begins in the decades leading up to the 1960s, as dramatic cultural shifts set the stage for a decade defined by racial tension, riots, surges in crime, and extraordinary legal change. The urbanization and immigration attendant to the Industrial Revolution transformed the United States from a "rural agrarian, Anglo-Protestant society" into a more racially, ethnically, and religiously diverse society.[1] This cultural shift

> produced great uncertainly in the minds of those whose more traditional ways of life were being challenged by the changes that accompanied this more diverse and industrial society. One of the by-products of these changes was an increase in criminal activity, probably partly because of an ever-increasing population density. The increase in crime combined with fears of people from different races and cultures led to great increases in police power with a focus on "law and order" crime control.[2]

By the 1960s, however, civil rights activists focused public consciousness on both social and legal equality. Part of these efforts cast light on how abuse of police power disproportionally affected the poor, the uneducated, and people of color.[3]

Under the direction of Chief Justice Earl Warren, the U.S. Supreme Court began to "constitutionalize" much of criminal procedure with a focus on individual rights and liberties—a shift in policy generally referred to as the *due process revolution*.[4] Much of the Court's attention in this area of the law focused on creating public policy designed to ensure that police honored the constitutional rights of criminal suspects.

Indeed, "[t]ired of the steady stream of abuses that continued to filter up from the states, the Supreme Court of the 1960s made policing the police, as well as state courts, a distinctly federal concern."[5]

Terry v. Ohio stands among the most enduring and recognizable of the many landmark criminal procedure cases decided by the U.S. Supreme Court in the 1960s.[6] *Terry* set the legal parameters for police to conduct brief, limited, investigatory detentions (known as "stops") and attendant pat-downs for weapons (known as "frisks").

> A stop is a police practice involving the temporary detention and questioning of a person initiated on a reasonable suspicion (less than probable cause) of criminal activity for the purposes of crime prevention and investigation. A frisk is a limited search, for the protection of the law enforcement officer carrying out the investigation, of a stopped person who is reasonably believed to be armed and dangerous.[7]

Collectively, we refer to the process of stopping, questioning, and (potentially) frisking someone as "SQF." But the practice of SQF far predates *Terry*. This chapter explores the foundations of SQF in two ways. First, we set the stage for understanding the complexities of the law governing SQF by outlining basic Fourth Amendment principles. Second, we review the legal status of SQF practices prior to the decision in *Terry*.

The Fourth Amendment

The Fourth Amendment provides as follows:

> The right of the people to be secure in their persons, houses, papers, and effects, against unreasonable searches and seizures, shall not be violated, and no Warrants shall issue, but upon probable cause, supported by Oath or affirmation and particularly describing the place to be searched, and the persons or things to be seized.[8]

The first part of the Fourth Amendment is referred to as the Reasonableness Clause, given its general proscription against "unreasonable searches and seizures." The second part of the Fourth Amendment is known as the Warrants Clause because of its directive that "no Warrants shall issue, but upon probable cause."

> Reconciling the clauses requires balancing the citizenry's privacy interest against the government's power to intrude in pursuing important government objectives. If the Court assigns the Warrant Clause the greater role in Fourth Amendment analysis, the warrant and probable cause requirements will restrict the government's right to intrude. On the other hand, if the Court primarily relies on a general reasonableness standard, the obstacles of obtaining a warrant and proving probable cause are removed, and the scope of valid government intrusions broadens. The two clauses thus strike different balances between the citizenry's privacy interests and the government's police power, and emphasizing one clause or the other will reflect the different balances. In many ways, to decide how the two clauses interrelate is to determine the Fourth Amendment's values and purposes.[9]

The framers likely had several motivations for including the Fourth Amendment in the Bill of Rights. First and foremost, they wanted to ban the use of "general warrants"—warrants that lacked any specificity with regard to the people or places to be searched or the items to be seized—from justifying arbitrary intrusions.[10] The term "general warrant" was also commonly applied in the framers' era to a "warrant lacking a complaint under oath or an adequate showing of cause."[11] Such general warrants were frequently used during the colonial period preceding the American Revolution, especially for the purposes of searching for goods subject to tariffs and for items related to what the English crown considered to be seditious libel.[12]

Thomas Davies, professor emeritus of law at the University of Tennessee, pointed out, however, that the usual "general warrants" explanation does not fully address why the Fourth Amendment starts with the Reasonableness Clause. It appears that the framers generally feared warrants—even those that were sufficiently specific or particularized. Accordingly, they were more concerned with the overall reasonableness of all searches and seizures, including warrantless ones.[13] Yale law professor Akhil Amar posited, therefore, that the Reasonableness Clause should be interpreted as providing a "freestanding reasonableness standard" that is supposed "to be the 'global' standard by which all government searches or seizures should be judged."[14] Even those who disagree with Amar that the two clauses should be read independently of each other appear to accept the importance and perhaps even paramountcy of the concept of reasonableness in the execution of search and seizures, largely as a function of the fact that the framers distrusted—even disdained—"the character and judgment of ordinary officers."[15]

> Indeed, the Framers' perception of the untrustworthiness of the ordinary officer was reinforced by class-consciousness and status concerns. It was disagreeable enough for an elite or middle-class householder to have to open his house to a search in response to a command from a high status magistrate acting under a judicial commission; it was a gross insult to the householder's status as a "freeman" to be bossed about by an ordinary officer who was likely drawn from an inferior class.[16]

Unfortunately, the precise ways the Reasonableness Clause and Warrants Clause interrelate remain unclear. Seemingly, the Reasonableness Clause and the Warrants Clause are directed at different parts of the investigative process.[17] Yet the language in the latter clause has clearly influenced judicial interpretation of the former. Indeed, the U.S. Supreme Court has often (but not always) required that probable cause support warrantless searches and seizures (including arrests, which are seizures of people). As the Court explained in *Wong Sun v. United States* (1963), if the requirements for warrantless arrests, searches, and seizures were less stringent than those for warrants, "a principal incentive now existing for the procurement of . . . warrants would be destroyed."[18]

Placing the Fourth Amendment in Evidentiary Context: Burdens of Persuasion

Unfortunately, the phrase "burden of proof" has become common parlance. But the burden of proof actually refers to two distinct concepts. The first is known as the *burden of production* (also referred to as the burden of coming forward). This responsibility requires the party bearing the burden to produce sufficient evidence to warrant going forward with the judicial process. In other words, courts do not waste precious time and valuable resources adjudicating disputes that are not supported by enough evidence to warrant a trial. Once the party with the burden of production meets this burden, the rest of the adjudicatory process focuses on the *burden of persuasion*—the obligation to prove facts in dispute by a certain quantum of evidence that may be conceptualized on a continuum ranging from no proof (0 percent) to proof to an absolute certainty (100 percent), as illustrated in figure 2.1. Neither extreme on the ends of this continuum are used in the U.S. system of justice. Rather, courts require specific levels of persuasion that lie in between these two extremes, depending on the specific legal context.

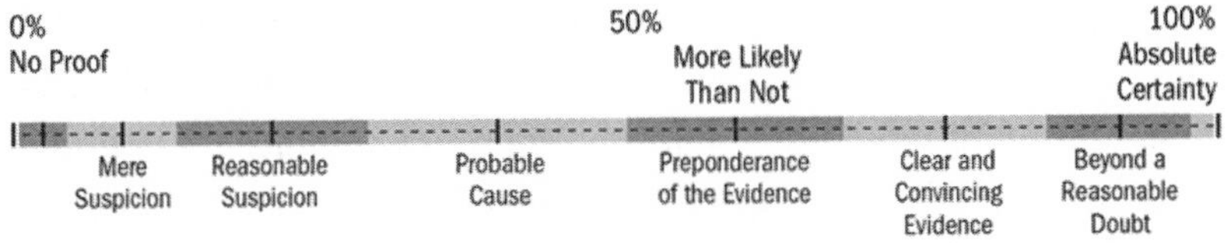

0% No Proof			50% More Likely Than Not		100% Absolute Certainty
Mere Suspicion	Reasonable Suspicion	Probable Cause	Preponderance of the Evidence	Clear and Convincing Evidence	Beyond a Reasonable Doubt

FIGURE 2.1. Burden of Persuasion Continuum

"Mere suspicion" lies at the low end of the scale. Mere suspicion can be conceptualized as a hunch based on intuition. "Although intuitively knowing something is undoubtedly a skill that serves law enforcement officers well, mere suspicion is insufficient proof of any fact in a court of law."[19]

At some point, a law enforcement officer's hunch or intuition might be supported by reasons that he or she can articulate to a third party, such as a judge. Although the quantum of evidence is only slightly higher than mere suspicion, the ability to articulate reasonable grounds for being suspicious of someone is legally important. "Instead of just having a hunch or an intuitive feeling, a person can articulate the reasons *why* he or she is suspicious. Moreover, the explanations offered as the bases for the suspicion are objectively reasonable—clearly understandable to another person who hears the explanations."[20] Put another way, reasonable suspicion involves "a particularized and objective basis" for suspecting the person of criminal activity.[21] This level of proof forms the evidentiary backbone of SQF procedures in the United States due to the U.S. Supreme Court's decision in *Terry v. Ohio*.

Probable cause sits just above reasonable suspicion on the continuum of proof scale. Defining probable cause is no easy task: "It is differentiated from reasonable, articulable suspicion by the existence of facts—independently verifiable factual information that supports the conclusion that there is a 'fair probability' that a crime occurred or that a particular person was involved in a crime."[22]

The only burden of persuasion that is easily and properly reduced to the quantitative is known as a preponderance of the evidence. This level of proof sits just above the 50 percent mark on the continuum; it represents a sufficient amount of evidence that something is more likely than not. The preponderance of the evidence standard is the burden of persuasion in most civil trials. In the criminal justice process, preponderance of the evidence is the "standard of proof used to establish the validity of waivers of constitutional rights, as well as the burden for proving that exceptions to the exclusionary rule apply."[23]

At some point, there is a level of proof that renders a fact at issue not just "more likely than not," but so clear that the trier-of-fact (a judge or a jury) believes the facts to have been clearly and convincingly established, although there is room for some reasonable doubt. Such clear and convincing evidence is required in a narrow range of civil cases and is also the level of proof to which defendants must establish certain affirmative defenses, such as insanity.[24]

The highest level of proof used in American jurisprudence is the "beyond a reasonable doubt" standard. It is reserved for determinations of guilt in criminal trials as an evidentiary means of honoring the presumption of innocence accorded those accused of crimes in the United States. In their textbook on courts, Professors David Neubauer and Henry F. Fradella explain how this standard of proof operates:

> The prosecution bears this burden of proving all the elements of the crime(s) charged beyond a reasonable doubt; defendants are not required to prove themselves innocent. If the prosecution fails to meet this burden of proof on any element of a crime, the defendant must be acquitted.[25] A specific definition for the "beyond a reasonable doubt" standard has not been adopted by the U.S. Supreme Court, leading to some confusion among jurists and jurors alike. In fact, jury instructions explaining reasonable doubt are often the basis for appeal. It is sufficient to say that proof beyond a reasonable doubt requires that the guilt of the defendant be established to a reasonable, but not absolute or mathematical, certainty. Probability of guilt is not enough. In other words, to satisfy the standard of "beyond a reasonable doubt," the jury must be satisfied that the charges against the defendant are almost certainly true. A challenged definition of beyond a reasonable doubt that was upheld by the U.S. Supreme Court reads as follows: "A reasonable doubt is an actual and substantial doubt arising from the evidence, from the facts or circumstances shown by the evidence, or from the lack of evidence."[26] Keep in mind that reasonable doubt is an inherently qualitative concept; it cannot be quantified, and any attempt to do so for a jury is likely to result in reversible error.[27]

As previously mentioned, the reasonable suspicion standard constitutes the salient burden of persuasion for SQF activities and, therefore, this book. Although the reasonable suspicion standard will be explored in more detail in chapter 3, it is important to note that the quantum of proof that demarcates mere suspicion from reasonable suspicion (or, for that matter, reasonable suspicion from probable cause) is one of degree and not one of kind. The bases on which these evidentiary standards may be satisfied are seemingly endless, but most frequently include a law enforcement officer's personal observations of a suspect, as well as the logical inferences and deductions that stem from those observations in light of the officer's knowledge, training, and experience;[28] information gathered from known informants that carries indicators of reliability;[29] information gathered from anonymous informants that carries indicators of reliability as verified through independent corroboration by the investigating officer(s);[30] and information from police flyers, bulletins, or radio dispatches.[31]

Basic Fourth Amendment Concepts

The Reasonableness Clause of the Fourth Amendment limits governmental authority to conduct "searches and seizures," but does not define what those terms mean. It will undoubtedly be helpful to provide definitions at the outset of our Fourth Amendment discussion with the caveat that this chapter will elaborate on the meaning of these terms.

- A search occurs when governmental actors either
  - physically intrude (trespass) onto a person's property to obtain information or discover something;[32] or
  - violate a person's reasonable expectation of privacy.[33]
- A seizure of property occurs "when there is some meaningful interference with an individual's possessory interests" with property.[34]
- A seizure of a person occurs when his or her freedom of movement is restrained by means of physical force or show of authority, and under the circumstances, a reasonable person would believe that he was not free to leave or otherwise terminate the encounter.[35]

The law of search and seizure can only be understood within the framework of four basic Fourth Amendment concepts: property, privacy, reasonable suspicion versus probable cause, and reasonableness.

Before examining these concepts, we note that the technicalities of the Fourth Amendment can be waived when a person voluntarily grants consent for a law enforcement officer "to search his or body, premises, or belonging."[36] The U.S. Supreme Court has repeatedly validated such consent searches: "Officers may seek consent-based encounters [from citizens] if they are lawfully present in the place where the consensual encounter occurs. If consent is freely [voluntarily] given, it makes no difference that an officer may have approached the person with the hope or expectation of obtaining consent."[37]

In spite of their seemingly voluntary nature and a long history of judicial approval, consent searches can be controversial for two reasons. First, "voluntary" simply means the absence of coercion; it does not mean "knowing." Thus, unlike in the Fifth Amendment context—in which *Miranda v. Arizona* (1966) dictates that suspects be warned about their rights before a custodial interrogation occurs—the person being asked by police to grant consent to a search does not need to be told that they may decline consent.[38] Second, research suggests that, as with SQF, significant racial disparities exist regarding those whom officers ask for consent to search.[39] These factors are salient because consent forms the basis of between 53 percent and 90 percent of searches.[40] Nonetheless, because this book examines SQF behaviors in the absence of consent, we now turn to an examination of the four foundational concepts in Fourth Amendment jurisprudence: property, privacy, probable cause, and reasonableness.

Property

The Fourth Amendment stresses the importance of property rights by its inclusion of both personal and real property in its text, guaranteeing the right of people "to be secure in their persons, houses, papers, and effects, against unreasonable searches and seizures." Indeed, security in one's property has been a hallmark of common-law rights for centuries:

The great end for which men entered into society was to secure their property. That right is preserved sacred and incommunicable in all instances where it has not been taken away or abridged by some public law for the good of the whole. . . . By the laws of England, every invasion of private property, be it ever so minute, is a trespass. No man can set foot upon my ground without my license but he is liable to an action though the damage be nothing.[41]

Given the historical importance of property rights, it is unsurprising that the U.S. Supreme Court grounded Fourth Amendment jurisprudence in a property-rights framework. Such an approach posits that a "search," for Fourth Amendment purposes, occurs when governmental authorities physically intrude into a constitutionally protected area. The landmark Prohibition-era case of *Olmstead v. United States* (1928)[42] illustrates this principle.

The defendants in *Olmstead* were convicted of "conspiracy to violate the National Prohibition Act by unlawfully possessing, transporting and importing intoxicating liquors and maintaining nuisances, and by selling intoxicating liquors."[43] The key evidence was obtained through wiretaps of the defendants' home telephones and their principal place of business. Because the wiretaps were installed without any physical trespass onto the defendants' property, the Court ruled that neither a search nor a seizure had occurred. "There was no entry of the houses or offices of the defendants."[44] The Court applied the same logic in *Goldman v. United States* (1942),[45] when it ruled that no search or seizure had occurred when police had placed a listening device against a wall in an office that adjoined the defendant's office. Again, the lack of a physical intrusion was key to the Court's reasoning.

In contrast, when law enforcement physically intruded onto a suspect's property without a valid warrant, the Court routinely held that such trespass to property constitutes an illegal search and seizure. That was the result in *Silverman v. United States* (1961), a case in which law enforcement officers pushed a "spike mike" through a common wall until it hit a heating duct in the defendant's home.[46] Because the microphone had physically invaded the target premises, even though the invasion was slight, the Court ruled that the intrusion violated the Fourth Amendment.

As the next subsection should make clear, the property-rights approach to the Fourth Amendment declined in the 1960s as a result of the U.S. Supreme Court's decision in *Katz v. United States* (1967), which stressed that invasions of privacy—even in the absence of any physical trespass to property—violated the Fourth Amendment.[47] Nonetheless, in *United States v. Jones* (2012), the U.S. Supreme Court made clear that *Katz*'s privacy-rights approach supplemented, but did not replace, the property-rights approach.[48] In *Jones*, the FBI and Washington, DC, police jointly investigated a nightclub owner they suspected of drug trafficking. Initially, their investigation used techniques that the U.S. Supreme Court had previously ruled did not constitute a search or seizure for Fourth Amendment purposes, such as visual surveillance of the nightclub, the use of a video camera, and a pen register that recorded the numbers dialed from and received by the defendant's cell phone. Using the information obtained from these techniques, the police obtained a warrant to place an electronic monitoring device on a vehicle registered to Jones's wife. The warrant authorized the installation of the device in the District of Columbia and gave police ten days to install it. On the eleventh day, and while in Maryland, not DC, police installed a global positioning satellite (GPS) device on the vehicle, which was used to monitor Jones's movements for twenty-eight days. Thus, both the installation of the GPS device and its subsequent monitoring fell outside the scope of the warrant, placing the actions of the police outside the protections of the Fourth Amendment's Warrants Clause.

After Jones was charged, his lawyers moved to exclude all of the evidence obtained via the GPS monitoring. The Supreme Court held that "the Government's installation of a GPS device on [Jones's] vehicle, and its use of that device to monitor the vehicle's movements, constitutes a 'search'" under the Fourth Amendment.[49] As the U.S. Supreme Court explained in its decision in *Jones*, the key to reaching this conclusion was that the law enforcement officers had physically intruded on Jones's property when they installed the GPS device on his wife's car:

> It is important to be clear about what occurred in this case: The Government physically occupied private property for the purpose of obtaining information. We have no doubt that such a physical intrusion would have been considered a "search" within the meaning of the Fourth Amendment when it was adopted. . . .
>
> [W]e must assure preservation of that degree of privacy against government that existed when the Fourth Amendment was adopted. . . . [F]or most of our history the Fourth Amendment was understood to embody a particular concern for government trespass upon the areas ("persons, houses, papers, and effects") it enumerates. . . . [W]hen the Government does engage in physical intrusion of a constitutionally protected area in order to obtain information, that intrusion may constitute a violation of the Fourth Amendment. We have embodied that preservation of past rights in our very definition of "reasonable expectation of privacy" which we have said to be an expectation "that has a source outside of the Fourth Amendment, either by reference to concepts of real or personal property law or to understandings that are recognized and permitted by society."[50]

Privacy

Even in the absence of a trespass to property, law enforcement officers can still run afoul of the Fourth Amendment if they violate a suspect's reasonable expectation of privacy. In *Katz v. United States* (1967), FBI agents had attached an electronic listening and recording device to the outside of a public telephone booth to overhear telephone conversations. They used this device to record the defendant obtaining gambling-related information and placing illegal bets. These conversations were then transcribed and used against Katz at trial. Even though the FBI agents had not violated Katz's privacy rights by trespassing on his property, the U.S. Supreme Court nonetheless determined that the agents' actions violated the Fourth Amendment:

[T]his effort to decide whether or not a given "area," viewed in the abstract, is "constitutionally protected" deflects attention from the problem presented by this case. For the Fourth Amendment protects people, not places. What a person knowingly exposes to the public, even in his own home or office, is not a subject of Fourth Amendment protection. . . . But what he seeks to preserve as private, even in an area accessible to the public, may be constitutionally protected.[51]

The Court ruled that the placement of the recording device on the outside of the booth constituted a search and seizure for Fourth Amendment purposes. "The fact that the electronic device employed to achieve that end did not happen to penetrate the wall of the booth can have no constitutional significance."[52]

Since *Katz*, courts have analyzed Fourth Amendment claims under the privacy-rights approach using the criteria Justice Harlan set forth in his concurring opinion in *Katz*. Harlan said that "there is a twofold requirement, first that a person has exhibited an actual (subjective) expectation of privacy and, second, that the expectation be one that society is prepared to recognize as [objectively] 'reasonable.'"[53]

The courts have decided numerous cases ruling on the circumstances under which people possess or lack a reasonable expectation of privacy. Consider the following sampling of cases:

- People reasonably expect the highest levels of privacy in their homes. Thus, *Payton v. New York* (1980) held that unless exigent circumstances justify an immediate warrantless entry into one's home, or unless the resident grants consent for state actors to enter the home, the plain text of the Fourth Amendment protects against searches of homes without a warrant.[54] Similarly, *United States v. Kyllo* (2001) held that the privacy expectation in one's home is so special that the Fourth Amendment protects people's homes from warrantless scans using thermal imaging devices.[55]

- People also reasonably expect privacy in the curtilage, or area immediately around their homes, such as on their porches and patios. But
the greater the distance from the dwelling and its immediately adjacent
living spaces, the less likely an area is to be deemed within the curtilage
of a home. For example, structures, like barns, on a landowner's private
property that are located many yards away from the main house are not
within the curtilage of the home, according to *United States v. Dunn*
(1987).[56] Similarly, open fields around one's home are also not protected
by the Fourth Amendment under *Katz's* reasonable expectation of privacy logic—even if "no trespassing" signs are posted, according to *Oliver
v. United States* (1984).[57]

- *California v. Greenwood* (1988) held that one does not have a reasonable
expectation of privacy in one's garbage because trash constitutes abandoned property—property in which the owner has given up his or her
possessory interest and discarded on the street, where anyone could rum-
mage through it.[58]

- One does not have a reasonable expectation of privacy in the numbers
dialed from one's telephone, according to *Smith v. Maryland* (1979),
because they are used in the regular course of conducting the phone company's business.[59] Similarly, one does not have a reasonable expectation of
privacy in one's bank records, according to *United States v. Miller* (1976),
because bank records are not private papers, but rather constitute information a person voluntarily shared with a third party—namely, a bank,
such that the information becomes a part of a bank's business records.[60]

- *United States v. White* (1971) held that people cannot hold reasonable expectations of privacy in face-to-face conversations with others that they
believe to be private.[61] Absent a privileged conversation protected by
law, such as with one's attorney, clergy member, psychotherapist, or the
like, people should expect that others in whom they confide might break
that confidence by telling other third parties, including law enforcement
officers.

- Although people may reasonably expect privacy in the contents of their
computers under certain circumstances, the reasonableness of that expectation of privacy evaporates when one connects to a peer-to-peer network
or when one's hard drive is transported when entering the United States

on an international flight or cruise. Indeed, *United States v. Arnold* (2008) held that because the government has a duty to ensure the safety of its interior, one should not reasonably expect privacy when crossing international borders.[62] Thus, searches of hard drives at the border are reasonable simply by virtue of the fact that they occur at the border.

Determinations regarding reasonable expectations of privacy are made by judges, not juries, because the question of whether something constitutes a "search" or "seizure" for Fourth Amendment purposes is a pure question of law, not a question of fact. Yet judges are supposed to make this legal determination with deference to what "society" considers reasonable. How do judges know what "society" thinks? Unfortunately, judges rarely rely on empirical data to make such determinations, and as a result, many of the rulings previously summarized appear to be at odds with the actual views of the American public. Criminologists have surveyed people's levels of agreement with key Fourth Amendment precedents and found significant levels of public agreement with cases in which the courts had protected privacy rights under the Fourth Amendment, but significant levels of public disagreement with cases in which the courts had allowed a range of invasions of privacy over Fourth Amendment challenges.[63] As a result, they concluded that "courts often misjudge what 'society' is prepared to embrace as a reasonable expectation of privacy."[64]

Probable Cause

Discerning any precise point at which the law distinguishes between reasonable suspicion and probable cause is impossible. Even the U.S. Supreme Court has admitted as much:

> Articulating precisely what "reasonable suspicion" and "probable cause" mean is not possible. They are commonsense, non-technical conceptions that deal with the factual and practical considerations of everyday life on which reasonable and prudent men, not legal technicians, act. . . . As

such, the standards are "not readily, or even usefully, reduced to a neat set of legal rules. . . ." We have described reasonable suspicion simply as "a particularized and objective basis" for suspecting the person stopped of criminal activity . . . , and probable cause to search as existing where the known facts and circumstances are sufficient to warrant a man of reasonable prudence in the belief that contraband or evidence of a crime will be found. . . . We have cautioned that these two legal principles are not "finely-tuned standards," comparable to the standards of proof beyond a reasonable doubt or of proof by a preponderance of the evidence. . . . They are instead fluid concepts that take their substantive content from the particular contexts in which the standards are being assessed.[65]

Reasonable suspicion is best understood by examining the facts of *Terry v. Ohio* (1968), which is explored in chapter 3. In *Carroll v. United States* (1925), the U.S. Supreme Court explained that probable cause to search exists when "the facts and circumstances within their [the officers'] knowledge and of which they had reasonably trustworthy information [are] sufficient in themselves to warrant a man of reasonable caution in the belief that [seizable property would be found in a particular place or on a particular person]."[66] In 1983 the Court succinctly restated this definition of probable cause as "a fair probability that contraband or evidence of a crime will be found in a particular place."[67]

Nearly twenty-five years after the decision in *Carroll*, the Court paraphrased *Carroll* when explaining that probable cause to arrest exists when "facts and circumstances within [the officers'] knowledge and of which they had reasonably trustworthy information [are] sufficient in themselves to warrant a man of reasonable caution in the belief that an offense has been or is being committed [by the person to be arrested]."[68]

Probable cause can be established in a number of ways, including through the collective knowledge of police,[69] through the individual knowledge of a particular officer,[70] and from informants.[71] It is important to note, however, that any single factor may be insufficient to establish probable cause on its own. Rather, probable cause is determined under the "totality of the circumstances" known at the time and must include consideration of whether the information is reasonably trustworthy.[72]

Reasonableness

Because the Fourth Amendment prohibits "unreasonable searches and seizures," the reasonableness of governmental actors' conduct is always key to any constitutional question regarding their actions. Indeed, "the central inquiry under the Fourth Amendment [is] the reasonableness in all the circumstances of the particular governmental invasion of a citizen's personal security."[73]

As with the concepts of reasonable suspicion and probable cause, there "is no formula for the determination of reasonableness. Each case is to be decided on its own facts and circumstances."[74] Determining the reasonableness under the unique circumstances of each case involves a two-step inquiry. First, courts consider "whether the . . . action was justified at its inception," and second, courts "must determine whether the search as actually conducted was reasonably related in scope to the circumstances which justified the interference in the first place."[75] Indeed, "a search which is reasonable at its inception may violate the Fourth Amendment by virtue of its intolerable intensity and scope."[76]

Reasonableness is a nebulous standard; what is reasonable to one person may be unreasonable to the next. It is also a highly deferential standard that typically results in courts upholding the actions of governmental actors.[77] Some scholars see such deference as a problem, since the framers of the U.S. Constitution were so concerned about arbitrary searches that they included the Fourth Amendment in the Bill of Rights.[78]

The Reasonableness Clause does not bar law enforcement officers from using a reasonable amount of force when needed to conduct a search or seize evidence—even if such searches and seizures involve searches of the body—provided that the force must generally be minimally invasive and necessary to achieve the goals of a valid search. For example, police may seize hair samples by plucking hair;[79] seize a DNA sample by swabbing someone's mouth;[80] or seize biological evidence by scraping under someone's fingernail.[81] Police may even have medical personnel forcibly draw a blood sample from a driving-under-the-influence suspect without a warrant if there are exigent circumstances that prevent the arresting officer from obtaining a warrant.[82] Strip searches may even be permissible, if there is a legitimate reason for conducting such a search and it is carried out in a reasonable manner, such as when performed by a trained professional on an arrestee upon arrival at a jail's intake area.[83] But if excessive force were used, an otherwise legitimate search can be rendered unreasonable. Consider that in *Evans v. Stephens* (2005), a federal appeals court ruled a strip search unreasonable when the officer "inserted the same baton or club—without intervening sanitation—in each Plaintiff's anus and used the same baton or club to lift each man's testicles" due to the unsanitary nature of the actions taken, among other factors, such as the use of "threatening and racist" language and a lack of privacy.[84]

The Court has also made it clear that some type of bodily invasions are so intrusive that they that are, per se, unreasonable. Thus, for instance, *Rochin v. California* (1952) invalidated pumping an arrestee's stomach in a hospital environment as part of a search for pills believed to be drugs.[85] Similarly, *Winston v. Lee* (1985) ruled impermissible the surgical removal (under general anesthesia) of a bullet from the suspect's chest, finding the process too invasive and too risky to be reasonable under the Fourth Amendment.[86] And the Reasonableness Clause has been used to invalidate a host of actions that involve the use of unnecessary, unjustifiable, or excessive force. For instance, a series of U.S. Supreme Court cases, decided since the mid-1980s, teach that it is unreasonable for police to use deadly force to stop a fleeing suspect unless the circumstances indicate that the suspect is dangerous and poses an immediate threat of safety to the officers or others.[87] At the other end of the scale, however, *Terry v. Ohio* (1968) and case law in its progeny sanctioned SQF—brief, limited investigatory detentions of people under suspicious circumstances for the purposes of discovering whether criminal activity is afoot—reasoning that such practices are so minimally intrusive that they are "reasonable" under the Fourth Amendment, even in the absence of probable cause.

Summary

The text of the Fourth Amendment says nothing about suspicion. The only standard of proof mentioned in the amendment is "probable cause," and a plain-text reading suggests that the requirement of probable cause concerns the issuance of warrants, not all searches and seizures—which only need to be "reasonable." Perhaps that is part of the reason why legal scholars criticize reliance on the concept of suspicion in the Fourth Amendment context. As law professor Fabio Arcila Jr. said, "Suspicion is a siren. It has lured us into misguided Fourth Amendment waters, obscuring a more rational search jurisprudence."[88]

History provides at least some explanation for the concepts of "reasonableness" and "suspicion" becoming inextricably linked in the search and seizure context. Thus, we turn to a brief review of SQF practices in early English common law.

SQF in a Pre-*Terry* World

A law enforcement officer's legal authority to detain and question a suspicious person dates back to the common law of England. English common law had very strict rules governing formal arrests.[89] Legal proscriptions on investigation of crime, however, were significantly more lax.

English Common Law

English constables and "watchmen" were permitted to detain "nightwalkers"—suspicious people encountered at night.[90] Indeed, according

to Sir Matthew Hale's (1736/1847) authoritative treatise on English common law, *Historia Placitorum Coronæ* (*The History of the Pleas of the
Crown*), those on the night watch could legally "arrest such as pass by
until the morning, and if no suspicion, they are then to be delivered
[released], and if suspicion be touching them, they shall be delivered to
the sheriff."[91] Even private citizens could "arrest any suspicious night-
walker, and detain him till he give a good account of himself."[92] Note
that the authority of watchmen and citizens alike rested on the existence
of "suspicion"—a somewhat nebulous term. Lord Hale cautioned that
"mere suspicion" was insufficient to justify any apprehension; rather, the
suspicion had to be "founded upon some probable reason."[93]

The English common-law tradition of allowing a detention based
on suspicion differed from the law of other European countries. "It is
quite common even in the most liberal and democratic of Continental
countries for a suspect to lie in prison for many months, without a defi-
nite charge, while the police are building up the case against him."[94] In
contrast, a "detention for questioning" in England under night-walker
provisions was limited to a few hours—until morning came. Nonetheless, it is clear that English police abused this authority, as it was not
uncommon for suspicious people to be detained for up to four days.[95]
But as the common law evolved, any "detention for questioning" that
went beyond detaining a suspicious night-walker came to be viewed as
an illegal false imprisonment unless the circumstances satisfied the requirements for a true, valid arrest.[96] It is therefore unsurprising that in
the United States, the concept of reasonable suspicion eventually came
to be linked to brief detentions by police for the purposes of questioning
whether criminal activity is afoot.

The Uniform Arrest Act

Until 1939, there was considerable variation in the ways U.S. law handled
police-initiated contacts with citizens that did not amount to arrests. In
some states, it was unclear whether American common law, borrowing

from its English antecedents, conferred a right to detain and question suspects when the requirements for a full arrest were clearly absent.[97] In other jurisdictions, the right to detain and question suspects was conferred on police by state statute or by municipal ordinance. In these states, detentions for questioning "were generally left to the discretion of individual officers and were not subject to constitutional protections or judicial oversight."[98] That state of the law, however, came to be viewed as "entirely inadequate to meet the modern needs for questioning and detaining suspects."[99]

In 1939 the Interstate Commission on Crime authorized a study to examine how arrests were made across the United States. The study examined the feasibility of creating a model law that states could adopt to harmonize the law of arrest across the country and to bring the actions of police into alignment with constitutional mandates.[100] Once drafted, that model law became known as the Uniform Arrest Act. Its provisions dealt with nine types of police-initiated contacts with citizens, the first two of which were "questioning and detaining suspects" and "searching suspects for weapons."[101]

STOP AND QUESTION

Section 2 of the Uniform Arrest Act provided as follows:

(1) A peace officer may stop any person abroad [outside the home] whom he has reasonable ground to suspect is committing, has committed or is about to commit a crime, and may demand of him his name, address, business abroad and whither he is going.

(2) Any person so questioned who fails to identify himself or explain his actions to the satisfaction of the officer may be detained and further questioned and investigated.

(3) The total period of detention provided for by this section shall not exceed two hours. Such detention is not an arrest and shall not be recorded as an arrest in any official record. At the end of the detention the person so detained shall be released or be arrested and charged with a crime.

Harvard law professor Sam B. Warner, one of the drafters of the Uniform Arrest Act, explained that the above-quoted provisions were "essential to proper policing,"[102] especially in urban areas, for the following reasons:

> A man climbing into a window late at night may be the householder who has forgotten his key and does not want to disturb his wife, or he may be a burglar. A man who looks round furtively, tries the door of an automobile, steps in and seems unfamiliar with its mechanism, may or may not have a right to drive the car. Under such circumstances, a passing officer ought to question the suspicious behavior.[103]

Notably, section 2 of the act was broader than the authority conferred on constables and watchmen under English common law because its provisions empowered police to act at any time, not just at night. Nonetheless, the act was careful to use words like "stop" and "detain" to differentiate such encounters from arrests. Warner (and, presumably, the other drafters of the act) asserted that although the constitutionality of such provisions had yet to be determined, the stop and question provisions of the act would likely be deemed constitutional because they were "reasonable" in light of the needs of law enforcement and citizen safety, especially in large cities.

SEARCHING FOR WEAPONS

Section 3 of the Uniform Arrest Act provided as follows:

> A peace officer may search for a dangerous weapon any person whom he has stopped or detained to question, as provided in section 2, whenever he has reasonable ground to believe that he is in danger if the person possesses a dangerous weapon. If the officer finds a weapon, he may take and keep it until the completion of the questioning, when he shall either return it or arrest the person. The arrest may be for the illegal possession of the weapon.

This provision differed substantially from the common-law authority of English constables and watchmen, who had no right to search a suspect until an arrest was made. Sam Warner defended the expansion of police authority under such circumstances by arguing that there was "no reason why such a right should have been granted" under English common law because "hoodlums with four-inch pistols were centuries in the future."[104] In contrast to policing methods of the past, when weapons were likely to be a "sword, staff, or bow and arrow," modern policing required officers to have the ability to "frisk a suspect before questioning him, that is, to pass his hands over the latter's outer clothing to make sure that no dangerous weapons are concealed on his person" if there were some reason to believe that the person was carrying a concealed weapon.[105]

Warner argued that the frisk provision contained in section 3 of the Uniform Arrest Act was "undoubtedly constitutional."[106] He based that conclusion on two arguments. First, he reasoned by analogy that because police had the legal authority to conduct a search of a person upon a lawful arrest, by logical extension, a frisk that occurred during lawful questioning prior to arrest should similarly be deemed "reasonable" and therefore constitutional under the Fourth Amendment.[107] Second, Warner relied on the one case-on-point that had been adjudicated in the United States as of that time—a California Court of Appeals case decided in 1908. That decision reversed a lower court judgment for false arrest when an officer conducted a stop and frisk of a suspect. The court noted that the frisk "was a precaution which the officer might well take under the circumstances of the meeting, given the conduct of the plaintiff, whether plaintiff was under arrest or not."[108] In contrast, the court cases decided by the date that had rejected such frisks for weapons involved more full-scale searches for contraband other than weapons.[109]

In 1941 the legislatures of New Hampshire and Rhode Island adopted the Uniform Arrest Act as the laws of their states.[110] Delaware followed suit in 1951.[111] Other states enacted statutes authorizing some SQF practices, but did not adopt the Uniform Arrest Act as the law of their states.[112] New York was one such state. In 1964 New York enacted a "stop and frisk" statute that purported "to authorize police officers to 'stop' people, 'demand' explanations of them and 'search them for dangerous weapons' in certain circumstances upon 'reasonable suspicion' that they are engaged in criminal activity and that they represent a danger to the policeman."[113] Notably, the New York law empowered police to engage in SQF activity for past, present, or potential criminal conduct[114] just two years after the U.S. Supreme Court extended the exclusionary rule to the states in *Mapp v. Ohio*.[115] Civil libertarians and criminal defense attorneys predicted that the law would diminish the civil rights of New Yorkers, especially racial and ethnic minorities.[116] Consider the commentary offered by civil rights leader Bayard Rustin:

> Whatever its provisions or its purposes, this law is a nefarious example of class legislation, for its effect is to permit harassment of the poor. No police are going to stop and frisk well-dressed bankers on Wall Street— but they don't hesitate to stop well-dressed Negro businessmen in Harlem and go through their attaché cases. That kind of brusque police action is reserved for the poor and minorities like Negroes and Puerto Ricans.[117]

New York's stop and frisk statute was upheld by the highest court in the state.[118] Nonetheless, as chapter 3 explores in more detail, the statute was sharply criticized in the landmark case of *Sibron v. New York*.[119]

Conclusion

By the mid-1960s, most courts that had considered the constitutionality of SQF laws had upheld them under the Fourth Amendment.[120] Notably, even when courts found that the actions of police may have exceeded their constitutional authority, they limited their rulings to how SQF laws had been applied in specific cases, often mentioning—albeit in portions of decisions not central to their holdings or rationale—that the laws themselves appeared to pass constitutional muster. For example,

People v. Simon (1955) upheld the authority of law enforcement to detain and question people loitering around a warehouse at night, but invalidated the convictions in the case because the police had exceeded the scope of their authority by searching the suspects, yielding a marijuana cigarette.[121] Similarly, *People v. Henneman* (1937) upheld the authority of police to stop and question suspicious people, but reversed convictions in the case because the police had ordered the defendants out of their car and, after searching the vehicle, found two guns.[122]

Prompted by the need to clarify the scope of permissible conduct during SQF procedures, the U.S. Supreme Court issued three landmark rulings in 1968 that set federal constitutional benchmarks for SQF within the framework of the Fourth Amendment: *Terry v. Ohio, Sibron v. New York*, and *Peters v. New York*. These three cases adopted formal rules governing police-initiated street encounters with citizens under circumstances amounting to less than full arrests and searches.

3

The Contemporary Legal Context

Though civil rights advocates had won several hard-fought battles by the mid-1960s, racial tensions between police and minority groups ran high for many reasons.[1] Indeed, a series of urban riots occurred between 1964 and 1967, which led President Johnson to establish the National Advisory Commission on Civil Disorders, more commonly known as the Kerner Commission. The Kerner Commission began its final report by stating its basic conclusion: "Our Nation is moving toward two societies, one Black, and one White—separate and unequal."[2] The commission warned that the country faced a system of apartheid in its major cities unless a host of conditions brought about by racism, segregation, and poverty were remedied, including massive improvements in housing, education, municipal services, consumer and credit practices, employment, and the administration of justice.

The Kerner Commission members devoted a significant portion of their final report to discussing the particularly strained relations between police and the urban communities they were supposed to serve. In fact, the commission singled out the "deep hostility between police and ghetto communities as a primary cause" of the civil unrest the commission was established to study.[3] As Columbia University law professor and federal court of appeals judge Debra Livingston stated,

The Kerner Commission criticized various police practices as contributing to hostile relations between police and African Americans in the inner city. Aggressive, "stranger" patrol—including the use of roving task forces "which move[d] into high-crime districts without prior notice and conduct[ed] intensive, often indiscriminate, street stops and searches"— caused community resentment, while the patrol car removed the officer from the street, contributing to his alienation from citizens. Significantly, however, the Commission also observed that the intensity of inner city residents' anger about hostile police conduct in their communities might even be exceeded by the animosity that they expressed over another matter: "the conviction that ghetto neighborhoods [were] not given adequate police protection."[4]

The following year, the Warren Court issued decisions in *Terry v. Ohio*,[5] *Sibron v. New York*,[6] and *Peters v. New York*[7]—three cases that adopted formal rules governing police-initiated street encounters with citizens under circumstances amounting to less than full arrests and searches. This chapter is devoted to an extensive discussion of the seminal *Terry*, *Sibron*, and *Peters* cases, as well as the subsequent court cases that, over the next several decades, served to expand police authority to stop, question, and frisk U.S. citizens.

The Foundational Cases of *Terry*, *Sibron*, and *Peters*
Terry v. Ohio

Terry v. Ohio set the legal parameters for SQF in the United States. The key facts of the case were summarized by the U.S. Supreme Court as follows:

> Petitioner Terry was convicted of carrying a concealed weapon and sentenced to the statutorily prescribed term of one to three years in the penitentiary. Following the denial of a pretrial motion to suppress, the prosecution introduced in evidence two revolvers and a number of bullets seized from Terry and a codefendant, Richard Chilton, by Cleveland Police Detective Martin McFadden. At the hearing on the motion to suppress this evidence, Officer McFadden testified that, while he was patrolling in plain clothes in downtown Cleveland at approximately 2:30 in the afternoon of October 31, 1963, his attention was attracted by two men, Chilton and Terry, standing on the corner of Huron Road and Euclid

Avenue. He had never seen the two men before, and he was unable to say precisely what first drew his eye to them. However, he testified that he had been a policeman for 39 years and a detective for 35, and that he had been assigned to patrol this vicinity of downtown Cleveland for shoplifters and pickpockets for 30 years. He explained that he had developed routine habits of observation over the years, and that he would "stand and watch people or walk and watch people at many intervals of the day." He added: "Now, in this case, when I looked over, they didn't look right to me at the time."

His interest aroused, Officer McFadden took up a post of observation in the entrance to a store 300 to 400 feet away from the two men. "I get more purpose to watch them when I seen [sic] their movements," he testified. He saw one of the men leave the other one and walk southwest on Huron Road, past some stores. The man paused for a moment and looked in a store window, then walked on a short distance, turned around and walked back toward the corner, pausing once again to look in the same store window. He rejoined his companion at the corner, and the two conferred briefly. Then the second man went through the same series of motions, strolling down Huron Road, looking in the same window, walking on a short distance, turning back, peering in the store window again, and returning to confer with the first man at the corner. The two men repeated this ritual alternately between five and six times apiece—in all, roughly a dozen trips. At one point, while the two were standing together on the corner, a third man approached them and engaged them briefly in conversation. This man then left the two others and walked west on Euclid Avenue. Chilton and Terry resumed their measured pacing, peering, and conferring. After this had gone on for 10 to 12 minutes, the two men walked off together, heading west on Euclid Avenue, following the path taken earlier by the third man.

By this time, Officer McFadden had become thoroughly suspicious. He testified that, after observing their elaborately casual and oft-repeated reconnaissance of the store window on Huron Road, he suspected the two men of "casing a job, a stick-up," and that he considered it his duty as a police officer to investigate further. He added that he feared "they may have a gun." Thus, Officer McFadden followed Chilton and Terry and saw them stop in front of Zucker's store to talk to the same man who had conferred with them earlier on the street corner. Deciding that the situation was ripe for direct action, Officer McFadden approached the three men, identified himself as a police officer and asked for their names. At this point, his knowledge was confined to what he had observed. He was not acquainted with any of the three men by name or by sight, and he had received no information concerning them from any other source. When the men "mumbled something" in response to his inquiries, Officer Mc-Fadden grabbed petitioner Terry, spun him around so that they were facing the other two, with Terry between McFadden and the others, and patted down the outside of his clothing. In the left breast pocket of Terry's overcoat, Officer McFadden felt a pistol. He reached inside the overcoat pocket, but was unable to remove the gun. At this point, keeping Terry between himself and the others, the officer ordered all three men to enter Zucker's store. As they went in, he removed Terry's overcoat completely, removed a .38 caliber revolver from the pocket and ordered all three men to face the wall with their hands raised. Officer McFadden proceeded to pat down the outer clothing of Chilton and the third man, Katz. He discovered another revolver in the outer pocket of Chilton's overcoat, but no weapons were found on Katz. The officer testified that he only patted the men down to see whether they had weapons, and that he did not put his hands beneath the outer garments of either Terry or Chilton until he felt their guns. So far as appears from the record, he never placed his hands beneath Katz' outer garments. Officer McFadden seized Chilton's gun, asked the proprietor of the store to call a police wagon, and took all three men to the station, where Chilton and Terry were formally charged with carrying concealed weapons.

On the motion to suppress the guns, the prosecution took the position that they had been seized following a search incident to a lawful arrest. The trial court rejected this theory, stating that it "would be stretching the facts beyond reasonable comprehension" to find that Officer McFadden had had probable cause to arrest the men before he patted them down for weapons. However, the court denied the defendants' motion on the ground that Officer McFadden, on the basis of his experience, "had reasonable cause to believe . . . that the defendants were conducting themselves suspiciously, and some interrogation should be made of their action."

Purely for his own protection, the court held, the officer had the right to pat down the outer clothing of these men, who he had reasonable cause to believe might be armed. The court distinguished between an investigatory "stop" and an arrest, and between a "frisk" of the outer clothing for weapons and a full-blown search for evidence of crime. The frisk, it held, was essential to the proper performance of the officer's investigatory duties, for, without it, "the answer to the police officer may be a bullet, and a loaded pistol discovered during the frisk is admissible."[8]

The U.S. Supreme Court upheld the convictions and the lower courts' rationale. In doing so, the Court sanctioned the notions that a stop is distinct from an arrest and a frisk is different from a search, even though the Fourth Amendment applies to all such police activities. But "instead of applying the probable cause standard to stops and frisks, the Court applied the fundamental test of the Fourth Amendment: the reasonableness under all the circumstances of the particular governmental invasion of a citizen's personal security."[9] In doing so, the Court disentangled the Fourth Amendment's Reasonableness Clause from the Warrants Clause:

We do not retreat from our holdings that the police must, whenever practicable, obtain advance judicial approval of searches and seizures through the warrant procedure . . . or that, in most instances, failure to comply with the warrant requirement can only be excused by exigent circumstances. . . . But we deal here with an entire rubric of police conduct—necessarily swift action predicated upon the on-the-spot observations of the officer on the beat—which historically has not been, and, as a practical matter, could not be, subjected to the warrant procedure. Instead, the conduct involved in this case must be tested by the Fourth Amendment's general proscription against unreasonable searches and seizures.[10]

The significance of this disentanglement cannot be overstated. In deciding to analyze the reasonableness of Officer McFadden's conduct, the Court sanctioned a line of inquiry that is distinct from questions of probable cause. Indeed, rather than weighing the quantum and reliability of evidence along a continuum like that presented earlier, the Court analyzed the "reasonableness of Officer McFadden's conduct as a general proposition" by balancing "the need to search or seize against the invasion which the search or seizure entails."[11] Moreover, this balancing test depends not on whether probable cause exists, but rather on whether a law enforcement officer can "point to specific and articulable facts which, taken together with rational inferences from those facts, reasonably warrant that intrusion."[12]

After adopting the aforementioned balancing test, the Court explained that "effective crime prevention and detection" served as a general interest whenever police encounter suspicious behavior.[13] With that governmental interest in mind, the Court endorsed Officer McFadden's decision to stop and question Terry, Chilton, and Katz because— according to the Court—he had observed them

go through a series of acts, each of them perhaps innocent in itself, but which, taken together, warranted further investigation. There is nothing unusual in two men standing together on a street corner, perhaps waiting for someone. Nor is there anything suspicious about people in such circumstances strolling up and down the street, singly or in pairs. Store windows, moreover, are made to be looked in. But the story is quite different where, as here, two men hover about a street corner for an extended period of time, at the end of which it becomes apparent that they are not waiting for anyone or anything; where these men pace alternately along an identical route, pausing to stare in the same store window roughly 24 times; where each completion of this route is followed immediately by a conference between the two men on the corner; where they are joined in one of these conferences by a third man who leaves swiftly, and where the two men finally follow the third and rejoin him a couple of blocks away. It would have been poor police work indeed for an officer of 30 years' experience in the detection of thievery from stores in this same neighborhood to have failed to investigate this behavior further.[14]

The Court then turned to the constitutionality of McFadden's patdown of the suspects to see whether they were armed. Again, the Court approved of McFadden's actions, reasoning that more was at stake than some generalized governmental interest in investigating crime:

[T]here is the more immediate interest of the police officer in taking steps to assure himself that the person with whom he is dealing is not armed with a weapon that could unexpectedly and fatally be used against him. Certainly it would be unreasonable to require that police officers take unnecessary risks in the performance of their duties. American criminals have a long tradition of armed violence, and every year in this country many law enforcement officers are killed in the line of duty, and thousands more are wounded. Virtually all of these deaths and a substantial portion of the injuries are inflicted with guns and knives.

In view of these facts, we cannot blind ourselves to the need for law enforcement officers to protect themselves and other prospective victims of violence in situations where they may lack probable cause for an arrest. When an officer is justified in believing that the individual whose suspicious behavior he is investigating at close range is armed and presently dangerous to the officer or to others, it would appear to be clearly unreasonable to deny the officer the power to take necessary measures to determine whether the person is, in fact, carrying a weapon and to neutralize the threat of physical harm.[15]

The Court then balanced the above needs against the nature of the intrusion that a frisk for weapons engenders and, in doing so, described the protective search for weapons as "a brief, though far from inconsiderable, intrusion upon the sanctity of the person."[16] In ruling that McFadden's actions were reasonable and, therefore, permissible under the Fourth Amendment, the Court emphasized the limited nature of the frisk:

> Officer McFadden patted down the outer clothing of petitioner and his two companions. He did not place his hands in their pockets or under the outer surface of their garments until he had felt weapons, and then he merely reached for and removed the guns. He never did invade Katz' person beyond the outer surfaces of his clothes, since he discovered nothing in his pat-down which might have been a weapon. Officer McFadden confined his search strictly to what was minimally necessary to learn whether the men were armed and to disarm them once he discovered the weapons. He did not conduct a general exploratory search for whatever evidence of criminal activity he might find.[17]

Sibron v. New York

On the same day that the U.S. Supreme Court decided *Terry v. Ohio*, the Court also issued rulings in two other cases that were consolidated and decided in a single opinion: *Sibron v. New York* (1968) and *Peters v. New York* (1968). Like *Terry*, these cases presented questions about the scope of police authority to conduct SQFs. The Court summarized the key facts of the *Sibron* case as follows:

> Sibron . . . was convicted of the unlawful possession of heroin. He moved before trial to suppress the heroin seized from his person by the arresting officer, Brooklyn Patrolman Anthony Martin. After the trial court denied his motion, Sibron pleaded guilty to the charge, preserving his right to appeal the evidentiary ruling. At the hearing on the motion to suppress,

Officer Martin testified that while he was patrolling his beat in uniform on March 9, 1965, he observed Sibron "continually from the hours of 4:00 P.M. to 12:00, midnight . . . in the vicinity of 742 Broadway." He stated that during this period of time he saw Sibron in conversation with six or eight persons whom he (Patrolman Martin) knew from past experience to be narcotics addicts. The officer testified that he did not overhear any of these conversations, and that he did not see anything pass between Sibron and any of the others. Late in the evening Sibron entered a restaurant. Patrolman Martin saw Sibron speak with three more known addicts inside the restaurant. Once again, nothing was overheard and nothing was seen to pass between Sibron and the addicts. Sibron sat down and ordered pie and coffee, and, as he was eating, Patrolman Martin approached him and told him to come outside. Once outside, the officer said to Sibron, "You know what I am after." According to the officer, Sibron "mumbled something and reached into his pocket." Simultaneously, Patrolman Martin thrust his hand into the same pocket, discovering several glassine envelopes, which, it turned out, contained heroin.[18]

The state attempted to justify Patrolman Martin's actions under New York's stop and frisk statute, referred to in the relevant appellate decisions as § 180-a. That statute contained the following provisions:

1. A police officer may stop any person abroad in a public place whom he reasonably suspects is committing, has committed or is about to commit a felony or any of the offenses specified in section five hundred fifty-two of this chapter, and may demand of him his name, address and an explanation of his actions.

2. When a police officer has stopped a person for questioning pursuant to this section and reasonably suspects that he is in danger of life or limb, he may search such person for a dangerous weapon. If the police officer finds such a weapon or any other thing the possession of which may constitute a crime, he may take and keep it until the completion of the questioning, at which time he shall either return it, if lawfully possessed, or arrest such person.[19]

The U.S. Supreme Court expressly refused to determine the constitutionality of the above-quoted statute: "We decline . . . to be drawn into what we view as the abstract and unproductive exercise of laying the extraordinarily elastic categories of § 180-a next to the categories of the Fourth Amendment in an effort to determine whether the two are in some sense compatible."[20] Instead, the Court interpreted Sibron's appeal as an "as applied" challenge to the law. Nonetheless, the Court expressed great skepticism about the scope of § 180-a's grant of authority:

> The operative categories of § 180-a are not the categories of the Fourth Amendment, and they are susceptible of a wide variety of interpretations. New York is, of course, free to develop its own law of search and seizure to meet the needs of local law enforcement, . . . and in the process it may call the standards it employs by any names it may choose. It may not, however, authorize police conduct which trenches upon Fourth Amendment rights, regardless of the labels which it attaches to such conduct. The question in this Court upon review of a state-approved search or seizure "is not whether the search [or seizure] was authorized by state law. The question is rather whether the search was reasonable under the Fourth Amendment. Just as a search authorized by state law may be an unreasonable one under that amendment, so may a search not expressly authorized by state law be justified as a constitutionally reasonable one."[21]

Then, in a footnote containing dicta, the Court further expressed incredulity about the statutory language in § 180-a:

> It is not apparent, for example, whether the power to "stop" granted by the statute entails a power to "detain" for investigation or interrogation upon less than probable cause, or if so what sort of durational limitations upon such detention are contemplated. And while the statute's apparent grant of a power of compulsion indicates that many "stops" will constitute "seizures," it is not clear that all conduct analyzed under the rubric of the statute will either rise to the level of a "seizure" or be based upon

less than probable cause. In No. 74, the *Peters* case, for example, the New York courts justified the seizure of appellant under § 180-a, but we have concluded that there was in fact probable cause for an arrest when Officer Lasky seized Peters on the stairway. . . . In any event, a pronouncement by this Court upon the abstract validity of § 180-a's "stop" category would be most inappropriate in these cases, since we have concluded that neither of them presents the question of the validity of a seizure of the person for purposes of interrogation upon less than probable cause.

The statute's other categories are equally elastic, and it was passed too recently for the State's highest court to have ruled upon many of the questions involving potential intersections with federal constitutional guarantees. We cannot tell, for example, whether the officer's power to "demand" of a person an "explanation of his actions" contemplates either an obligation on the part of the citizen to answer or some additional power on the part of the officer in the event of a refusal to answer, or even whether the interrogation following the "stop" is "custodial" [triggering *Miranda* protections]. There are, moreover, substantial indications that the statutory category of a "search for a dangerous weapon" may encompass conduct considerably broader in scope than that which we approved in *Terry v. Ohio* . . . . At least some of the activity apparently permitted under the rubric of searching for dangerous weapons may thus be permissible under the Constitution only if the "reasonable suspicion" of criminal activity rises to the level of probable cause. Finally, it is impossible to tell whether the standard of "reasonable suspicion" connotes the same sort of specificity, reliability, and objectivity which is the touchstone of permissible governmental action under the Fourth Amendment. . . . In this connection we note that the searches and seizures in both *Sibron* and *Peters* were upheld by the Court of Appeals of New York as predicated upon "reasonable suspicion," whereas we have concluded that the officer in *Peters* had probable cause for an arrest, while the policeman in *Sibron* was not possessed of any information which would justify an intrusion upon rights protected by the Fourth Amendment.[22]

The Court invalidated Sibron's conviction on the ground that the officer lacked reasonable suspicion that he was involved in any criminal activity. The officer

> merely saw Sibron talking to a number of known narcotics addicts over a period of eight hours. It must be emphasized that Patrolman Martin was completely ignorant regarding the content of these conversations, and that he saw nothing pass between Sibron and the addicts. So far as he knew, they might indeed have been talking about the World Series. The inference that persons who talk to narcotics addicts are engaged in the criminal traffic in narcotics is simply not the sort of reasonable inference required to support an intrusion by the police upon an individual's personal security.[23]

Not only did the Court reject the officer's authority to stop Sibron under such circumstances, but it also rejected the subsequent search on three distinct grounds.

First, "[b]efore he places a hand on the person of a citizen in search of anything, he must have constitutionally adequate, reasonable grounds for doing so."[24] In other words, the fact that the officer lacked reasonable suspicion to stop and question Sibron invalidated the officer's subsequent actions.

Second, the Court specifically determined that the officer lacked reasonable suspicion that Sibron was armed and dangerous. In fact, the Court reasoned that the officer's "opening statement to Sibron—'You know what I am after'—made it abundantly clear that he sought narcotics" and did not believe that Sibron was reaching for a weapon.[25]

Third, the Court criticized the officer's actions, likening them more to a search than to a frisk:

> The search for weapons approved in *Terry* consisted solely of a limited patting of the outer clothing of the suspect for concealed objects which might be used as instruments of assault. Only when he discovered such

objects did the officer in *Terry* place his hands in the pockets of the men he searched. In this case, with no attempt at an initial limited exploration for arms, Patrolman Martin thrust his hand into Sibron's pocket and took from him envelopes of heroin. His testimony shows that he was looking for narcotics, and he found them. The search was not reasonably limited in scope to the accomplishment of the only goal which might conceivably have justified its inception—the protection of the officer by disarming a potentially dangerous man. Such a search violates the guarantee of the Fourth Amendment, which protects the sanctity of the person against unreasonable intrusions on the part of all government agents.[26]

Peters v. New York

The Court summarized the key facts of *Peters v. New York* (1968) as follows:

Peters . . . was convicted of possessing burglary tools under circumstances evincing an intent to employ them in the commission of a crime. The tools were seized from his person at the time of his arrest, and like Sibron he made a pretrial motion to suppress them. When the trial court denied the motion, he too pleaded guilty, preserving his right to appeal. Officer Samuel Lasky of the New York City Police Department testified at the hearing on the motion that he was at home in his apartment in Mount Vernon, New York, at about 1 P.M. on July 10, 1964. He had just finished taking a shower and was drying himself when he heard a noise at his door. His attempt to investigate was interrupted by a telephone call, but when he returned and looked through the peephole into the hall, Officer Lasky saw "two men tiptoeing out of the alcove toward the stairway." He immediately called the police, put on some civilian clothes and armed himself with his service revolver. Returning to the peephole, he saw "a tall man tiptoeing away from the alcove and followed by this shorter man, Mr. Peters, toward the stairway." Officer Lasky testified that he had lived in the 120-unit building for 12 years and that he did not recognize either of the men as tenants. Believing that he had happened upon the two men in the course of an attempted burglary, Officer Lasky opened his door, entered the hallway and slammed the door loudly behind him. This precipitated a flight down the stairs on the part of the two men, and Officer Lasky gave chase. His apartment was located on the sixth floor, and he apprehended Peters between the fourth and fifth floors. Grabbing Peters by the collar, he continued down another flight in unsuccessful pursuit of the other man. Peters explained his presence in the building to Officer Lasky by saying that he was visiting a girlfriend. However, he declined to reveal the girlfriend's name, on the ground that she was a married woman. Officer Lasky patted Peters down for weapons, and discovered a hard object in his pocket. He stated at the hearing that the object did not feel like a gun, but that it might have been a knife. He removed the object from Peters' pocket. It was an opaque plastic envelope, containing burglar's tools.[27]

In contrast to *Sibron*, the Court affirmed the conviction in *Peters*. The Court reasoned that by the time the officer caught Peters in the staircase, he had probable cause to arrest Peters for attempted burglary.

The officer heard strange noises at his door which apparently led him to believe that someone sought to force entry. When he investigated these noises he saw two men, whom he had never seen before in his 12 years in the building, tiptoeing furtively about the hallway. They were still engaged in these maneuvers after he called the police and dressed hurriedly. And when Officer Lasky entered the hallway, the men fled down the stairs. It is difficult to conceive of stronger grounds for an arrest, short of actual eyewitness observation of criminal activity.[28]

In light of the existence of probable cause to arrest, the search of Peters could be justified as a search incident to arrest—a more complete search than the limited frisk/pat-down for weapons authorized under *Terry*.

Arriving at the Decisions in *Terry*, *Sibron*, and *Peters*

The U.S. Supreme Court heard oral arguments from nine lawyers across two days in the *Terry*, *Sibron*, and *Peters* cases.[29] *Peters* was a unanimous decision. Only one justice dissented in *Sibron* because he thought that there was "probable cause for the policeman to believe that when Sibron reached his hand to his coat pocket, Sibron had a dangerous weapon which he might use if it were not taken away from him."[30] And only one justice also dissented in *Terry*. In a strongly worded dissent, Justice Douglas rejected the notion that the Reasonableness Clause of the Fourth Amendment could provide a basis to support SQF outside the usual probable cause standard:

> The opinion of the Court disclaims the existence of "probable cause." If loitering were in issue and that was the offense charged, there would be "probable cause" shown. But the crime here is carrying concealed weapons; and there is no basis for concluding that the officer had "probable cause" for believing that that crime was being committed. Had a warrant been sought, a magistrate would, therefore, have been unauthorized to issue one, for he can act only if there is a showing of "probable cause." We hold today that the police have greater authority to make a "seizure" and conduct a "search" than a judge has to authorize such action. . . .
>
> The requirement of probable cause has roots that are deep in our history. The general warrant, in which the name of the person to be arrested was left blank, and the writs of assistance, against which James Otis inveighed, both perpetuated the oppressive practice of allowing the police to arrest and search on suspicion. Police control took the place of judicial control, since no showing of "probable cause" before a magistrate was required. That philosophy [rebelling against these practices] later was reflected in the Fourth Amendment. And as the early American decisions both before and immediately after its adoption show, common rumor or report, suspicion, or even "strong reason to suspect" was not

adequate to support a warrant for arrest. And that principle has survived to this day. . . .

To give the police greater power than a magistrate is to take a long step down the totalitarian path. Perhaps such a step is desirable to cope with modern forms of lawlessness. But if it is taken, it should be the deliberate choice of the people through a constitutional amendment. Until the Fourth Amendment, which is closely allied with the Fifth, is rewritten, the person and the effects of the individual are beyond the reach of all government agencies until there are reasonable grounds to believe (probable cause) that a criminal venture has been launched or is about to be launched.

There have been powerful hydraulic pressures throughout our history that bear heavily on the Court to water down constitutional guarantees and give the police the upper hand. That hydraulic pressure has probably never been greater than it is today.

Yet if the individual is no longer to be sovereign, if the police can pick him up whenever they do not like the cut of his jib, if they can "seize" and "search" him in their discretion, we enter a new regime. The decision to enter it should be made only after a full debate by the people of this country.[31]

The published decisions in *Terry*, *Sibron*, and *Peters* do not tell the whole story. In 2012 St. John's University law professor John Q. Barrett used the notes left by deceased justices to reconstruct the Court's consideration of *Terry*, *Sibron*, and *Peters*.[32] The documentary evidence suggests that the justices saw the issues in *Terry* very differently at the start of the case. Their views morphed as consideration of the case unfolded. For example, most of the justices originally viewed the facts of *Terry* as giving Officer McFadden probable cause to search Terry, Chilton, and Katz; the justices did not even discuss the status of the "frisks" because, in their minds—at least at first—McFadden had searched the three suspects.[33] Accordingly, there was no discussion during their original vote on how to decide *Terry* with regard to the Reasonableness Clause of the Fourth Amendment playing any independent role in justifying SQF practices short of probable cause.

As Chief Justice Warren drafted evolving versions of the decision in *Terry*, it became difficult to fit the facts of the case into a traditional probable cause framework. Indeed, the first draft of the *Terry* opinion to be circulated among the justices explained that "the probable cause required to justify a search for weapons is probable cause to believe that someone is armed and dangerous, even though that belief does not constitute probable cause to make an arrest."[34] Several justices, most notably Abe Fortas, questioned whether the draft was creating a "new kind of probable cause."[35] The justices also disagreed over what the rule should be if there were going to be a new, lesser standard of probable cause (short of probable cause to arrest) and what that would mean if a person did not satisfactorily answer a police officer's questions. After several drafts on which the justice worked over a nearly four-month period, and with considerable input from Justice Brennan and Chief Justice Warren's law clerk, Earl C. Dudley Jr., the Court ultimately adopted an approach that Justice Harlan had proposed in what was originally to be his concurring opinion in *Terry*.

Notably, as the justices exchanged feedback on the draft opinion, Chief Justice Warren came to be of the opinion that he needed to write a model stop and frisk statute in much the same way they provided model language for Fifth Amendment warnings prior to custodial interrogations in the Court's 1966 *Miranda v. Arizona* decision.[36] But Justice Harlan's proposal prompted Chief Justice Warren to abandon this approach and embrace, at least in part, Justice Harlan's ideas in order to preserve a majority of the Court's justices signing on to his opinion.

In Harlan's view, the real constitutional issue that the stop-and-frisk cases raised was whether police officers may stop persons when the officers do not have probable cause to arrest them. Harlan wrote that the Court had correctly answered that question in the affirmative, but it had not explained why or when such stops were permitted by the Constitution. Harlan then answered these questions directly. Although Harlan saw stops as less intrusive than formal arrests, he also recognized that they nonetheless are "seizures" that must be "reasonable" under the Fourth Amendment. Because "probable cause" is the constitutional standard for a reasonable arrest, Harlan said the Court should use different phraseology to define a reasonable stop. His proposed standard was "reasonable suspicion."[37]

Justice Harlan's concurring opinion in *Terry* particularly set forth helpful guidance for law enforcement. He made it clear that police officers have the authority to engage in SQFs so long as such actions are "reasonable under the circumstances as the officer credibly relates them in court."[38] But he cautioned that this authority to frisk is predicated on the antecedent authority to stop based on "an articulable suspicion of a crime."[39] Of course, the Court asserted that the stop in *Terry* was reasonable, although that conclusion is questionable in light of facts surrounding Officer McFadden's stop of Terry, Chilton, and Katz that the Court either omitted from or glossed over in the *Terry* decision.

The result of Justice Harlan and Brennan's influence on the stop and frisk cases produced decisions in *Terry*, *Sibron*, and *Peters* that were generally applauded for their "sensitivity to the safety interests of law enforcement officers."[40] Many celebrated the decision as a middle ground compromise "that a frisk is not a 'search' at all and therefore outside the Fourth Amendment and the competing claim (embraced by a dissenting Justice Douglas) that a frisk is a full-fledged constitutional event, governed by the Fourth Amendment's probable cause requirement."[41]

Not everyone, however, lauded the stop and frisk decisions. Indeed, the cases "encountered a firestorm of criticism" from liberals for "granting the police excessively broad discretion that threatens the liberty of the innocent and which facilitates discrimination against minorities and others that the police are all too likely to view as suspicious."[42] And Justice Douglas's dissent in *Terry* expressed the concern from conservatives who saw the case's reasonable suspicion standard as whittling away constitutional protections from governmental intrusion absent probable cause. Indeed, in a subsequent U.S. Supreme Court case, Justice Scalia noted that although the common law granted legal authority for English watchmen and constables to stop suspicious persons under night-walker statutes, there was no "precedent for physical search of a person thus temporarily detained for questioning."[43] Scalia went on to say that he doubted "whether the fiercely proud men who adopted our Fourth Amendment would have allowed themselves to be subjected, on mere *suspicion* of being armed and dangerous, to such indignity."[44] Scalia likely overstated the point, however, because, as previously explained, the night-walker statutes authorize custodial arrests for at least overnight, based on suspicion.[45] Nonetheless, *Terry* clearly authorized a broader, more general investigative detention authority than night-walker statutes, which, by the terms, were confined to night-time detentions to prevent breaches of the peace.[46] Moreover, those who made arrests under night-walker statutes were subject to liability for false imprisonment if the overnight detention was not justified. As Rosenthal noted, "[u]nder the contemporary qualified immunity doctrine, in contrast, officers face no personal liability even if they violate Fourth Amendment standards, as long as their judgment under the circumstances is considered reasonable."[47]

The Impact of *Terry*, *Sibron*, and *Peters*

In *Dunaway v. New York* (1979), the U.S. Supreme Court explained its view of what *Terry* had accomplished in legal terms:

> *Terry* for the first time recognized an exception to the requirement that Fourth Amendment seizures of persons must be based on probable cause. . . . *Terry* departed from traditional Fourth Amendment analysis in two respects. First, it defined a special category of Fourth Amendment "seizures" so substantially less intrusive than arrests that the general rule requiring probable cause to make Fourth Amendment "seizures" reasonable could be replaced by a balancing test. Second, the application of this

balancing test led the Court to approve this narrowly defined less intrusive seizure on grounds less rigorous than probable cause, but only for the purpose of a pat-down for weapons.[48]

Terry's legal impact quickly expanded law enforcement authority by applying the reasonable suspicion standard to a range of police actions:

[C]iting *Terry*, the Court has upheld the detention of property when there was reasonable suspicion that contraband was inside; "protective sweeps" of a house when there was reasonable suspicion that the suspect's armed associates might be present; searches of a car when there was reasonable suspicion that weapons were present there; and search of a probationer's home on basis of reasonable suspicion.[49]

The impact of *Terry* in practical terms is more debatable. On one hand, the constitutional authority for police to conduct stops and frisks has been credited for contributing to the significant reductions of violent crime in the United States since the early 1990s.[50] Yet only a small fraction of people stopped are arrested; the majority of people stopped are innocent of wrongdoing.[51] Moreover, only about 2.6 percent of stop and frisks yielded either a weapon or contraband, a figure that undercuts arguments that aggressive stop and frisk practices reduced the number of weapons and the amount of drugs available on the streets.[52]

On the other hand, abundant evidence demonstrates that police use SQF against racial and ethnic minorities at much higher rates than they do against Whites.[53] Consider that of the people stopped in New York City in 2011, "53% were Black, 34% were Hispanic, 9% were white, and about 4% were Asian."[54] Jeffrey Bellin, a professor at William and Mary law school, noted a parallel between these data on stops and misdemeanor marijuana arrests in New York City during the 1990s:

From the perspective of officers seeking guns, misdemeanor arrests and stop-and-frisks look very similar. They begin by accosting a pedestrian with the goal of conducting a search. If during the encounter, the officer learns that the person was smoking marijuana (or committing some other crime), the officer can make an arrest and conduct a lawful search for weapons incident to that arrest. If the encounter reveals no basis for arrest, the officer may still be able to lawfully conduct a frisk if she can articulate reasonable suspicion that the person is armed and potentially dangerous. Either way, the encounter achieves its purpose once the officer obtains lawful (or at least quasi-lawful) grounds to search or determines that a search would be pointless. The distinction between arrest and stop, while certainly important to the individual, is irrelevant to the officer's underlying goal: detecting guns.[55]

Aggressive SQF tactics did not yield many weapons. Police found weapons in only 1.5 percent of frisks, and only a subset of those weapons were guns.[56] In contrast, 16 percent of the arrests following stops in New York—the highest percentage of arrests for any offense—were for marijuana possession.[57] Notably, not only is possession of marijuana not tied to crimes of violence, but also, simple possession of marijuana was decriminalized in New York in 1977. Yet such possession became the leading cause of arrest under the "proactive" policing strategies in New York City.

New York City politicians and NYPD officials argued that the data concerning weapons demonstrated the effectiveness of SQF insofar as the policy deterred people from carrying weapons and using them to commit robberies and homicides—especially in high-crime neighborhoods.[58] But focusing aggressive SQF tactics in crime "hot spots" led to disproportionately high rates of stops against minorities, some of which were unconstitutional because they were not based on individualized suspicion.[59] It is impossible to determine the precise numbers of unconstitutional stops from the available official data because NYPD reports do not capture all stops, as evidenced not only by the testimony of citizens who alleged that suspicionless stops violated their constitutional rights, but also by officers who provided statements like this: "We frisk

20, maybe 30 people a day. Are they all by the book? Of course not."[60] Indeed, according to criminologist and lawyer Delores Jones-Brown and colleagues, one high-ranking police commander in the NYPD estimated that the UF-250 form, on which SQF data were to be recorded by NYPD officers, was completed in only one out of ten stops.[61] Thus, at a minimum, some percentage of stops in New York violate the Fourth Amendment vis-à-vis *Terry*. If these unconstitutional stops are motivated by demographic characteristics such as perceived race or ethnicity—and some undoubtedly were—then they also violate the Fourteenth Amendment's Equal Protection Clause.[62]

Many scholars posit that *Terry*'s reasonable suspicion standard invites racial profiling.[63] Indeed, data suggest that "[m]inority group members can be not only stopped, but subjected to a frisk without any evidence that they are armed or dangerous, just because . . . [of] the neighborhoods in which they work or live."[64] Although racism and its attendant purposeful bias against minorities partially explain such findings, it is important to understand that unconscious bias also contributes to such racial and ethnic disparities in stop and frisk practices. In fact, the reasonable suspicion standard itself invites unconscious bias to play a major role in determining who gets stopped through the actions of what has been termed the *suspicion heuristic*—a concept developed by law professor L. Song Richardson and psychologist Phillip Atiba Goff "to explain the predictable errors in perception, decision-making, and action that can occur when individuals make judgments of criminality."[65] Drawing on a wealth of scientific and psychological data on both decision making and implicit racial bias, Richardson and Goff developed the suspicion heuristic primarily to explain the unconscious biases that operate when split-second judgments are made regarding whether another person poses a threat based on ambiguous actors or behaviors—most notably when determining the reasonableness of using force in self-defense. Unlike the split-second decision making that is typically required in deadly force incidents, law enforcement officers have an obligation under *Terry* to deliberate before making a stop. Some may even argue that officers should make careful observations to corroborate their suspicions prior to approaching a pedestrian on the public streets. Nonetheless, given the ways the psychology of unconscious bias operates, we believe that the suspicion heuristic has relevance in the context of stop and frisk.

Racial animus is not a necessary precursor for people to hold racial biases.[66] Research has consistently demonstrated that, even in the twenty-first century, a majority of Americans maintain implicit biases against Blacks.[67] Psychologists Anthony G. Greenwald and Mahzarin Banaji defined implicit biases as "introspectively unidentified (or inaccurately identified) traces of past experience that mediate favorable or unfavorable thought, feeling, or action toward social objects."[68] Importantly, these implicit racial biases can trigger "conscious attitudes that are activated automatically, and which influence behavior depending on how much behavioral control can be brought to bear."[69] Alternatively, racial biases *unconsciously* cause discriminatory behaviors[70] such as

non-verbal negativity toward out-group members; severity of criminal sentencing decisions; and greater likelihood of mistaking a harmless tool for a gun when it is held by a Black man. Implicit race biases may thus have morally relevant outcomes that most people would not explicitly endorse.[71]

Even 40 percent of African Americans demonstrate implicit pro-White biases.[72] The key to understanding these implicit racial biases rests on understanding that they operate "below the level of conscious awareness" and therefore are very difficult to control.[73] In other words, unconscious cognitive processes often lead people of *all* races to view young Black men with suspicion.[74] This suspicion heuristic associates young African American males in particular with a stereotype linked to dangerousness and violent criminality.[75] Consider research by psychologists Joshua Correll and colleagues.[76] They used a computer program and asked participants to either push the "shoot" button if the suspect was armed, or push the "don't shoot" button if the suspect held something neutral. They found that participants were not only quicker to shoot a Black suspect than a White suspect, but also that the two most common errors involved shooting an unarmed Black man and failing to shoot an armed White man. To the extent that police officers have such implicit biases, there may be disparities in police use of force and SQFs. In fact, several teams of researchers implemented versions of the "shoot/ don't shoot" research protocol and found evidence of race-based implicit biases in police officers.[77]

The reasonable suspicion standard for SQF serves to perpetuate the hegemonic nature of implicit racial bias vis-à-vis the suspicion heuristic. For instance, appellate courts are supposed to give deference to trial court determinations of reasonableness because they were supported by inferences drawn from an officer's "own experience."[78] But experience is influenced by the suspicion heuristic. Consider the *Terry* decision itself; nowhere in any of the opinions does any Justice mention that both Terry and Chilton were Black men.[79] Yet, according to the transcript of the trial court's suppression hearing,[80] Officer McFadden testified that when he saw the men standing on the street, "they didn't look right to me at the time."[81] Criminologists suggest that McFadden's attention may have been drawn to the men on account of their race.[82] This conclusion is bolstered by a number of ambiguities and inconsistencies in Officer Mc-Fadden's account of the case, as law professor Lewis R. Katz explained:

> [McFadden] was not acquainted with either man by name or sight, and he had received "[a]bsolutely no information regarding [the] men at all." Officer McFadden did not explain what about the two men "didn't look right" to him. The two men were dressed in topcoats, the standard dress of the day. They were engaged in no unusual behavior when they initially attracted McFadden's attention. When pressed on what about the two men attracted his interest and whether he would pursue them as he did if he saw them that day across from the court house, Officer McFadden replied, "I really don't know."
>
> What happened as McFadden studied Terry and Chilton depends upon which version of Officer McFadden's statement of the facts one

reads and in which court opinion the facts appear. McFadden watched the men over a period of ten minutes. He watched as one of the two men left the other and walked down the street and looked inside a shop window and continued walking, and then walked back to the other man, again looking in the shop window. The second man then repeated the same behavior. That behavior is the critical conduct which gives rise to the stop in this case. If they did it once or twice each, their behavior was pretty unremarkable. So, how many times they looked in the store window is crucial. In the police report filed the same day as the incident, Officer McFadden wrote that the men did this "about three times each." Between the day of the event when he wrote the police report and his memory was freshest, and the suppression hearing, which was almost one year to the day after the event, Officer McFadden's memory changed. At the suppression hearing three times each became "at least four or five times apiece," which later turned into four to six trips each. Moreover, at trial, when asked how many trips he observed, Officer McFadden replied, "about four trips, three to four trips, maybe four to five trips, maybe a little more, it might be a little less. I don't know, I didn't count the trips." The Ohio Court of Appeals decision in the case picked up on the uncertainty and asserted that the men separated and looked in the window "at least two to five times" each. However, by the time the fact worked its way into Chief Justice Warren's majority opinion in the Supreme Court, the number expands exponentially. He wrote that the men did this "between five or six times apiece—in all roughly a dozen trips." Later in the majority opinion, Chief Justice Warren came up with still another number when he described Terry and Chilton's behavior: "where these men pace alternately along an identical route, pausing to stare in the same store window roughly twenty-four times." The body of law which stems from *Terry* is dependent upon this single fact.

Officer McFadden was never sure which store was the subject of the suspects' attention. At the suppression hearing he admitted he had no experience in observing the activities of individuals who were "casing" a store for a robbery. In the police report, Officer McFadden indicated that they were looking in an airline ticket office; at the suppression hearing, the Detective mentioned an airline office or a jewelry store.[83]

In light of these facts—especially McFadden's inability to explain why he was initially suspicious of the men, the ever-changing number of trips the men made up and down the street, and the uncertainty of the type of store into which the men were looking—the reasonableness of the initial stop in *Terry* may be open to debate. Yet the U.S. Supreme Court's decision glossed over these key facts. The failure of the Court to address the questionable reasonableness of the stop in *Terry* illustrates how the very foundation of the reasonable suspicion standard in American constitutional law masks racially disparate SQF practices with the cloak of race neutrality in much the same way that "Stand Your Ground" laws mask racially disparate successes in self-defense claims as illustrated by the outcome in George Zimmerman's trial for the fatal shooting of Trayvon Martin in 2012.[84] At minimum, the facts surrounding the initial stop in the *Terry* case demonstrate that the undercurrent of racial injustice attendant to stop and frisk practices is rooted in the very precedent that constitutionally justified stop and frisk based on suspicion instead of probable cause. Others understandably view the foundational shortcomings of the *Terry* case in a more damning light. Indeed, the racial disparities evident in "modern" stop and frisk practices have led numerous commentators to condemn *Terry* as a "truly disastrous" decision[85] that "authorized a police practice that was being used to subvert the Fourth Amendment rights of Blacks nationwide."[86]

Key Cases after 1968

It took eleven years after the decisions in *Terry*, *Sibron*, and *Peters* before the U.S. Supreme Court had the opportunity to revisit stop and frisk. In both of the first two cases, the Court invalidated police actions and reiterated the seemingly narrow authority granted under *Terry*.

Police stopped the defendant in *Brown v. Texas* (1979) because they saw him in an area with a "high incidence of drug traffic."[87] Because police did not recall seeing Brown in the area before, they felt that the "situation looked suspicious."[88] Brown refused to identify himself and was charged for that refusal. In overturning his conviction, the Court ruled the initial stop invalid. The fact that Brown "was in a neighborhood frequented by drug users, standing alone, is not a basis for concluding that appellant himself was engaged in criminal conduct. In short, the appellant's activity was no different from the activity of other pedestrians in that neighborhood."[89] *Brown v. Texas* stood with *Sibron* as examples that reasonable suspicion required more than presence in a high-crime area or association with persons known to be involved in criminal conduct.

That same year, the Court decided *Ybarra v. Illinois* (1979). In that case, officers had obtained a search warrant to search a bar and a bartender for evidence of narcotics crimes. When they executed the warrant, the police frisked all of the customers in the bar. In explaining why the multiple frisks violated the Fourth Amendment, the Court stated, "The 'narrow scope' of the *Terry* exception does not permit a frisk for weapons on less than reasonable belief or suspicion directed at the person to be frisked [i.e., a bar customer], even though that person happens to be on premises where an authorized narcotics search is taking place."[90]

In the early 1980s, courts began to interpret *Terry* as providing significant leeway to law enforcement officers to conduct stops. Additionally, the U.S. Supreme Court directed the lower courts to assess the validity of stops based on "the whole picture"[91]—or what came to be known as the "totality of the circumstances." Perhaps more importantly, the Court told lower courts to defer to the professional judgment and experience of police when assessing the totality of the circumstances:

> In other words, courts hearing motions challenging the introduction of evidence obtained during *Terry* stops should view the facts brought before them to support the stop from the position of the police. Courts should ask whether a police officer—a person engaged in what the Court has

called elsewhere "the often competitive enterprise of ferreting out crime" would feel that all of the circumstances "raise a suspicion that the particular individual being stopped is engaged in wrongdoing."

Cortez thus sent a strong signal to lower courts that deference to the police and their trained crime-fighting sensibilities would henceforth be the order of the day.[92]

Exempting Some Stops

Terry suggests that although a stop is a distinct, less intrusive form of seizure than an arrest, the Fourth Amendment applies to both. But the Court pulled back from *Terry* when it qualified that only some stops— those in which a reasonable person stopped by police would not feel free to leave—constitute seizures for Fourth Amendment purposes.

In *United States v. Mendenhall* (1980), federal agents approached the defendant in the open concourse area of an airport.[93] The agents neither wore uniforms nor displayed weapons. They requested, but did not demand, to see the defendant's ticket and identification. Under these circumstances, the U.S. Supreme Court found that the encounter did not constitute a stop that qualified as a seizure for Fourth Amendment purposes, but rather a voluntary and cooperative encounter, because at no time should a reasonable person in the defendant's situation have ever felt that she could not leave. The Court went on to explain the "free-to-leave test" that has since served as the hallmark for determining when a Fourth Amendment seizure of a person takes place:

Examples of circumstances that might indicate a seizure, even where the person did not attempt to leave, would be the threatening presence of several officers, the display of a weapon by an officer, some physical touching of the person of the citizen, or the use of language or tone of voice indicating that compliance with the officer's request might be compelled. In the absence of some such evidence, otherwise inoffensive contact between a member of the public and the police cannot, as a matter of law, amount to a seizure of that person.[94]

The circumstances explained in *Mendenhall* are now considered "shows of authority" by law enforcement officers—shows that indicate that a stop constitutes a seizure. For example, in *Florida v. Royer* (1983), agents approached the defendant near a boarding area in an airport.[95] The defendant had purchased a one-way ticket for a flight under an assumed name—conduct that suggested he fit a "drug courier profile." The agents confronted him with this suspicion, kept his license and airline ticket, and asked the suspect to accompany them to a room just off the concourse.

> Asking for and examining Royer's ticket and his driver's license were no doubt permissible in themselves, but when the officers identified themselves as narcotics agents, told Royer that he was suspected of transporting narcotics, and asked him to accompany them to the police room, while retaining his ticket and driver's license and without indicating in any way that he was free to depart, Royer was effectively seized for the purposes of the Fourth Amendment. These circumstances surely amount to a show of official authority such that a reasonable person would have believed he was not free to leave.[96]

Nonetheless, the U.S. Supreme Court has decided several cases finding that no seizure occurred even though it strains credibility under the facts to think that the people interacting with law enforcement officers would have felt "free to leave." For example, *I.N.S. v. Delgado* (1984) held that when immigration authorities entered a factory to determine whether any employees were undocumented, no Fourth Amendment seizure occurred.[97] Yet agents wore badges and were armed; some agents were positioned near the building exits, while others roamed the factory questioning people about their immigration status.

> Persons such as [defendants] who simply went about their business in the workplace were not detained in any way; nothing more occurred than

> that a question was put to them. While persons who attempted to flee or evade the agents may eventually have been detained for questioning, [defendants] did not do so and were not in fact detained. The manner in which defendants were questioned, given its obvious purpose, could hardly result in a reasonable fear that [defendants] were not free to continue working or to move about the factory.[98]

Thus, *Delgado* morphed the "free-to-leave test" into something even more restrictive on personal liberty: free to continue working and moving about the factory.

The Court further narrowed *Terry* and *Mendenhall*'s free-to-leave test when it clarified that law enforcement officers have the authority to stop and ask basic investigatory questions—including requests to examine identification or to search luggage—without there being a seizure for Fourth Amendment purposes "as long as the police do not convey the message that compliance with their requests is required."[99] In *Bostick*, police questioned the defendant while he was seated on a bus. The Court all but abandoned *Mendenhall*'s free-to-leave test by changing the inquiry to one of coercive police tactics through shows of authority:

> [T]he mere fact that Bostick did not feel free to leave the bus does not mean that the police seized him. Bostick was a passenger on a bus that was scheduled to depart. He would not have felt free to leave the bus even if the police had not been present. Bostick's movements were "confined" in a sense, but this was the natural result of his decision to take the bus; it says nothing about whether or not the police conduct at issue was coercive.[100]

Since the early 1990s, the only cases in which the U.S. Supreme Court has found that stops amounted to seizures involve cases in which there are true shows of authority that police intentionally apply. For example, when police stop a motor vehicle using lights and/or sirens, both the driver and the passengers are seized for Fourth Amendment purposes.[101] Notably, however, the intentional show of authority must actually result in the detention of the suspect. If the person police seek to stop fails to submit to the show of authority (i.e., the suspect does not, in fact, stop), then no seizure occurs.[102]

Expanding Frisk Authority

Recall that *Terry* authorized a pat-down of a suspect's outer clothing if the officer had reason to believe that the person was armed and therefore might pose a danger to the officer or others nearby. In *Michigan v. Long* (1983), however, the Court upheld more expansive protective searches for weapons.[103] *Long* sanctioned conducting a brief search of the places in which a weapon might be hidden inside the passenger compartment of a car. Any contraband, such as drugs, that are viewed during such a sweep of a vehicle for weapons may be seized without a warrant and used at trial.

In contrast, if the illegal nature of the items in plain view is not immediately apparent without some further manipulation of the object, the scope of a valid pat-down is exceeded; a duly authorized search warrant (or some recognized warrant exception) would be necessary to conduct a more thorough inspection of the object. Consider the case of *Minnesota v. Dickerson* (1993).[104] During a valid frisk, an officer felt a lump in the suspect's pocket. The officer then placed his hands inside the suspect's pocket and manipulated the lump with his fingers until he determined that it was likely drugs. In overturning the defendant's conviction, the Court reasoned that because the officer could determine that the item was "contraband only after conducting a further search [involving manipulation of the object]—one not authorized by *Terry* or by any other exception to the warrant requirement," the drugs were seized in violation of the defendant's Fourth Amendment rights.[105]

Expanding Reasonable Suspicion

The decision in *Sibron* suggested that reasonable suspicion needed to be based on more than just hunches. But by the early 1990s, courts upheld

SQF practices with seemingly lower and lower levels of evidence. For example, *Alabama v. White* (1990) upheld a stop of a vehicle based on an anonymous tip even though there was no indication of the reliability of the tip.[106] The Court reasoned that the fact that the car described in the tip departed at the time and place specified and travelled toward the described destination was sufficient corroboration to suspect that criminal activity (in this case, drug trafficking) was afoot. It appeared to be of little consequence that such a tip could have been a fabrication motivated by revenge, a desire to harass, or even for entertainment value as a prank. Nonetheless, the suspicion in *Alabama v. White*, however weak, was still particularized in that it applied to one person's car. As the following paragraphs should make clear, the Court has even sanctioned stops without any individualized suspicion at all.

In the name of protecting motorists from drunk drivers, *Michigan Department of State Police v. Sitz* (1990) authorized sobriety checkpoints at which police stopped drivers without any particularized suspicion of driving while impaired.[107] As with the *Terry* case itself, the decision in *Sitz* was premised on the Fourth Amendment's Reasonableness Clause. Ultimately, the Court balanced "the state's interest in preventing accidents caused by drunk drivers, the effectiveness of sobriety checkpoints in achieving that goal, and the level of intrusion on an individual's privacy caused by the checkpoints" and concluded that roadblocks were reasonable and, therefore, constitutional.[108] Interestingly, however, it turns out that sobriety checkpoints are not, in fact, particularly efficient. As Justice Stewart's dissent in *Sitz* explained, suspicion-based stops would be far more effective:

> Over a period of several years, Maryland operated 125 checkpoints; of the 41,000 motorists passing through those checkpoints, only 143 persons (0.3%) were arrested. The number of man-hours devoted to these operations is not in the record, but it seems inconceivable that a higher arrest rate could not have been achieved by more conventional means. Yet, even if the 143 checkpoint arrests were assumed to involve a net increase in the

number of drunk driving arrests per year, the figure would still be insignificant by comparison to the 71,000 such arrests made by Michigan State Police without checkpoints in 1984 alone.

Any relationship between sobriety checkpoints and an actual reduction in highway fatalities is even less substantial than the minimal impact on arrest rates. As the Michigan Court of Appeals pointed out, Maryland had conducted a study comparing traffic statistics between a county using checkpoints and a control county. The results of the study showed that alcohol-related accidents in the checkpoint county decreased by ten percent, whereas the control county saw an eleven percent decrease; and while fatal accidents in the control county fell from sixteen to three, fatal accidents in the checkpoint county actually doubled from the prior year.

In light of these considerations, it seems evident that the Court today misapplies the balancing test . . . [by] overvalu[ing] the law enforcement interest in using sobriety checkpoints [and] undervalue[ing] the citizen's interest in freedom from random, unannounced investigatory seizures.[109]

Given the "whole picture" or totality of the circumstances test, there are few, if any, factors that are not relevant when assessing whether a law enforcement officer's suspicion was reasonable. Several factors, however, reappear in many cases.[110] Behavioral cues include nervous or evasive behavior, unprovoked flight, and "furtive gestures," such as avoiding eye contact, providing conflicting answers to questions, repeatedly looking over one's shoulder, unexpected leaning or bending over, attempting to hide something from an officer's line of sight, or otherwise gesturing in a way that might convey nervousness or having something to hide.[111] Notably, however, the concept of "furtive gestures" is so ambiguous that several jurisdictions have limited the use of that term in establishing reasonable suspicion or probable cause.[112]

Evidentiary cues include obvious factors, such as an officer observing a bulge in the suspect's pocket that might be a weapon,[113] knowledge of a suspect's prior criminal record or association with other known criminals,[114] or a suspect matching a photo on a wanted flier or a description in a recent report of a violent crime.[115] But one of the most vexing situational evidentiary cues concerns geography—specifically, location in or proximity to a high-crime area.

Although *Illinois v. Wardlow* (2000) held that presence in a high-crime area "standing alone, is not enough to support a reasonable, particularized suspicion that the person is committing a crime,"[116] location nonetheless is a key factor when assessing the reasonableness of suspicion under the totality of the circumstances.[117] Note, however, that this factor has the potential of transforming everyone in poor, urban neighborhoods into suspicious people given the possibility of criminal activity in such locations.[118] Because high-crime areas are perceptually and statistically associated with ethnic minorities,[119] police may have elevated levels of suspicion in minority neighborhoods.[120] To the extent that the police have elevated levels of suspicion in these neighborhoods, it may exacerbate and reinforce racial/ethnic inequalities in the practice of law enforcement, or as the minority threat perspective highlights, the subjugation of ethnic minorities.[121]

Sociologists Lincoln Quillian and Devah Pager found that the prevalence of young Black men affected urban residents' perceptions of crime in their neighborhood, even after controlling for neighborhood characteristics and crime rates.[122] Extrapolating on this research, police may have distorted perceptions of ethnic minorities in neighborhoods where they are heavily concentrated.[123] Consequently, police officers likely develop a perceptual shorthand that associates certain races and ethnicities with specific kinds of people who are perceived as "symbolic assailants."[124] Such a suspicion heuristic contributes to racial and ethnic disparities in SQF rates and associated use of force by police because these symbolic assailants are viewed as the enemy.[125]

But the suspicion heuristic is not limited to police perceptions and the actions they take pursuant to them. The lower courts give enormous weight to this neighborhood factor. "Thus, 'high crime area' becomes a centerpiece of the *Terry* analysis, serving almost as a talismanic signal justifying investigative stops. Location in America, in this context, is a proxy for race or ethnicity."[126]

> By sanctioning investigative stops on little more than the area in which the stop takes place, the phrase "high crime area" has the effect of criminalizing race. It is as though a [B]lack man standing on a street corner or sitting in a legally parked car has become the equivalent to "driving while [B]lack" for motorists.[127]

It is commonplace for police to pull over a car for a routine traffic offense "as a pretext for investigating other crimes, particularly drug offenses . . . and Blacks and Hispanics are disproportionately targeted by the practice."[128] Such a practice allows police to stop and question people without reasonable suspicion. In *Whren v. United States* (1996), the U.S. Supreme Court held that pretextual stops were constitutional; so long as a stop is supported by a legitimate reason, no matter how minor—such as a failure to signal, driving with a nonfunctioning taillight, exceeding the speed limit by a mile or two per hour, and so on—then the stop is permissible under the Fourth Amendment.[129] According to *Whren*, the fact that police may have used such a minor infraction as a means of investigating other criminal activity for which a stop would not have been authorized (on account of a want of reasonable suspicion) is simply irrelevant.

The *Whren* Court rejected the fact that racial profiling might underlie a pretextual stop as being of consequence to the law of search and seizure. "[T]he constitutional basis for objecting to intentionally discriminatory application of laws is the Equal Protection Clause, not the Fourth Amendment. Subjective intentions play no role in ordinary . . . Fourth Amendment analysis."[130] Thus,

> *Whren* creates a reality in which it is possible to separate a police officer's racial bias from his or her observations and account of alleged criminality, thereby making it possible for the reviewing judge at a suppression

hearing to uphold the officer's actions as resting upon neutral facts un-
tainted by racial bias.[131]

Of course, *Whren* completely misses the mark with regard to the role
of race in the suspicion heuristic, as well as other cognitive schemas
and stereotypes[132] that affect criminal justice system actors.[133] In other
words, *Whren* sanctioned racial profiling under the Fourth Amendment.

The problems with *Whren's* rationale notwithstanding, it remains the
law as of the writing of this book. The problems with *Whren* were compounded by the U.S. Supreme Court's decision in *Hiibel v. Sixth Judicial
Dist. Ct. of Nev., Humboldt County* (2004).[134] The defendant in *Hiibel*
was stopped by a police officer who was investigating an assault. He
was arrested and subsequently convicted under a state "stop and identify" statute because he declined to tell the officer his name. The Court
upheld the conviction, reasoning that the Fourth Amendment permits
a state to require a suspect to disclose his name in the course of a stop
and frisk. When considered together, *Whren* permits pretextual stops
that, in turn (under *Hiibel*), can then be used to force people to identify
themselves; if they refuse to cooperate, they can be taken into custody
and, at that point, the arresting officer may conduct a full search of the
person incident to arrest—a far more complete search than the type of
frisk authorized in *Terry v. Ohio*.

Conclusion

Terry and most of the SQF cases decided since 1980 collectively ignore
the fundamental problems with using a low standard of proof that
invites the use of racial, ethnic, and socioeconomic class stereotypes as
part of a calculus of suspicion while simultaneously cloaking the standard in race-neutral language. Importantly, such bias need not be a
product of intentional discrimination. The suspicion heuristic explains
how deeply held cognitive biases affect split-second decision making
that use stereotypes as the basis for developing unconscious suspicion

against racial and ethnic minorities—even by decision makers who are, themselves, members of those racial or ethnic groups. In spite of its significant shortcomings, we believe that SQF can and should be a valuable crime-control tool for twenty-first-century police departments—if the practice is retooled and managed in ways that rely on the proper exercise of discretion. The remaining chapters of this book explore our ideas for doing so.

4

Crime-Control Benefits and Collateral Consequences

WITH WESTON MORROW

Since the 1968 decision in *Terry v. Ohio*,[1] stop and frisk activities have become an important crime-fighting tool for many police departments across the United States. Notably, police departments in Philadelphia, Boston, Chicago, and New York City have all implemented some form of order-maintenance policing in conjunction with stop and frisk tactics to preserve law and order.[2] Despite the widespread adoption of SQF, the consensus about its effectiveness in reducing crime is mixed. For proponents, SQFs are believed to be a major factor underlying crime declines in some urban cities. In New York City, for instance, crime rates have been steadily declining for decades, and the decline began at about the same time the stop and frisk program was implemented.[3] Such observations have led some departmental and political leaders to identify SQFs as precipitating New York City's crime decline and creating a greater sense of safety among citizens. According to former police commissioner Raymond Kelly, "Police stops are just one component of multiple efforts by the Department that have saved lives and driven the murder rate to record lows. In the first 11 years of Mayor Bloomberg's tenure there were 7,363 fewer murders in New York City compared to the 11 years prior to the Mayor taking office."[4] Former mayor Michael Bloomberg stated, "New York is the safest big city in the nation, and our crime reductions have been steeper than any other big cities. For instance, if New York City had the murder rate of Washington, D.C., 761 more New Yorkers would have been killed last year."[5] Despite the adoption of SQF practices by police departments and the optimism expressed by Kelly and Bloomberg, researchers and social activists have been more skeptical about the effectiveness of these stops, claiming that their impact on crime is minimal to modest at best.[6] Not only are these scholars and activists suspicious of their effectiveness, they are also concerned that the strategy generates social, political, constitutional, and human costs that offset any potential crime-control benefits. We believe that these concerns are well-founded.

The confluence of media coverage, legal proceedings, and public opinion related to stop and frisk has resulted in the strategy becoming one of the most controversial and contested topics in the United States. To facilitate further discussion about their impact on crime, this chapter examines the implementation, impact, and consequences of SQF in New York and elsewhere. Although the New York Police Department is not the only law enforcement agency to use stop and frisk, it is one of the few departments to receive attention from researchers about its reliance on the practice. As a result, much of the chapter focuses on the NYPD experience with stop and frisk.

Stop and Frisk: A New York City Preface

Since the early 1990s, New York City has experienced a major decrease in crime. Although various explanations have been put forth to account for this decline, the NYPD continues to be a focal point of controversy. Central to this debate are the changes that Commissioner William Bratton instituted under his tenure—most notably, the adoption of order-maintenance policing (OMP) to address disorder and low-level crime, widespread use of SQF, and CompStat (a computer management system "defined by timely and accurate information, rapid deployment of resources, effective tactics, follow-up and assessment"[7]). These changes, however, did not occur independently of events in the city and the department.

New York City, like many cities across the United States, faced a major spike in violence, crime, and disorder in the 1980s.[8] Many attributed the rise in crime rates to the emergence of crack cocaine.[9]

Crack cocaine is a smoked version of cocaine that provides a short, but extremely intense high. The invention of crack represented a technology innovation that dramatically widened the availability and use of cocaine in inner cities. Virtually unheard of prior to the mid-1980s, crack spread quickly across the country, particularly within Black and Hispanic communities. . . . Sold in small quantities in relatively anonymous street markets, crack provided a lucrative market for drug sellers and street gangs. . . . Much of the violence [associated with crack] is attributed to attempts to establish property rights not enforceable through legal means.[10]

The crack cocaine epidemic contributed to a significant rise in New York City's homicide rate.[11] In fact, the number of homicides in the city increased exponentially, from 1,392 in 1985 to 2,262 in 1990. The streets of New York City, along with the subway system, were also flooded with social and physical disorder. Drug dealers became a widespread problem on street corners and in city parks, where they were openly selling marijuana, heroin, and cocaine—especially in crack form. Drug use and transactions were readily observable on the street. The crack cocaine epidemic in New York City was of particular concern because selling crews relied on guns and violence to maintain their clientele and territory.[12] In addition to the flourishing drug market, New York City was also rife with beggars and panhandlers, especially in the subways. Although some were passive and peaceful, others would aggressively solicit subway users for money. The beggar and panhandler problem became so pronounced that "[a]pproximately 1,200 to 2,000 persons a night were sleeping in the subway. . . . Following on the heels of disorder and petty crimes, robbery and felonies started a steep increase in 1987."[13]

In response to the crime and disorder problems in the subway system, the New York Transit Authority appointed William Bratton chief of the Transit Police in 1990. Bratton was tasked with addressing the "underworld's" disorderly behavior and crime problems. He tapped criminologist George Kelling as a consultant. Through the use of a broken windows–based enforcement strategy, officers began remedying social and physical disorder by arresting and ejecting panhandlers, homeless, and low-level offenders from the subway system. Over the next two years, felony crimes dropped by 30 percent and riders began feeling a sense of safety in the subway system.[14] Given the success of Chief Bratton's enforcement strategy in the subway system, newly elected Mayor Rudolph Giuliani named Bratton the NYPD commissioner in 1994.

Bratton immediately set about altering the NYPD to reflect the theoretical underpinnings of the broken windows theory. This perspective argues that minor forms of disorder have a contagious effect that facilitates the onset of more serious crime problems. If the police do not address various forms of social and physical disorder, law-abiding citizens will refrain from exercising informal social control and community regulation, which will ultimately invite more serious offenders to settle into the neighborhood.[15] Consequently, disorder that is not addressed (e.g., broken windows) engenders a cycle that breeds more disorder, leading to the breakdown of community standards and the onset of crime. In order to restore the neighborhood to normalcy, the police aggressively focus efforts on minor forms of social and physical disorder so that law-abiding citizens can strengthen the dynamics of social regulation and social control, and the disorder-crime cycle will be broken.[16]

Broken windows theory served as the foundation for the NYPD's "order-maintenance policing" (OMP) philosophy.[17] OMP applies a zero tolerance mindset with regard to social disorder (e.g., public drunkenness, vandalism, loitering, panhandling, etc.), but it can also embrace central tenets of community policing. In theory, this means that OMP can combat disorder while minimizing coercive encounters with citizens on the street, and engaging the community as partners in controlling crime and disorder. The problem, however, is that "New York moved in a very different direction, exchanging amelioration of physical disorder for interdiction of social disorder."[18] Hence, instead of adhering to a new set of standards premised on positive social interactions and partnerships with law-abiding citizens, the NYPD focused exclusively on the aggressive pursuit of disorderly people through indicators of stops and arrests.[19]

The NYPD's OMP philosophy was defined, in large part, by two written policy documents. First, *Reclaiming the Public Spaces of New York* reconstructed the broken window theory such that streets were targeted through systematic and aggressive enforcement strategies aimed at low-level social disorder.[20] The second policy, described in *Getting Guns off the Streets of New York*,[21] sought to reduce gun violence by thoroughly investigating incidents and arrests involving guns, following up on leads in those cases, and aggressively targeting illegal gun carrying.[22] Stop and frisk became a primary tactic defining both initiatives: combatting social disorder and targeting gun violence. The combination of OMP with "gun-oriented policing" was thought to act as a potential deterrent to gun-related crimes because "[s]topping people on minor infractions also made it riskier for criminals to carry guns in public."[23] By 1998, the NYPD had confiscated more than 50,000 guns, resulting in 40,000 gun-related arrests.[24] Though SQF has been used primarily as a tool in the NYPD efforts to seize guns and address social disorder, it also emerged as a central component of the department's targeted effort against marijuana. Criminologists Amanda Geller and Jeffrey Fagan reported that in 2006 alone there were 32,000 arrests for marijuana possession, a 500 percent increase from the previous decade.[25]

Bellin notes that the development of SQF as a massive enforcement program has its origins in the initial gun interdiction efforts devised by the NYPD.[26] Quickly after becoming commissioner, William Bratton had identified gun crime as one of the primary sources of violent crime in the city, and in fact, the NYPD's *Getting Guns off the Streets* report stated that, from 1960 to 1992, the number of murders committed with a handgun in New York had increased by 2,000 percent.[27] In order to achieve the goals laid out in the *Getting Guns off the Streets* document, the department tripled the size of the Street Crime Unit in 1997, and tasked the unit with aggressive gun interdiction in violent crime hot spots.[28] Though the Street Crime Unit relied on a variety of tactics, stop and frisk became increasingly common. In 1998 the Street Crime Unit (approximately 380 officers) alone generated 27,000 stop and frisks.[29] By the time the NYPD disbanded the SCU in 2002 (as part of the original *Daniels* settlement), SQF had already been integrated into the department's CompStat and hot spot strategies as a quantitative indicator of officer activity and as an overall measure of the NYPD's performance in terms of generating reductions in crime.[30] This development is largely consistent with criminologists Skolnick and Fyfe's articulation of the "numbers game," where a focus on quantitative indicators of internal activity overtakes a department's concern with more appropriate measures of officer (and department) performance.[31]

The two aforementioned policies resulted in policing tactics that strayed from the original contentions of broken windows theory. First, the NYPD's version of policing social disorder emphasized arresting and prosecuting individuals who committed disorder offenses. During police stops, individuals were often questioned and checked for outstanding police warrants.[32] In short, rather than preventing disorder from snowballing into more serious crime, the focus on disorder offenses became a way to remove weapons, wanted criminals, and disorderly people from the community. Second, community engagement was virtually absent from the NYPD's crime-control efforts. Instead, the department embraced an internally focused management style from the private sector[33] that stressed innovative approaches to management accountability, prioritization, and information-based decision making.[34] The outcome of such changes included various structural modifications and the development and implementation of CompStat. Essentially, the NYPD relied upon its data-driven accountability system to identify community needs, rather than engaging and asking the citizens who reside in the community.[35]

CompStat, coupled with aggressive OMP and stop and frisk in high-crime areas, would for the next two decades serve as the foundation of the NYPD's crime-control effort. This effort, particularly stop and frisk, intensified under Operation Impact, which focused police resources on identified areas where crime was concentrated (i.e., "impact zones" or hot spots). Based on data from crime analysts, commanders identified twenty-four impact zones where they would deploy additional police resources.[36] In January 2003, the NYPD deployed approximately 1,500 recent academy graduates to the newly identified impact zones, and the new officers were encouraged to enforce misdemeanor laws and aggressively employ SQF.[37] Criminologist John MacDonald and colleagues noted that impact zones evolved over time, as some were temporary and others were more permanent: "Seventy-five of the 76 precincts in NYC had an impact zone on at least a few blocks between 2004 and 2012. However, the share of impact zones was devoted largely to high crime precincts where a majority of the residents are Black and Latino."[38] Once Operation Impact started, the number of SQFs grew exponentially over the next decade,[39] and it seems clear that the strategy became a quantitative measure of both individual officer and department-wide performance (i.e., Skolnick and Fyfe's "numbers game").[40]

The Crime Decline in New York

The crime decline in New York was large in magnitude and long in duration. The extent to which the New York City crime decline was larger and longer than declines in other cities in the United States and abroad remains a subject of debate. Comparing New York's 2009 crime rates to their highest historic levels, law professor Franklin Zimring found a reduction in homicide, rape, robbery, assault, burglary, auto theft, and theft rates equivalent to 82 percent, 77 percent, 84 percent, 67 percent, 86 percent, 94 percent, and 63 percent, respectively.[41] Putting these differentials in perspective, New York's homicide and theft rates in 2009 were 18 percent and 6 percent of its 1990 total. Zimring argues that, even when compared to New York's less extreme crime periods, there were still reductions in crime trends that make New York a statistical anomaly. Not only was New York's crime decline large in magnitude, but it was "twice the length of the national downward trend and the longest big-city decline that has yet been documented

TABLE 4.1. Crime Patterns in Six Cities, 1990–2009

	Homi-cide	Rape	Robbery	Assault	Burglary	Auto theft	Larceny
New York	-82%	-77%	-84%	-67%	-86%	-94%	-63%
Los Angeles	-71%	-59%	-69%	-78%	-68%	-68%	-58%
Houston	-64%	-56%	-37%	20%	-51%	-74%	-30%
San Diego	-75%	-39%	-63%	-57%	-66%	-67%	-56%
San Jose	-36%	-49%	-19%	-46%	-47%	-66%	-54%
Boston	-68%	-54%	-65%	-52%	-73%	-89%	-52%

Source: Federal Bureau of Investigation. See also Zimring, *The City That Became Safe.*

with reliable crime statistics."[42] Indeed, New York's downward trend continued through the end of 2009. Between 2000 and 2009, homicide, rape, robbery, assault, burglary, larceny, and auto theft rates declined 33 percent, 51 percent, 46 percent, 38 percent, 52 percent, 23 percent, and 72 percent, respectively.[43] Although the magnitude was not as substantial as the 1990–2000 era, it was still robust relative to other cities across the United States.

The magnitude and duration of the New York City crime decline cannot be fully understood without comparison to other large U.S. cities. From 1990 through 2009, New York's declines in the rates of homicide, rape, robbery, assault, burglary, auto theft, and larceny were greater than those in Los Angeles, Houston, San Diego, San Jose, and Boston, with assault in Los Angeles being the one exception (see table 4.1). The only big city to rival New York's crime decline was Los Angeles, but as Zimring explains, New York's crime decline was greater in magnitude if the two cities were compared to their 1990 levels of crime.[44] Some researchers have questioned the use of official police reports to examine the crime decline, given known limitations with citizen reporting, as well as the potential for data falsification and tampering with reports.[45] In an effort to address this concern, criminologists Janet Lauritsen and Robin Schaum cross-referenced data from the Uniform Crime Report (UCR) with the National Crime Victimization Survey (NCVS) and found consistency for burglary and robbery rates, with less agreement for aggravated assault rates.[46] Similar degrees of convergence have also been documented when contrasting UCR data against health statistics and insurance company data.[47]

Other researchers, however, have found that New York's crime rates did not decline at exceptional levels.[48] In perhaps the most comprehensive study to date, criminologists Eric Baumer and Kevin Wolff examined the uniqueness of the New York City crime decline by comparing the trends in New York to trends in other American cities, as well as other countries across the globe.[49] The authors assert that the crime decline actually started in New York during the early 1980s before being interrupted by an "aberrant, relatively brief violence epidemic" during the late 1980s and early 1990s; that much of the crime decline in cities across the United States is part of a "shared trend" as well as national-level conditions; and that most cross-national examinations of crime also show substantial declines (Canada, England and Wales, Netherlands, Finland, France, Australia, and Scotland), albeit slighter later than the decreases documented in the United States.[50]

The NYPD's Use of Stop and Frisk

SQF encounters in New York are recorded on UF-250 forms (figure 4.1). The information from these UF-250 forms provides the basis for the NYPD's official statistics on SQFs. Because an officer may not record a stop on a UF-250 form, the official data available on the NYPD's website may not capture all SQFs. Some estimate that the NYPD may only be documenting approximately 70 percent of all SQFs.[51] Other estimates suggest that the non-reporting problem may be much larger. For example, in 2012 the Civilian Complaint Review Board found that 20 percent of the complaints it received regarding *Terry* stops did not have an accompanying UF-250 form (up from 5 percent in 2008).[52] And, as stated previously, one NYPD commander suggested that the non-reporting rate could be as high as 90 percent.[53] Regardless, the NYPD's

(COMPLETE ALL CAPTIONS)

STOP, QUESTION AND FRISK REPORT WORKSHEET
PD344-151A (Rev. 11-02)

Pct.Serial No.		
Date		Pct. Of Occ.

Time Of Stop	Period Of Observation Prior To Stop	Radio Run/Sprint #

Address/Intersection Or Cross Streets Of Stop

☐ Inside ☐ Transit	Type Of Location
☐ Outside ☐ Housing	Describe:

Specify Which Felony/P.L. Misdemeanor Suspected	Duration Of Stop

What Were Circumstances Which Led To Stop?
(MUST CHECK AT LEAST ONE BOX)

☐ Carrying Objects In Plain View Used In Commission Of Crime e.g., Slim Jim/Pry Bar, etc.
☐ Fits Description.
☐ Actions Indicative Of "Casing" Victim Or Location.
☐ Actions Indicative of Acting As A Lookout.
☐ Suspicious Bulge/Object (Describe)
☐ Other Reasonable Suspicion Of Criminal Activity (Specify)

☐ Actions Indicative Of Engaging In Drug Transaction.
☐ Furtive Movements.
☐ Actions Indicative Of Engaging In Violent Crimes.
☐ Wearing Clothes/Disguises Commonly Used In Commission Of Crime.

Name Of Person Stopped	Nickname/ Street Name	Date Of Birth
Address	Apt. No.	Tel. No.

Identification: ☐ Verbal ☐ Photo I.D. ☐ Refused
☐ Other (Specify) _____

Sex:☐ Male Race:☐ White ☐ Black ☐ White Hispanic ☐ Black Hispanic
☐ Female ☐ Asian/Pacific Islander ☐ American Indian/Alaskan Native

Age	Height	Weight	Hair	Eyes	Build

Other (Scars, Tattoos, Etc.)

Did Officer Explain Reason For Stop ☐ Yes ☐ No	If No, Explain:

Were Other Persons Stopped/ Questioned/Frisked?	☐ Yes ☐ No	If Yes, List Pct. Serial Nos.

If Physical Force Was Used, Indicate Type:
☐ Hands On Suspect
☐ Suspect On Ground
☐ Pointing Firearm At Suspect
☐ Handcuffing Suspect
☐ Suspect Against Wall/Car
☐ Drawing Firearm
☐ Baton
☐ Pepper Spray
☐ Other (Describe)

Was Suspect Arrested? ☐ Yes ☐ No	Offense	Arrest No.
Was Summons Issued? ☐ Yes ☐ No	Offense	Summons No.
Officer In Uniform? ☐ Yes ☐ No	If No, How Identified? ☐ Shield ☐ I.D. Card ☐ Verbal	

Was Person Frisked? ☐ Yes ☐ No   IF YES, MUST CHECK AT LEAST ONE BOX

☐ Inappropriate Attire - Possibly Concealing Weapon   ☐ Furtive Movements   ☐ Refusal To Comply With Officer's Direction(s)
☐ Verbal Threats Of Violence By Suspect   ☐ Actions Indicative Of   Leading To Reasonable Fear For Safety
☐ Knowledge Of Suspects Prior Criminal   Engaging In Violent   ☐ Violent Crime Suspected
   Violent Behavior/Use Of Force/Use Of Weapon   Crimes   ☐ Suspicious Bulge/Object (Describe)
☐ Other Reasonable Suspicion of Weapons (Specify)

Was Person Searched? ☐ Yes ☐ No   IF YES, MUST CHECK AT LEAST ONE BOX ☐ Hard Object ☐ Admission Of Weapons Possession
☐ Outline Of Weapon   ☐ Other Reasonable Suspicion of Weapons (Specify)

Was Weapon Found? ☐ Yes   ☐ No   If Yes, Describe: ☐ Pistol/Revolver ☐ Rifle/Shotgun ☐ Assault Weapon ☐ Knife/Cutting Instrument
☐ Machine Gun ☐ Other (Describe)

Was Other Contraband Found?   ☐ Yes ☐ No If Yes, Describe Contraband And Location _____
Demeanor Of Person After Being Stopped _____
Remarks Made By Person Stopped

Additional Circumstances/Factors: (Check All That Apply)

☐ Report From Victim/Witness   ☐ Evasive, False Or Inconsistent Response To Officer's Questions
☐ Area Has High Incidence Of Reported Offense Of Type Under Investigation ☐ Changing Direction At Sight Of Officer/Flight
☐ Time Of Day, Day Of Week, Season Corresponding To Reports Of   ☐ Ongoing Investigations, e.g., Robbery Pattern
   Criminal Activity   ☐ Sights And Sounds Of Criminal Activity, e.g., Bloodstains, Ringing
☐ Suspect Is Associating With Persons Known For Their Criminal Activity   Alarms
☐ Proximity To Crime Location
☐ Other (Describe)

| Pct. Serial No. _____ | Additional Reports Prepared: Complaint Rpt.No. _____ | Juvenile Rpt. No. _____ | Aided Rpt. No. _____ | Other Rpt. (Specify) _____ |

REPORTED BY: Rank, Name (Last, First, M.I.)   REVIEWED BY: Rank, Name (Last, First, M.I.)
Print _____ Tax# _____   Print _____ Tax# _____
Signature _____ Command _____   Signature _____ Command _____

FIGURE 4.1 *(opposite and above).* Front and back of NYPD UF-250 Form.
Source: Jones-Brown et al., *Stop, Question, and Frisk Policing Practices in New York City.*

use of the practice increased substantially beginning in 2003. As figure 4.2 illustrates, the number of SQFs more than quadrupled from 2003 through 2011, where it peaked at 685,724 stops. As public pressure and litigation mounted in 2012, the NYPD's use of SQFs started to decline. This decline accelerated with the federal court ruling in the *Floyd v. City of New York* case in 2013 and the subsequent mayoral election.[54] The

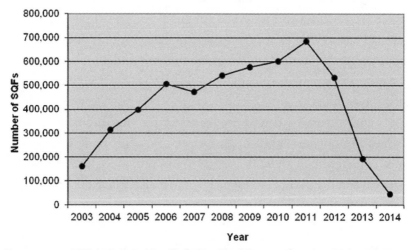

FIGURE 4.2. SQF Activity in New York City: Total Stops, 2003–2014. Source: Morrow, "Examining the Potential for Racial/Ethnic Disparities in Use of Force during NYPD Stop-and-Frisk Activities."

most recent estimates suggest that the NYPD generated just 45,787 SQFs in 2014, which marks a 93.3 percent decrease from the 2011 numbers.

The effectiveness of stop and frisk in producing gun seizures and arrests was modest and declined notably over time. In 2003, for instance, the NYPD recovered 627 guns through 160,851 stops, meaning that 0.3 percent of stops resulted in gun seizures. In 2011, at the SQF policy's peak, the discovery of illegal firearms declined even further. The NYPD found 780 guns through 685,724 stops; in other words, 0.1 percent of stops led to confiscated firearms.[55] Similarly, the number of arrests resulting from stop and frisk activities has also remained relatively flat over the years. The rate of stop and frisks resulting in arrest in 2008, 2009, 2010, 2011, and 2012 hovered between 5 and 6 percent (5.9 percent, 6.1 percent, 6.8 percent, 5.9 percent, and 6.1 percent, respectively).[56]

The Theoretical Rationale

Justification for the increased use of SQFs, especially between 2003 and 2011 in New York, is primarily grounded in a deterrence-based philosophy. Deterrence theory stems from early classical theorists, such as Cesare Beccaria and Jeremy Bentham, who posited that people are rational actors who choose to engage in behavior only after performing a cost–benefit analysis, weighing the pros and cons by balancing the pleasure to be gained from the behavior against the potential pain that the conduct might engender, especially if punishment follows.[57] The logic underlying deterrence theory is that stop and frisk prevents crimes from occurring through two mechanisms. First, in line with specific deterrence, there is a reduction in crime because individuals who have in the past been stopped by the police will avoid engaging in behavior in the future that will again draw the attention of the police. As a result, potential offenders will not carry a gun and they will refrain from engaging in suspicious or criminal behavior.[58] Second, through the general deterrence perspective, individuals may refrain from criminal behavior because they are aware of (or witness) SQF activities and they want to avoid the possibility of being stopped by the police themselves.[59] Whether a deterrence-based rationale is reasonable is still subject to debate, as research that examines deterrence more generally is mixed.[60]

The low arrest and confiscation rates of NYPD stops is often debated in the deterrence context. Critics argue that the low "return" rates are an indicator of the ineffectiveness of the tactic and strongly suggest racial discrimination.[61] For example,

> In 2003, the second year of Mayor Michael R. Bloomberg's first term, police officers confiscated 627 guns through 160,851 stop-and-frisk encounters: a success rate of one gun for every 266 stops. Last year [(2011)], the police seized 780 guns through 685,724 stop-and-frisk encounters [a success rate of one gun for every 879 stops].[62]

New York City officials and the NYPD, however, have argued the opposite: that the low rates of arrest and gun confiscations demonstrate the deterrent value of stop and frisk. "Knowing there is a strong likelihood they will be stopped by the police, the argument goes, deters would-be offenders from carrying weapons and contraband or otherwise engaging in criminal activity."[63]

Studies That Examine the Role of the NYPD in the New York Crime Decline

There is no consensus among scholars who examine the impact of the NYPD on New York City crime levels. Several studies have found an association between NYPD activities and declines in crime. Corman and Mocan reported that misdemeanor arrests were associated with declines in robbery, motor vehicle theft, and grand larceny, but not homicide, assault, burglary and rape.[64] Kelling and Sousa found that misdemeanor arrest levels were significantly associated with reductions in violent crime, while controlling for several relevant community factors.[65] Smith and Purtell evaluated the NYPD's efforts to combat violent crime through Operation Impact.[66] Using panel data from 1990 through 2006 in an interrupted time-series evaluation, the authors found that Operation Impact had a significant effect on crimes against persons in impact zones. Research has also suggested an impact on gun-carrying and firearm injuries. Data from the Centers for Disease Control and the New York City Department of Health and Mental Hygiene show that gun carrying among New York City high school students declined from 4.2 percent in 1997 to 2.3 percent in 2011.[67] New York City data also show that hospitalizations for firearms injuries declined by 20 percent from 2000 to 2011.[68]

One of the biggest advocates of the NYPD's role in the crime decline has been Franklin Zimring. In his book *The City That Became Safe: New York's Lessons for Urban Crime and Its Control*, Zimring argues that New York's crime decline from 1990 through 2009 was largely attributable to the NYPD's policing practices, including CompStat, hot spots policing, and a more aggressive approach targeting public drug markets.[69] Taken together, these policing strategies and priorities led Zimring to draw the following conclusion about the NYPD's role in the city's crime decline:

> The package of changes in the quantity and quality of policing should get credit for what I have called "the New York difference"—a crime decline close to 35% for some offenses—by a process of elimination. There are simply no other changes in policy, social conditions, or economics that could plausibly explain the city's much better than typical performance in the crime drop years of the 1990s and in the nine years after the general crime decline stopped.[70]

Other studies have documented only weak or no effects. Rosenfeld, Fornango, and Rengifo explored this question with a rigorous methodology that controlled for a wide range of precinct-level characteristics, and found that the NYPD's order-maintenance policing strategy (OMP, measured as misdemeanor arrests and ordinance violations) was associated with small declines in robbery and homicide (4 and 10 percent);

the authors reported, however, that the reductions started before the NYPD initiated the police strategy.[71] Messner and colleagues found that OMP was significantly related to gun-related homicides, but not non–gun-related homicides, though again, the effect was relatively small.[72] Baumer and Wolff conducted a comprehensive analysis of crime trends in New York, other American cities, and cities in other countries; they concluded that much of the New York City crime decline is explained by national and global factors.[73]

Direct Tests of the SQF–Crime Decline Link

Paul Browne, a spokesman for the NYPD, has stated that the crime decline is at least "in part because of stop, question, and frisk."[74] Commissioner Bratton also recently said that "any police department in America that tries to function without some form of 'stop-question-frisk,' or whatever the terminology they use, is doomed to failure. It's that simple."[75] Despite the explosion in SQFs since 2003 (see figure 4.2), only a few studies have examined whether SQF activity has directly influenced crime rates, and the findings are, again, mixed.

Smith and Purtell conducted a follow-up to their Operation Impact study to more specifically examine the effects of SQF on crime in New York. They found that there was a significant inverse relationship between SQF rates and robbery, burglary, motor vehicle theft, and homicides rates.[76] Conversely, SQF activity was not associated with rates of assault, rape, or grand larceny. The authors also noted that there was a diminishing return over time.

Scholars have highlighted a number of methodological limitations in the Smith and Purtell article.[77] Criminologists Rosenfeld and Fornango addressed many of these methodological concerns, as the authors examined the "effects of total police stops and stops of Black, Hispanic, and white suspects on yearly precinct robbery and burglary rates over the period 2003–2010."[78] Rosenfeld and Fornango found virtually no effects of SQF on crime, with the exception of one "marginally significant" relationship between burglary and two-year lagged stop and frisk totals.[79] Rosenfeld and Fornango offer some cautionary thoughts about continued use of the strategy:

> But we can be more certain that, if there is an impact, it is so localized and dissipates so rapidly that it fails to register in annual precinct crime rates, much less the decade-long citywide crime reductions that public officials have attributed to the policy. If SQF is effective, but its effects are highly focused and fleeting, policy-makers must decide whether expansions in a policy that already produces 700,000 police stops a year are warranted, especially given the ongoing controversy regarding the disproportionate impact of SQF on racial and ethnic minorities and the possibility that it reduces police legitimacy, which may erode its crime-reduction effects over the long term.[80]

More recently, criminologist John MacDonald and colleagues conducted a comprehensive examination of the crime effects of Operation Impact (with a specific focus on SQF), and concluded that "Operation Impact was not a major contributor to crime reductions in NYC."[81] They note that the NYPD would have been better served by implementing a more limited SQF program that included stops based on more objective criteria.

Weisburd and colleagues took a different approach and examined whether the NYPD's use of SQF is consistent with the evidence-based strategy, "hot spots policing."[82] Hot spots policing is grounded in real-time crime analysis that identifies high concentrations of crime in relatively small areas (much smaller than NYPD precincts), and police then target resources to those areas (see chapter 6 for more discussion of hot spots). Given that the NYPD decreased in size by approximately 17 percent during a time when it significantly increased SQF activity, the authors concluded that the NYPD "was able to do more with less" by focusing *Terry* stops on crime hot spots.[83] The researchers do suggest that the NYPD could have maintained similar crime declines with less damage to relations with minority citizens if they had incorporated procedural justice and legitimacy into their strategies.[84]

Bellin makes an interesting and compelling case that the NYPD's SQF program did serve as an effective deterrent against illegal gun carrying, and as a consequence, the program played a role in the crime decline.[85] However, he argues that the effectiveness of the NYPD's SQF program was intimately tied to its unconstitutionality, arguing that the only way to produce a deterrent effect among illegal gun carriers, who will strive to avoid police attention by otherwise abstaining from suspicious or criminal conduct, is to engage in arbitrary (and unconstitutional) stops:

> NYC Stop and Frisk, if conceptualized as a program to deter gun-carrying, necessarily depends on stopping people without individualized suspicion. The theory justifying mass stop-and-frisk is that people will leave their guns at home to keep their weapons from being uncovered by an officer's frisk. In this scenario, the likelihood of a frisk determines the deterrent effect. If a frisk can be avoided by avoiding criminal activity such as trespassing, public marijuana smoking or public urination, people can comfortably carry guns unlawfully so long as they obey (or think they will obey) other laws while doing so. Thus, a high volume of arbitrary frisks is essential to effectively deter gun possession. The knowledge that a stop-and-frisk is almost inevitable powerfully deters gun possession.[86]

Bellin goes on to conclude that "a massive stop-and-frisk program can be constitutional or effective, but not both."[87] We find this conclusion to be compelling and worthy of serious consideration by police departments that are planning or maintaining stop and frisk programs.

Research on SQF and Crime Rates in Other Jurisdictions

Research evaluating the effectiveness of SQFs on crime in jurisdictions other than New York is extremely rare. An early study in San Diego examined the impact of field interrogations of citizens on crime, and results indicated that the tactic was associated with declines in burglary and petty theft in some areas of the city.[88] Two studies have documented a decrease in gun crimes following the implementation of aggressive enforcement strategies that included SQF. In Kansas City, criminologists Sherman and Rogan evaluated a focused gun enforcement strategy in a concentrated violent crime hot spot. Over a six-month study period, they found a 65 percent increase in firearms seizures and a 49 percent decrease in gun crimes.[89] In Pittsburgh, researchers reported a 70 percent decline in gunshot injuries following implementation of targeted patrols that increased police presence by 25–50 percent during high crime times, and they attributed the decrease to a deterrent effect that reduced gun carrying.[90]

Police scholars Ratcliffe and colleagues conducted a study to determine whether increased foot patrol in randomly selected hot spot areas would reduce violent crime counts.[91] The increase in foot patrol was mirrored by an increase in pedestrian stops, car stops, disturbances (e.g., disorderly crowds), narcotic incidents, disorder incidents, and arrests. The researchers found that foot patrol produced significant declines in violent crime in the most violent hot spots, but not in less crime-prone areas. Although Ratcliffe and colleagues did not look specifically at the impact of pedestrian stops on violent crimes, they did state in a footnote that "each violent crime reduction was associated with an additional 89 pedestrian stops, 8 vehicle stops, 4 arrests, 35 disturbance incidents, 4 disorder incidents, and an additional narcotics incident."[92] The authors, however, make no causal connection and did not use pedestrian stops independently to predict violent crime.

In sum, only two studies have directly assessed the impact of SQF on crime in New York, and virtually no research has examined this question in other jurisdictions. The two New York studies[93] produced contradictory results, and the difference in findings is likely attributable to variation in the methodologies employed by the authors. Regardless, the impact of SQF activity on crime is still largely uncertain, leading

Weisburd and colleagues to conclude that "there will simply be no un-ambiguous answer to the question of whether the police [and SQF specifically] contributed significantly to the New York City crime decline."[94] We agree with this assessment, and we return to two points made previously: first, that a massive SQF program is at great risk of devolving into routine unconstitutional stops of citizens; and second, that a more just, professional approach would involve the use of evidence-based alternatives with few collateral consequences.

The Diminishing Returns and Collateral Consequences of SQF

Many scholars have argued that the excessive use of stop and frisk has come at the cost of racial and ethnic tension, compromised police legitimacy, and devastating effects on citizens' emotional and physical well-being. These costs are in addition to the constitutional violations that occur when police use stop and frisk in a racially discriminatory manner.

Research clearly demonstrates that SQF tactics employed by the NYPD have disproportionately targeted minority citizens in mostly poor neighborhoods. An independent review by the office of the New York state attorney general Elliot Spitzer, released in 1999, concluded that 15 percent of the stops examined did not meet the reasonable suspicion threshold and as a result were unconstitutional.[95] The prevalence of unconstitutional stops was even higher (23 percent) for the NYPD's Street Crime Unit, which was responsible for the shooting death of Amadou Diallo earlier that year. Diallo, an unarmed African immigrant, was shot to death by four officers while he was standing at the entrance of his Bronx apartment building (the incident led to the initial state inquiry).[96] The attorney general's report also investigated racial disparities in SQF and found that Black and Hispanic citizens were disproportionately targeted for stops at rates that could not be explained by community demographics (racial makeup) or crime levels.[97] Similarly, Fagan and colleagues found that "[i]n a fifteen-month period from January 1998 through March 1999, non-Hispanic Black, Hispanic Black, and Hispanic White New Yorkers were three times more likely than their White counterparts to be stopped and frisked on suspicion of weapons or violent crimes."[98] Even in neighborhoods with low ethnic minority concentrations, Black and Hispanic stop rates were still well above their population percentage. The key question is whether this disproportionality is a result of racial discrimination, and both researchers and the federal courts have weighed in on this question.

In response to claims of racial bias in 2006, the NYPD asked the RAND Corporation to conduct a study on the issue. Its report found racial disparities in the more than 500,000 stops conducted in 2006.[99] Of those individuals who were stopped, 89 percent were non-White (53 percent were Black; 29 percent were Hispanic; 11 percent were White). Moreover, "forty-five percent of Black and Hispanic suspects were frisked, compared with 29 percent of white suspects; yet, when frisked, white suspects were 70 percent likelier than Black suspects to have had a weapon on them."[100] However, the RAND researchers concluded that although their more sophisticated analyses could not explain the racial disproportionality in stops, the disparities were small, and "a large-scale restructuring of NYPD SQF policies and procedures is unwarranted."[101]

Alternatively, other scholars found that the NYPD stopped minorities 1.5 to 2.5 times more often than Whites, even after controlling for crime rate.[102] Jones-Brown and colleagues found that, of the 540,320 stops in 2008, just 6.0 percent resulted in an arrest (and an additional 6.4 percent resulted in a summons).[103] It was also noted that the percentage of "innocent stops"—those not resulting in summons or arrest—has consistently remained between 86 and 90 percent, yet the percentage of stops resulting in the recovery of a gun has dropped by 60 percent (from 0.39 percent in 2003 to 0.15 percent in 2008), and the percentage of citizen complaints involving SQF has increased from 24.6 percent in 2004 to 32.7 percent in 2008.[104] Fagan and colleagues identified three notable findings in their study of NYPD SQF practices:

- First, stops within neighborhoods take place at rates in excess of what would be predicted from the separate and combined effects of population demography, physical and social conditions, and the crime rate. This excess seems to be concentrated in predominantly Black neighborhoods.
- Second, the excess stops in these neighborhoods persist over time, even as the Black population declines, crime rates remain low and effectively unchanged, the city's overall social and economic health improves, and housing and other investments increase across the city's neighborhoods, including its poorest and most segregated neighborhoods.
- Third, there appears to be a declining return in crime detection from marginal increases in enforcement, and this efficiency gap seems to grow over time.[105]

Moreover, New York City and NYPD leaders often made public comments that reflected the racial overtones of the department's SQF program. During his testimony in the *Floyd* case, state senator Adams attributed comments to Police Commissioner Kelly stating that SQF was effective because it created a fear among minority youth "that they could be stopped and frisked every time they leave their homes so that they are less likely to carry weapons."[106] Commissioner Kelly and Mayor Bloomberg both stated publicly that, according to the department's statistics on violent crime suspects, "we disproportionately stop whites too much and minorities too little."[107] And in 2013, an officer in the Fortieth Precinct recorded his commanding officer directing him to stop "the right people, at the right time, at the right location," described as "male [B]lacks, 14 to 20, 21."[108] The overt racially charged statements, along with clear racial disproportionality in the administration of the SQF program, provide an important backdrop for the decade-long litigation accusing the NYPD of discrimination.

Concern over the NYPD's aggressive enforcement practices, including SQF, have also extended to the department's relationship with the city's Arabic and Muslim communities. News reporter James Nislow noted that the 9/11 terrorist attacks fundamentally changed public perceptions of the police and racial profiling: "After years of enduring harsh criticism and suspicion from the public for alleged racial profiling practices, law enforcement in the aftermath of the World Trade Center disaster has suddenly found itself on the high road, as some who once considered the practice taboo are now eager for police to bend the rules when it comes to Middle Easterners."[109] Anthropologist Avram Bornstein highlighted the impact of the NYPD's increased scrutiny on Arabic and Muslim residents, echoing Nislow's point that many of the concerns associated with racial profiling of African Americans became increasingly evident in a new form of terrorist profiling:

> Before 9/11, the debate was if there was or was not systematic racial profiling by police of [B]lack people. Everyone agreed that it was wrong, but they did not agree that it occurred. After 9/11, the debate became *should* there be or not be profiling of Arabs and Muslims.[110]

Concerns about this new form of profiling increased notably in August 2011, when the Associated Press published a report detailing an NYPD "human mapping" program that employed undercover officers and surveillance techniques in Muslim communities.[111] The program, developed through a partnership with the CIA, drew significant criticism from Muslim leaders and legal advocacy groups, and raised serious questions about the pervasiveness of a racially insensitive mindset in the leadership of the NYPD.

The Federal Litigation over the NYPD's SQF Program

The widespread deployment of SQF by the NYPD resulted in two major lawsuits alleging racial profiling. In *Daniels v. City of New York*, the Center for Constitutional Rights (CCR) challenged the NYPD's use of SQF without reasonable suspicion under the Fourth and Fourteenth Amendments, and alleged that officers were selectively targeting individuals on the basis of their race and national origin in violation of the Equal Protection Clause of the Fourteenth Amendment to the U.S. Constitution.[112]

Of particular concern was the NYPD's Street Crime Unit (SCU). When the lawsuit was filed, the SCU was an elite commando unit comprising more than three hundred officers who patrolled the streets of New York City in unmarked cars and plain clothes. On one night in February 1999, a team of SCU officers shot and killed Amadou Diallo.[113] The death of Diallo not only ignited citywide demonstrations against police brutality, but also invited close scrutiny of the SCU.[114] Upon inspection, the New York state attorney general found that the SCU stopped sixteen African Americans for every arrest made.[115] Upon settling the civil suit, the NYPD agreed to maintain a written anti-racial profiling policy, whereby officers and their supervisors were audited to make sure that SQFs were properly documented and based on reasonable suspicion.[116]

Despite the settlement in the first case, the CCR continued to document racial disparities in SQF practices, leading to the filing of a second lawsuit against the NYPD in 2008, *Floyd v. City of New York*.[117] The named plaintiffs in the second lawsuit were David Floyd, Lalit Clarkson, David Ourlicht, and Deon Dennis, but they represented hundreds of thousands of New Yorkers who, according to the CCR, had been stopped because of their race or ethnicity. The allegations against the NYPD were based primarily on the expert reports of criminologist Jeffrey Fagan,[118] as well as analyses carried out by the CCR.[119] The CCR report revealed that 80 percent of the stops made by the NYPD involved Blacks and Latinos, who represented only 25 percent and 28 percent of the city's population, respectively.[120] Moreover, between 2005 and 2008, Blacks and Latinos were more likely to be frisked and to have had physical force used against them during their stops (compared to Whites). For example, force was used in 24 percent of encounters involving Black and Hispanic citizens, compared to 17 percent of stops of Whites.

Fagan's expert reports in the *Floyd* case analyzed the NYPD's SQF data from 2004 to 2009, and from January 2010 through June 2012.[121] Fagan concluded that the NYPD engaged in unconstitutional stop and frisk practices that targeted predominately Black and Latino New Yorkers. After controlling for crime, neighborhood context, and the concen-

TABLE 4.2. Summary of Findings from the Fagan Expert Opinion in the *Floyd* Case

Fourth Amendment Claim

- Nearly 150,000, or 6.71 percent, of all discretionary stops lack legal justification. An additional 544,252, or 24.37 percent, of all discretionary stops lack sufficiently detailed documentation to assess their legality.

- Officers rely heavily on two constitutionally problematic stop justifications for nearly half of all stops: furtive movements and proximity to a high-crime area.

- Documented stop justifications do little to explain overall variations in stop patterns and do not substantially influence the racial disparities that characterize stop practices between police precincts.

- The rate of gun seizure is .15 percent, or nearly zero, and arrests take place in less than 6 percent of all stops.

- Black and Hispanic suspects are treated more harshly once the decision is made that a crime has occurred. Black and Hispanic suspects are more likely to be arrested than issued a summons when compared to White suspects. They are more likely to be subjected to use of force.

Fourteenth Amendment Claim

- NYPD stop activity is concentrated in precincts with high concentrations of Black and Hispanic residents even after controlling for the influences of crime, social conditions, and the allocation of police resources.

- NYPD stops are significantly more frequent for Black and Hispanic citizens than for White citizens, even after adjusting for precinct crime rates, the racial composition, and other social and economic factors predictive of police activity.

- Blacks and Hispanics are more likely to be stopped than Whites even in areas where there are low crime rates and where residential populations are racially heterogeneous or predominantly White.

Source: *Floyd v. City of New York*, Report of Jeffrey Fagan, Ph.D., 3–4.

tration of police officers in specific areas, his analysis found that Blacks and Latinos were still disproportionately targeted by the NYPD's SQF program. Table 4.2 highlights Fagan's major findings with regard to *Floyd*'s Fourth and Fourteenth Amendment claims.

In August 2013, federal district court judge Shira Scheindlin ruled that the NYPD was engaging in unconstitutional SQF practices that targeted predominately Black and Latino New Yorkers.[122] In a separate decision, Judge Scheindlin ordered several remedies to address the NYPD's racially discriminatory SQF program.[123] First, the judge appointed a monitor, Peter L. Zimroth, to "serve the interests of all stakeholders, including the City, by facilitating the early and unbiased detection of non-compliance or barriers to compliance."[124] Compliance would be accomplished through reformation of policies, training, supervision, documentation, and disciplinary action, along with the publication of SQF reports that detail the NYPD's compliance with the ordered reforms. Second, Judge Scheindlin ruled that the individuals most affected by the NYPD's SQF program should be intimately involved in the department's reform efforts:

> The communities most affected by the NYPD's use of stop and frisk have a distinct perspective that is highly relevant to crafting effective reforms. No amount of legal or policing expertise can replace a community's understanding of the likely practical consequences of reforms in terms of both liberty and safety.[125]

The last ordered remedy centered on a one-year pilot study whereby police officers in the Seventy-Fifth Precinct would wear body cameras. Judge Scheindlin wrote that cameras

> will provide a contemporaneous, objective record of stop-and-frisks allowing for the review of officer conduct . . . [that] may either confirm or refute the belief of some minorities that they have been stopped simply as a result of their race, or based on the clothes they wore, such as baggy pants or a hoodie. . . . Thus, the recordings should also alleviate some of the mistrust that has developed between the police and the Black and Hispanic communities, based on the belief that stops and frisks are overwhelmingly and unjustifiably directed at members of these communities. Video recordings will be equally helpful to members of the NYPD who are wrongly accused of inappropriate behavior.[126]

Legal Challenges to SQF Practices in Other Jurisdictions

Several other police departments have been accused of using SQF in a racially and ethnically biased manner, including Newark, Chicago, and Philadelphia. In 2013 the American Civil Liberties Union of New Jersey (ACLU-NJ) conducted a six-month evaluation of SQF practices in

Newark. According to the ACLU-NJ, the Newark Police Department conducted an average of 2,093 stops per month from July to December 2013.[127] The authors note that this translates to a rate of 91 stops per 1,000 residents, a stop rate that was eleven times greater than the NYPD stop rate during the same time period. In fact, the Newark Police Department stop rate exceeded the NYPD rate during the height of the SQF program in New York (2011, when the NYPD rate was 84 stops per 1,000 residents). The ACLU-NJ report also discovered racial disproportionality in stops, as Blacks represented 52 percent of the population but 75 percent of those who were stopped by Newark police.[128]

The American Civil Liberties Union in Illinois (ACLU-IL) and Pennsylvania (ACLU-PA) also disseminated reports on SQF practices. In 2015 the ACLU-IL published a report claiming that the Chicago Police Department had "failed to train, supervise and monitor law enforcement in minority communities for decades, resulting in a failure to ensure that officers' use of stop and frisk is lawful."[129] As part of the report, the ACLU-IL presented data on SQFs in Chicago. Its results indicated that from May 1, 2014, through August 31, 2014, the Chicago Police Department made 93.6 stops per 1,000 residents. Like the Newark Police Department, the Chicago Police Department's stop rate exceeded the NYPD rate in 2011, when stops in New York City approached 700,000. When these stop rates are analyzed by racial/ethnic composition, the disparity is stark. In the Englewood district, a predominately minority community, Chicago police made 266 stops per 1,000 residents. In the predominately White district of Lincoln/Foster, Chicago police made only 43 stops per 1,000 people.[130] Furthermore, while Blacks represented 32 percent of Chicago's population, they made up 72 percent of those who were stopped during the ACLU-IL's study period.

The Philadelphia Police Department (PPD) stopped more than 250,000 citizens in 2009, prompting the American Civil Liberties Union of Pennsylvania to file a federal lawsuit in November 2010. The lawsuit, *Bailey v. City of Philadelphia*, alleged that the PPD was engaged in racial profiling.[131] The litigation resulted in a settlement agreement between the plaintiffs and the Philadelphia Police Department that centered on quarterly analyses of stop data by the ACLU, appointment of an independent monitor, retraining of officers, and new protocols governing SQF practices.[132] The ACLU-PA subsequently reported to the court and the settlement monitor that although the number of stops had declined by 15 percent,

> there has been no significant improvement in the quality of stops and frisks. By our analysis, pedestrian stops are being made without reasonable suspicion in approximately 43–47% of the cases. . . . Frisks are being conducted without reasonable suspicion in over 45% of the cases. . . . By race, 76% of the stops were of minorities (African Americans and Latinos) and 85% of the frisks were of minorities. The findings as to impermissible stops and frisks are particularly disturbing given the fact that the Police Department had the time and resources following the entry of the Agreement to re-train its officers on stop and frisk practices and to establish supervisory reviews to ensure accountability for practices that failed to meet clear mandates under the agreement.[133]

The ACLU-PA's most recent report as of the writing of this book continues to raise questions about the PPD's use of *Terry* stops. The 2015 report found that 37 percent of stops lacked reasonable suspicion; contraband was found in only 2 percent of stops and 5 percent of frisks; and Blacks comprised approximately 72 and 79 percent of all stops and frisks, respectively, while they made up only 43 percent of Philadelphia's population.[134]

The controversy surrounding SQF, its potential crime-control effects, and its association with racial discrimination has continued to generate both interest and concern with the strategy, especially in cities struggling with crime and violence. For example, an investigation into stop and frisk activities by the Miami Gardens Police Department found that, from 2008 to 2013, officers had stopped 65,328 individuals, and nearly 1,000 citizens had been stopped ten or more times. Moreover, only

13 percent of those stopped were arrested.[135] In chapter 1, the authors highlighted the experience in Detroit in 2013, where community opposition led to the decision to abandon an SQF program. A very similar story played out in San Francisco in 2012, when Mayor Ed Lee publicized adoption of an SQF program. After strong criticism from civil rights advocates and the San Francisco Board of Supervisors, the mayor shifted his attention to alternative policing strategies.[136] In July 2014, a city councilman in Cleveland advocated for the Cleveland Police Department to adopt an SQF program that would center on random stops of citizens in high-crime neighborhoods.[137] This proposal was immediately questioned based on the constitutionality of random stops without the requisite reasonable suspicion.[138]

The "Human Costs" of Misuse and Overuse of Stop and Frisk

Questions surrounding the NYPD's SQF practices have almost exclusively focused on racial and ethnic disproportionality in the rate of stops without necessarily considering what transpires during the stop, especially use of force by police. The lack of research on this issue is cause for concern, given the number of far-reaching consequences associated with police use of force, such as serious injury or death to the police officer or suspect, community upheaval, and the degradation of police-community relations. The civil disorder that followed Michael Brown's death in Ferguson and Freddie Gray's death in Baltimore highlights this point. Considering that law enforcement practices have historically been "conditioned by broader social forces and attitudes—including a long history of racism,"[139] there may be reason to believe that force is used disproportionately against racial and ethnic minority communities during *Terry* stops.

Some descriptive studies have shown that minority citizens are more likely to experience force during stop and frisks conducted by the NYPD. The Center for Constitutional Rights, for instance, found that force was used 24 percent of the time against Blacks and Latinos and only 17 percent of the time against Whites during stops from 2005 through 2008.[140] Similarly, in 2012 the NYPD used physical force in approximately 17.3 percent of all stop and frisk encounters, and minority citizens were more likely to experience use of force:, Black (17.6 percent), Hispanic (18.9 percent), White (12.5 percent), and Asian/Other (14.9 percent).[141] Morrow moved beyond descriptive statistics to determine whether a suspect's race or ethnicity would predict whether a NYPD officer uses force during a stop.[142] Controlling for suspect, situational, and precinct-level characteristics, Morrow found that Black and Hispanic individuals were more likely to have non-weapon force used against them than their White counterparts during stops.[143] Furthermore, Morrow found that living in a predominantly Hispanic precinct compounded the odds that Hispanic individuals would experience both non-weapon and weapon force by the NYPD during stops.[144]

The costs of SQF for minority citizens in New York far exceed the physical toll of use of force by police. Several studies have found that as a result of the disparate treatment of racial and ethnic minorities in New York, minority youth in New York City distrust the police, feel uneasy when they see the police, and view contact with the police as negative and adversarial.[145] As Weisburd states, "You can have a short-term effect on crime with stop and frisk, and crime goes down. But now you've alienated 260 kids that were stopped in ways that made them unhappy. It may lead to worse citizens in the future."[146] Other researchers have documented how negative interactions between police and citizens can create feelings of helplessness, resentment, and anger among disadvantaged minority groups. A recent study carried out by the Vera Institute of Justice examined the effects of being stopped by the NYPD on young people's perceptions of the police, and reported a number of noteworthy findings:

- 44 percent of young people surveyed indicated they had been stopped repeatedly—nine times or more.
- Less than a third—29 percent—reported ever being informed of the reason for a stop.

- 71 percent of young people surveyed reported being frisked at least once, and 64 percent said they had been searched.
- 45 percent reported encountering an officer who threatened them, and 46 percent said they had experienced physical force at the hands of an officer.
- One out of four said they were involved in a stop in which the officer displayed his or her weapon.
- 61 percent stated that the way police acted toward them was influenced by their age.
- 57 percent indicated that they were treated worse than others because of their race and/or ethnicity.[147]

In light of these findings, it is not surprising that "88 percent of young people surveyed believe that residents of their neighborhood do not trust the police."[148] Such views were further compounded if the youth is an ethnic or racial minority. Wilkinson and colleagues found that Black youth (ages sixteen to twenty-four) in East New York and Mott Haven held particularly negative views of the police.[149] Solis and colleagues reported similar findings from their interviews of Latino youth.[150] Interestingly, several studies have found that minority youth appreciated positive contacts with police, and in fact, wanted a police presence in their neighborhoods, but that their actual experiences with officers often were antagonistic and negative.[151]

The Center for Constitutional Rights conducted interviews with fifty-four citizens who had been the subject of a stop and frisk by the NYPD in order to paint a clearer picture of the "human impact" of the SQF program. Interviewees discussed a wide range of offensive behavior during SQFs, including inappropriate touching and sexual harassment, police brutality, trauma and humiliation, and improper arrests (which then led to other consequences such as loss of employment, housing, and public benefits). The CCR concluded,

> These interviews provide evidence of how deeply this practice impacts individuals and they document widespread civil and human rights abuses. . . . [T]he effects of these abuses can be devastating and often leave

behind lasting emotional, psychological, social, and economic harm. . . .
Residents of some New York City neighborhoods describe a police presence so pervasive and hostile that they feel like they are living in a state
of siege.[152]

The New York City Postscript

Events continued to unfold in New York City in the months following the landmark ruling in the *Floyd* case in August 2013. First, the city
appealed Judge Scheindlin's ruling to the U.S. Court of Appeals for the
Second Circuit and sought a stay of her remedies, pending the outcome
of the appeal. The Second Circuit granted the city's motion for a stay
pending appeal.[153] In that order, the Second Circuit also remanded the
case for the purpose of assigning a new judge because the appellate court
preliminarily determined that Judge Scheindlin had failed to avoid the
appearance of impropriety and impartiality.[154] Importantly, though, the
Second Circuit did not overturn the substance of Judge Scheindlin's rulings. Both the plaintiffs in the case and seventeen law professors as *amici
curiae* ("friends of the court") defended Judge Scheindlin in a motion to
reconsider her removal from the case, but the Second Circuit declined
to reconsider its order.[155] In an unprecedented action, Judge Scheindlin,
through counsel, moved to appear before the Second Circuit, seeking
reconsideration of the order of reassignment. Six retired U.S. district
court judges and thirteen professors of legal ethics filed an amicus brief
in support of that motion, as well as a related motion the plaintiffs filed
to have the Second Circuit, sitting *en banc*, reconsider the reassignment
order. The Second Circuit denied all of these motions.[156]

Second, several New York City police unions filed motions to intervene in the appeal, alleging that the district court "misconstrued
applicable burdens of proof, misapplied Fourth Amendment jurisprudence, applied Fourteenth Amendment theory that [p]laintiffs never
even presented, and accepted evidence that was insufficient as a matter
of fact and law to prove [p]laintiffs' claims."[157] These motions were

denied for three reasons: "the motions were untimely"; the unions had "no significant protectable interests relating to the subject of the litigation that would warrant intervention"; and "even if their alleged interests were cognizable, the [u]nions lack standing to vindicate those interests on appeal."[158] Though the NYPD police unions supported the hiring of William Bratton as commissioner, the union leadership has continued to be highly critical of the mayor's handling of the SQF litigation and its aftermath. On September 21, 2015, the NYPD was set to begin a pilot program where officers provide "stop and frisk receipts" to citizens they stop but do not arrest (the receipt includes the officer's badge number and requires the officer to provide a reason for the stop), and the Police Benevolent Association has questioned the value of the program."

Third, the NYPD's SQF program (and the *Floyd/Ligon* cases) became a defining feature of the New York City mayoral election in the fall of 2013, with candidates advocating both for and against the NYPD's use of the practice. In effect, the mayoral election became a referendum on SQF, and mayoral candidate William de Blasio was elected in part because of his opposition to the NYPD SQF program.

Fourth, upon taking office, Mayor de Blasio replaced NYPD Commissioner Raymond Kelly with former (and then new-again) Commissioner William Bratton. Although Bratton was the original architect of the NYPD's SQF program, his new term as commissioner has been clearly defined in terms of community engagement, improved police-minority community relations, and greatly reduced reliance on SQF. Mayor de Blasio stated, "The idea here is to have real reform, to only use stop and frisk when it's constitutionally warranted and constitutionally applied, and to show communities that we are respecting law abiding citizens."[159] Embracing the mayor's viewpoint, Commissioner Bratton pledged to address NYPD reform through the inclusion of "more oversight, more guidance, [and] more training; it's all for the good."[160] In an effort to foster reconciliation between the NYPD and citizens of New York, de Blasio dropped the city's appeal of the *Floyd* ruling and began working with Commissioner Bratton to implement the remedies ordered in Judge Scheindlin's original ruling. The police unions appealed the denial of their motion to intervene and sought to oppose the city's withdrawal of the appeal. In February 2014 the Second Circuit denied the unions' motions and remanded the case to the district court so that the city and the plaintiffs could come to a resolution.[161] On remand, the city sent a letter to Judge Analisa Torres, the U.S. district court judge to whom the case had been reassigned, suggesting

> a way for all five police unions to participate in the remedial process now. Under the City's approach, the City will share proposals with the unions before providing them to the Monitor and the Plaintiffs. The unions may then offer their comments, which the City will convey to the Monitor. The City will continue to confer with the unions about substantial revisions proposed by the Monitor and the Plaintiffs. This approach affords the unions "a practical opportunity" to inform the Monitor of their viewpoints before the Monitor reaches conclusions and submits Final Recommendations to the Court.[162]

Since de Blasio's election as mayor, the appointment of Bratton as commissioner of the NYPD, and the ongoing implementation of remedies to finally resolve the litigation, the use of SQFs has dropped off precipitously. In 2013 the NYPD engaged in under 200,000 stops, and in 2014 the number of stops dropped to 45,788 (marking a 91 percent decrease from 2012).

We agree with law professor Jeffrey Bellin's assertion that *Terry* stops were not designed as a blanket enforcement tool to be used on a large scale.[163] The focus of the initial U.S. Supreme Court stop and frisk cases centered on devising an investigative tactic that would be employed based on specific information indicating that an individual may be involved in criminal activity.[164] Bellin's overview of how the NYPD's use of SQF transformed from a case-by-case investigative tactic to a massive program is especially enlightening:

In summary, beginning in the mid- to late 1990s, mass stop-and frisk first surfaced as a tool employed by one specialized unit (SCU) to find guns, and later served midlevel supervisors citywide in responding to pressure to "do something" about persistent crime in their precincts. As the "program" grew and obtained disappointing "hit rates," it became increasingly justified as an effort to deter, rather than detect, gun-carrying. Consistent with this justification, proponents of NYC Stop and Frisk explained its disproportionate racial impact by highlighting the demographics of the group whose behavior the police were trying to deter. Violent crime suspects, the NYPD claimed, happened to be overwhelmingly [B]lack and Hispanic; stops designed to deter gun-carrying, and thus violent crimes, the NYPD contended, logically paralleled this demographic.[165]

This is an accurate assessment that offers an important cautionary tale for police departments that employ mass stop and frisk programs.

Conclusion

There are several important takeaway messages from this chapter. First, the role of the NYPD in the New York City crime decline remains largely unknown. Although there is some evidence to suggest that the NYPD (and SQFs) may have had an impact on crime, the limited research generally indicates that such an effect is minimal to modest, at best. Second, there is virtually no research examining the relationship between *Terry* stops and crime in other jurisdictions. Third, the NYPD's SQF program has produced significant collateral consequences for mostly minority citizens who have been disproportionately targeted by the practice. Litigation from the *Floyd* case demonstrates that the SQF program violated the constitutional protections guaranteed by the Fourth and Fourteenth Amendments for thousands of New Yorkers. Qualitative research by the Center for Constitutional Rights and the Vera Institute captured the human consequences of the overuse and misuse of stop and frisk, from emotional and psychological trauma to sexual harassment, physical injury, and loss of human dignity. The work of civil rights advocates in other jurisdictions shows that the aforementioned consequences were by no means limited to New York City.

The New York experience with SQF has generated a national dialogue over the proper role of the practice in American policing. In 2011 the Urban Institute convened a panel of police executives and researchers to discuss the challenges, benefits, and problems associated with widespread use of stop and frisk.[166] The panelists highlighted the importance of SQF as a deterrent to crime, particularly activities associated with narcotics and illegal gun carrying, but they also identified a number of concerns. Most notably, the panelists acknowledged that widespread use of SQF in high-crime areas is likely to have a disproportionate impact on minority communities; and Black and Hispanic citizens in those communities are likely to view those stops as unfair and unjustified—a phenomenon witnessed in New York City, Philadelphia, and other jurisdictions.[167] La Vigne and colleagues urged police to be mindful of the disproportionate consequences of intensive stop and frisk activities on minority communities, and to consider the implications of those consequences for their efforts to achieve legitimacy in the eyes of minority citizens. They also recommended that police leaders adopt a community policing lens when thinking about use of SQF.

The discriminatory treatment of racial and ethnic minorities during stop and frisk adversely affects citizen trust and faith in the police. Research strongly demonstrates that procedural justice—the manner in which police treat citizens—is crucial to achieving police legitimacy.[168] Furthermore, the President's Task Force on 21st Century Policing recently concluded that "[t]rust between law enforcement agencies and the people they protect is essential in a democracy."[169] To foster trust and legitimacy, police officers must be impartial and consistent in their decisions, and must treat all people with dignity, fairness, and respect. The community policing and police legitimacy frameworks provide an important lens for consideration of the role of stop and frisk going forward.

5

Beyond a Few Bad Apples

[H]istory teaches that if reform is to last, it must change the
systems and values to which officers adhere rather than just
the officers themselves.
—Jerome Skolnick and James Fyfe, 1993[1]

At its core, stop and frisk is an exercise in police discretion.[2] An officer witnesses something that generates reasonable suspicion—a bulge
in the waistband, furtive movements, clothing that seems out of place,
or behavior suggesting potential criminal activity—and the officer ini-
tiates the stop. The decision to stop the citizen, and consequently to
conduct a pat-down frisk (or even a search), is discretionary based on
the officer's training, expertise, and field experience. Stop and frisks
that are discriminatory or otherwise fail to meet the constitutionally
required threshold (i.e., reasonable suspicion) are also discretionary.
This, in fact, is the core controversy surrounding police-initiated stops
of citizens: Are police exercising discretion in an appropriate and just
manner when making *Terry* stops (i.e., are they conducting stops based
on reasonable suspicion that can be articulated)? Or are police stopping
citizens based on race/ethnicity or some other extralegal factor? The
central question addressed in this chapter involves how police departments can control their officers' decisions to initiate stops of citizens,
and to ensure that such stops meet constitutional standards and do not
violate citizens' rights.

To explore the potential for a police department to properly control
its officers' stop and frisk activities, we draw on the body of research
that has examined how police departments can effectively control their
officers' behavior—or misbehavior—in the field. For more than forty

years, researchers have investigated how to control officers' discretionary decision making during encounters with citizens, from arrest and use of force (including deadly force) decisions to automobile pursuits and use of canines. As the quote from criminologists Jerome Skolnick and James Fyfe above suggests, these are complex issues that go far beyond simply removing a few bad apples who consistently make poor decisions, or adding a few extra hours of training in the academy or at roll call. Research has consistently demonstrated the powerful nature of the informal police culture, particularly with regard to how it can shape officer behavior in the field, and how difficult it is to change.[3] Clearly, the challenges surrounding this question are daunting, and they must be addressed in the context of the larger historical backdrop of racial injustice in American policing. Also clear, however, is that the larger body of research on police discretion offers numerous lessons on accountability strategies that can effectively reduce poor decision making by officers.

Careful Selection of Personnel

Nearly fifty years ago, the President's Commission on Law Enforcement and Administration of Justice recommended proper screening of applicants to identify those who are ill-suited for the policing profession.[4] Though the traditional approach to recruit selection has been focused on "screening out" those who are mentally (or otherwise) unfit to be a police officer, this important process also involves efforts to identify candidates with sought-after qualities who should be "screened in" during the application process. This dialogue over screening out (and in) job applicants has typically occurred in the context of concerns over corruption and brutality, but the lessons are equally relevant for abuse of discretion in stop and frisk. The overriding goal of the recruit selection process is to identify and hire individuals who will behave lawfully and appropriately when given tremendous discretion to carry out their duties as police officers.

Most police leaders and researchers would agree on two key points: (1) there are certain characteristics that should serve as red flags for potential employment; and (2) police departments should conduct extensive background examinations to determine whether applicants possess those characteristics. In fact, numerous misconduct scandals (e.g., in Miami, Washington, DC, and Los Angeles) have been linked to "mass hiring," where departments hired hundreds of officers in a short period of time and did not carry out thorough selection processes.[5] Background investigations typically include a criminal history check, credit check, and interviews of family members, neighbors, and former employers. Well-established red flags include prior criminal behavior, drug use, poor performance in prior employment, and questionable morality (e.g., lying on the job application). Departments should also be looking for any evidence that a candidate possesses prejudicial attitudes that could lead to discriminatory actions on the job.

Background examinations are costly and time-consuming, but research continues to highlight their importance for screening out poor applicants based on certain characteristics (the old axiom "One of the best predictors of future behavior is past behavior" remains true).[6] In one of the few large-scale studies of police misconduct, researchers found that records of dismissal in prior jobs and military discipline were associated with internal police rules violations.[7] More recently, the Mollen Commission (created in 1992 to investigate misconduct in the NYPD) found a relatively high prevalence of prior arrests among suspended and dismissed officers.[8] In their study of career-ending misconduct in the NYPD, criminologists Robert Kane and Michael White highlighted the importance of "screening out" processes:

Perhaps the most salient policy implications of the present study relate to departmental screening processes. Because of the low visibility of police work, the unique opportunities for misconduct presented to police officers, and the conflict that often exists between the police and the public in certain communities, it seems clear that police departments should continue to exclude people from policing who have demonstrated records of criminal involvement and employee disciplinary problems. These represent evidence-based policy recommendations for which criminological perspectives developed for the general population (i.e., outside of policing) produced support (e.g., control theories, opportunity theories, and perhaps even routine activities theory).[9]

Performance in the police academy has also been found to predict likelihood of getting into trouble later on after graduation.[10] White and Kane examined predictors of career-ending misconduct over time to assess whether there is some variation among early-, mid- and late-career predictors of failure. They found that termination is a complex, long-term process with distinct patterns that emerge over police officers' careers. More specifically, a number of variables were significantly associated with termination regardless of an officer's career stage, such as race and prior criminal history, while others were significant only at certain career stages.[11] For example, promotion only protected against termination early in an officer's career, while military service was a predictor of misconduct only after ten years of service.[12]

Nevertheless, both empirical research and practical experience have demonstrated that it can be difficult to identify individuals who are unfit for the police profession.[13] For example, many officers who have gotten into trouble possessed none of the aforementioned red flags. One study concluded that "efforts to improve the quality of police officer performance by screening out those recruits who will not make good police officers have generally been unsuccessful."[14] As a result, "screening out" mechanisms should be supplemented with intensive processes designed to identify individuals with specific characteristics or qualities that "predict" good policing ("screening in").

The interest in identifying those best-suited for police work (rather than those who are ill-suited) gained traction in the 1960s, particularly with the passage of the Civil Rights Act of 1964, amid concerns that prevailing "screening out" processes disproportionately affected minority and female applicants.[15] Kane and White highlighted this aspect of the application process as well, noting that their "findings also suggest the importance of screening *in* or identifying potential police officers whose presence in police organizations may have the effect of making them better behaved."[16]

Though efforts at identifying predictors of good policing have had limited success,[17] relevant personal attributes would certainly include good judgment, an even temperament, respect and appreciation for diversity, creativity and problem-solving skills, ability to think on one's feet and handle pressure, and leadership skills. Many scholars have pointed to the need for a college education to develop the relevant skills to be an effective police officer. Though early research on the impact of college education on police performance is mixed,[18] recent studies suggest that it is important for reducing the likelihood of misconduct.[19] Shjarback and White found that departments with an associate's degree requirement for applicants experienced fewer citizen complaints of police use of force and fewer citizen assaults on their officers.[20]

The required skill set for good policing can be traced back to the very earliest writings on the profession by Sir Robert Peel in the mid-nineteenth century, who stated that recruits should be intelligent, in good physical condition, of good moral character, and in possession of an even temperament.[21] These qualities have been a mainstay in discussions of good policing since that time,[22] though few have captured the complexity of these qualities better than William K. Muir in his book *Police: Streetcorner Politicians*. Borrowing from Weber's model of the professional politician, Muir argued that the *professional policeman* possesses two important qualities: the officer is morally reconciled with the use of coercive force (called "passion"), and the officer understands the dignity and tragedy of the human condition (called "perspective," or empathy).[23] Within this framework, Muir also described three types of nonprofessional policemen: *enforcers* (those with passion but no perspective); *reciprocators* (those with perspective but no passion); and *avoiders* (those who lacked both passion and perspective).

In his book, Muir introduces three police officers who work on skid row: two who lacked the qualities to be professional policemen (Jim Longstreet and Bee Haywood), and one who was a professional (Mike Marshall). Muir uses their stories to highlight the consequences of poor policing, and these characterizations are especially relevant for consideration of the importance of recruit selection for reducing the prevalence of unjust and discriminatory *Terry* stops. The first officer, Jim Longstreet, was an *avoider* who lacked both passion and perspective. Muir observed that Longstreet worked hard to avoid "difficulty" and "hot situations."[24] Unfortunately, this avoidance/neglect strategy had dire consequences for the community, as those "who stood to profit from the policeman's absence—the strong-arm, the bully, the vicious" took control of Longstreet's beat.[25] The second officer, Bee Haywood, thrived on using physical violence. He was an *enforcer* who had passion but no perspective. Muir noted that officers like Haywood experienced a number of negative consequences from their brutal actions. First, the use of violence by police inevitably escalated police-citizen encounters, as residents soon learned what to expect and responded in kind. Second, residents learned to avoid the violence-prone officers and gave them little in the way of useful information. As a result, Haywood—and others like him—become completely disconnected from the goings-on in the neighborhood.

The third officer, Mike Marshall, had both passion and perspective. Unlike Longstreet and Haywood, Marshall had developed both eloquence and empathy in the way he carried out his work:

> Marshall's development of skid row had transformed the dispossessed of that community into "good citizens", into people who had something to lose and therefore something to protect—a line of credit, a decent friend-

ship, a good public servant, whatever it was that Marshall had come to represent through "a life spent in doing good before their eyes." One consequence of this professional response was that the community tended to develop confidence in the beat patrolman. It became more open, had a greater sense of security, and enjoyed a number of little productive happinesses. For the officer himself, one result was that he developed a feeling of safety, a more informed understanding of his beat, and considerable moral gratification from doing the job well.[26]

Marshall defused the fear and anger that characterized the beats worked by Longstreet and Haywood. The consequences of Marshall's efforts for both himself and his beat were profound.

Though the research by Muir is more than thirty years old, we believe that the principles of good policing that he described are still relevant today. Importantly, these principles—empathy, moral acceptance of coercive authority, protection of the vulnerable, and problem solving—reflect what some have called good craftsmanship.[27] These qualities are also central tenets of community-oriented and problem-oriented policing, the prevailing philosophies of good policing (or good craft) today. Quite simply, officers who possess these skills will be less likely to engage in racially biased and otherwise improper behavior during encounters of any kind with citizens, and departments should aggressively seek them out in their recruitment and selection processes. Applicants' personal characteristics can be assessed through standardized personality tests, through participation in community service and public engagements, through reference-check interviews that probe for such characteristics, and through in-person interviews that explore applicants' personal attributes. The President's Task Force on 21st Century Policing highlights how law enforcement agencies can instill the desired characteristics in their recruits through training that engages community members in the curriculum, and that covers cultural diversity, policing in a democratic society, implicit bias, the disease of addiction, social interactions, and crisis intervention training.[28]

Training

Careful recruit selection must be followed with effective training in the police academy, as well as later through field and in-service training. At the academy, the goal of training is to provide trainees with the basic skills and knowledge necessary to become a police officer. Cadets must receive a clear message at this early stage that racially biased stop and frisks are inappropriate and illegal, and will not be tolerated. Following graduation from the academy, officers are typically assigned to a veteran officer for a period of field training (the FTO program). The FTO experience is intended to bridge the gap between the classroom environment of the academy and the "real world" of policing on the street. This is a formative stage of a police officer's career, and it is critically important for field training officers to impart the message that racially biased *Terry* stops are not consistent with the principles of good policing. Police scholar James Fyfe highlighted the importance of the FTO role:

> When sergeants or older officers give young cops those fabled instructions to "forget what they told you in the police academy, kid, you'll learn how to do it on the street," formal training is instantly and irreparably devalued. Worse, when officers actually see firsthand that the behavioral strictures in which they were schooled are routinely ignored in practice, formal training is neutralized and the definitions of appropriate behavior are instead made in the secrecy of officers' locker rooms.[29]

The final form of training, called "in-service," where officers periodically receive additional training while on the job, can be used to "refresh" officers on ethical issues, such as avoiding discriminatory decision making, and to re-send the message that the department leadership denounces racial bias and expects the same from its officers.

In his review of how police training can be structured to reduce violence between police and citizens, Fyfe presented a number of key recommendations that are equally relevant for how training can reduce discriminatory, unjust stop and frisk activities.[30] These recommendations and how each applies to SQF practices are described below.

Effective Training Must Be Realistic

> Training for any endeavor should simulate as closely as possible the actual working conditions for which trainees are being prepared. . . . Although it cannot be eliminated, the artificiality of police training can be minimized. Perhaps the best way to do this is in role-play scenarios in facilities that duplicate as closely as possible the conditions officers encounter in the field, both indoors and outdoors.[31]

Police training should move away from the traditional pedagogical, lecture-based curriculum. Police scholars Bayley and Bittner stated that learning can be "accelerated and made more systematic" by relevant training that brings the reality of police work into the academy.[32] The question is how best to accomplish this. Andragogy has emerged as an effective adult learning technique in a variety of fields,[33] and several scholars have suggested that the approach could serve to increase the relevancy of police academy training.[34] Andragogy highlights self-directed learning with the instructor playing a facilitating role, with students participating in "self-directed group discussions and active debate," while the instructors "manage the classroom by allowing participants to share their experiences and knowledge, . . . integrate new knowledge, and . . . provide strategies that will allow transfer of learning back to the job."[35] Instead of listening to dry lectures and war stories, recruits learn through critical discussion and interaction with other recruits and instructional staff. The curriculum should include detailed instruction on Fourth Amendment law, preferably taught by law professors or lawyers. This training should also acquaint officers with the concepts of implicit bias and the suspicion heuristic. When this form of instruction is matched with the scenario-based role-plays described by Fyfe above, police instructors can develop valued, informative curricula that eliminate the traditional artificiality of training through "near real-world" SQF scenarios. Such realistic training will more sufficiently prepare recruits for the street; and most importantly, it will clearly convey the message that racially biased SQF practices will not be tolerated.

Training Should Be Tailored to the Officers' and Community's Needs

> Every community also possesses unique characteristics that create specific challenges for officers, and these must be taken into account in training. . . . One of the best ways to assure that training closely fits the actual needs of the community and the police is to base it on the real experience of the community and the police. Noteworthy police encounters with citizens—both those that have come to unhappy endings and those in which potential disaster was averted—should be documented and reviewed thoroughly for their training implications.[36]

As Fyfe suggests, training should prepare officers for the specific problems of the communities in which they will work. For years there have been calls for police to be racially and ethnically representative of the communities they serve (e.g., Commission on Accreditation for Law Enforcement Agencies standards[37]). There are a number of reasons why diversity in police departments is emphasized, most notably the perceived link between underrepresentation and long-term tense conflict between police and minority communities.[38] Moreover, many believe that increasing the diversity of the police force so that it reflects the community demographic trends will enhance police legitimacy, which will ultimately increase community cooperation and police effectiveness.[39] Logically, a representative police department is more likely to understand the culture and views of the community, and is more likely to be tolerant of those views. Importantly, this tolerance and understanding must be imparted early on to recruits during academy training.[40]

Moreover, police departments should include citizens as part of the academy training to give recruits a sense of the community's perspective, as well as an understanding of the consequences of SQF for citizens. This input will not only better prepare recruits for their future interactions with citizens, it can also help new officers to understand the role of *Terry* stops in the larger mission of the police department. More specifically, the department mission includes, of course, an emphasis on crime control, but it also likely highlights other central tenets such as public service, protecting citizens' rights, and compassion. For example, the International Association of Chiefs of Police statement of mission and values highlights that police will seek to make "communities safer by upholding the law fairly and firmly; preventing crime and antisocial behaviour; . . . investigating crime and bringing offenders to justice"; but it also states,

> We will act with integrity, compassion, courtesy and patience, showing neither fear nor favour in what we do. We will be sensitive to the needs and dignity of victims and demonstrate respect for the human rights of all. . . . We will work with communities and partners, listening to their views, building their trust and confidence, making every effort to understand and meet their needs.[41]

Citizen participation in SQF training can place the practice in its proper context and convey the importance of deploying the strategy in a manner consistent with the overall values of the department.

The debate over the role of local law enforcement in immigration enforcement also demonstrates the importance of this point on training. Arizona has been at the center of this debate over the last five years, particularly because of the state law passed in April 2010 (SB 1070) that authorized local police to engage in immigration enforcement.[42] Although the legislation had numerous provisions, the most controversial part of the law required local police to investigate the immigration status of suspects they had detained or arrested, if there was reasonable suspicion that the person had entered the country illegally. Many local law enforcement agencies, especially in Maricopa County, Arizona, viewed the law as a significant barrier to their officers' ability to successfully engage with the Hispanic population in their jurisdictions. As a result, several agencies developed training that was tailored to meet the mission of their department and the experiences of their community. For example, the Glendale (Arizona) Police Department begins its training with the following opening statements:

- It is the mission of the GPD to protect the lives and the property of the people we serve.
- We serve everyone in this community regardless of their immigration status.
- We have worked very hard to build a trusting relationship with our community.
- We are effective as a law enforcement agency because we do have the community's trust.
- It is important that we work to maintain this trust, which is the foundation of our community policing efforts.
- It is, however, equally important that we enforce the law. This duty is part of the oath that we took when we became police officers.[43]

These statements highlight the critical importance of community trust and convey the clear message that Glendale police officers, though required to enforce state law (including the new immigration law), must do so in a manner that is consistent with the primary mission of the department.

Training Must Be Continuous

Some of the most critical police violence prevention and reduction skills are needed so rarely that they are likely to atrophy into uselessness unless they are the subjects of frequent refresher training. . . . Thus, as in medicine and other emergency professions, constant in-service training is necessary to keep officers' most critical, but rarely employed skills at a useful level.[44]

We agree with Fyfe's assertion that the most important but rarely used skills will degrade if officers are not continually trained. The recommendation for continuous training in violence prevention is equally important for just and proper SQF practices, but his rationale is less applicable. Though use of force is rare and his concerns over skill atrophy are on the mark, the applicable skill set for avoiding racially biased behavior in *Terry* stops is employed by police much more regularly—potentially with each and every police-citizen encounter. As a result, the need for continuous training on issues related to race/ethnicity, cultural diversity and tolerance, and legal issues such as reasonable suspicion is even more critical. Besides the day-to-day use of these skills, there are a number of additional reasons why this is important. First, there may be changes in state or federal law that can impact police practice (e.g., SB 1070 in Arizona). Second, the racial and ethnic makeup of a community can change over time (sometimes very quickly), and failure on the part of the police department to recognize these changes can lead to significant conflict between police and those new population groups (e.g., Cuban immigration to Miami and the Liberty City riot in 1980; Los Angeles leading up to the riots in the early 1990s[45]). In simple terms, departments must remain aware of changes in their constituency, and they must ensure through proper training that their officers are prepared to handle those changes. Palmiotto highlighted the importance of this point: "Continuing police training throughout a police officer's career enables the officer to function more efficiently and safely, and is considered important in curtailing civil liability actions against an officer and his department."[46] Just as importantly, cultural awareness training can help to defuse tensions during stop and frisks, as officers are able to avoid language and behavioral cues that violate specific cultural norms.

Concentrate on Officers' Conduct Rather Than Incident Outcomes

Like assessments of surgeons' efforts, judgments about the propriety of officers' conduct and the adequacy of training should be based on what the officer *did*, rather than on the outcome of what they did. To do otherwise is to overlook inappropriate conduct until it results in disaster.[47]

Some scholars have maintained that police-citizen encounters are transactional events involving multiple decision points, with decisions made at earlier stages clearly affecting decisions made later in the encounter.[48] At each phase of the encounter, the police officer and the citizen make decisions and respond to the decisions of the other participant—much like a chess match. As a result, the decision by a police officer to conduct a more invasive search or to use force is the culmination of a series of earlier actions and reactions. The importance of this transactional perspective is that it underscores Fyfe's point above about process or conduct. How did the officer behave at each stage of the encounter? How could the officer have acted differently to achieve a more just outcome? With regard to deadly force incidents, Fyfe described police departments' tendency to focus on the final frame decision—what he called the split-second syndrome—while neglecting the earlier and equally important decisions that affected the final frame outcome where force was necessary.[49] To judge the appropriateness of police behavior based solely on the outcome—whether that outcome is a use of force or a search that led to confiscation of a small amount of marijuana—is shortsighted; in effect, allowing the ends to justify the means. As Fyfe suggests, this final-frame perspective is too limiting and will "overlook inappropriate conduct"; in simple terms, it gives officers "a pass" on mistakes they made earlier on in the encounter.[50]

The implications of the split-second syndrome for *Terry* stops of citizens are profound, as questions surrounding the lawfulness of a stop become irrelevant based on the results of the subsequent search. Grand juries determined that the NYPD officers who arrested Eric Garner and the Ferguson officer who shot and killed Michael Brown should not be criminally charged for their actions. But if we apply this transactional lens to the Eric Garner and Michael Brown cases, we can think about all the decisions made by officers in those encounters. Did Officer Wilson use foul language that showed disrespect to Michael Brown? Should Officer Wilson have waited for backup? Were there alternative methods to resolve an encounter involving the alleged selling of unlicensed cigarettes? The content of training on SQF practices should focus on all decision points during an encounter, and should highlight the vital importance of the process by which those activities are carried out. Why did the officer initiate the stop? Did the officer explain the reasons for the stop to the citizen? Did the officer use respectful language? Did the officer communicate effectively about the decision to engage in a pat-down or more invasive search? If the stop and frisk resulted in no formal action, did the officer use appropriate language and behavior to end the encounter in a procedurally just manner?

The overall goal of training is to provide officers with the skills and knowledge necessary to perform their duties effectively, lawfully, and humanely, and the principles outlined above by Fyfe offer an excellent road map for imparting those skills.[51]

> The development of successful boxers, diplomats, combat soldiers, and trial lawyers demonstrates that maintaining one's temper under stressful and confrontational conditions is a skill that can be taught. At the broadest level, police training designed to do so may involve providing students with what Muir[52] called *understanding*—a nonjudgmental sense that people's behavior, no matter how bizarre or provocative, may usually be explained by factors that go beyond the dichotomy of good and evil. . . . Even if genuine *understanding*, as defined by Muir, cannot be imparted to individuals who bring extremely narrow views to policing, officers can be made to know in training that they simply will not be permitted to act out their prejudices through violent, or even discourteous conduct.[53]

In plain terms, officers who are properly trained are less likely than poorly trained officers to engage in racially biased, unjust SQF practices. We can return to Fyfe's discussion of the impact of training on violence,[54] combined with Muir's professional policeman from the discussion above, to illustrate this point (again substituting stop and frisk of citizens in place of use of force).

Administrative Policy

Over the last forty years, administrative rule making has emerged as the dominant form of discretion control in American policing. Administrative guidance in the form of policies, rules, and procedures communicates to rank-and-file officers what the department expects, what is considered acceptable, and what will not be condoned.[55] Formal policy that is clearly articulated, disseminated widely in the organization, and enforced, can directly shape informal culture. Both the Commission on Accreditation of Law Enforcement Agencies (CALEA) and the American Bar Association (ABA) recommend written rules and policies as an effective way to structure police decision making. For example, a law enforcement agency can receive accreditation from CALEA if the agency successfully completes the five-phase, multi-year review process. The centerpiece of CALEA accreditation involves compliance with extensive requirements for administrative, written rules. "CALEA Accreditation requires an agency to develop a comprehensive, well thought out, uniform set of *written directives*. This is one of the most successful methods for reaching administrative and operational goals, while also providing direction to personnel."[56] The more than 450 written standards cover six general areas of organizational function: role, responsibilities, and relationships with other agencies; organization, management, and administration; personnel administration; law enforcement operations, operational support, and traffic law enforcement; detainee and court-related services; and auxiliary and technical services.

Police scholars Walker and Archbold articulate an administrative rule-making framework that has three basic components to ensure accountability with regard to critical incidents (use of force, automobile or foot pursuits, etc.).[57] First, agencies should develop written policies that specify what is (and what is not) appropriate behavior during given circumstances. Second, agencies should require officers to write a written report following a critical incident. Third, agencies should require supervisory review of critical incident reports to ensure that the officer acted within policy and law.[58] Walker and Archbold explain how their framework is grounded in the principles of confining, structuring, and checking discretion:

- Confining discretion involves having a written policy that clearly defines what an officer can and cannot do in a particular situation. This approach does not attempt to abolish discretion but only to limit its use to a narrow range of situations where judgment is still called for [use of deadly force policies that prohibit warning shots or shots fired at moving vehicles].
- Discretion is structured in the Davis model by allowing a certain amount of discretion while specifying the factors that an officer should consider in making a decision [vehicle pursuit policies that instruct officers to consider road conditions and the potential risk to pedestrians or other vehicles before initiating a pursuit].
- Discretion is checked in the Davis model by having incident reports reviewed by supervisors and other high command officers. The checking procedures . . . involve a commander or committee of supervisors of higher authority than an officer's immediate supervisor [an early intervention system that tracks officer-involved shootings to determine if there are any officers with unusually high rates of use of deadly force].[59]

Importantly, prior research has demonstrated that administrative rule making can effectively control police officer behavior in a number of misconduct and racial bias–prone areas. For example, research has consistently demonstrated that administrative policies—when enforced—can substantially curtail the rate of officer-involved shootings.[60] Alternatively, administrative permissiveness can also lead to *higher* rates of police shootings.[61] Police scholar Michael White, for example, found that the number of police shootings in Philadelphia increased significantly after a restrictive administrative policy was abolished in 1974.[62] Walker concluded that "administrative rules have successfully limited police shooting discretion, with positive results in terms of social policy. Fewer people are being shot and killed, racial disparities in shootings have been reduced, and police officers are in no greater danger because of these restrictions."[63] Similarly positive results have been documented with other types of formal police behavior, including high-speed pursuits, use of police dogs, foot pursuits, and responses to domestic violence incidents.[64] For example, police scholar Geoffrey Alpert found that the number of automobile pursuits, accidents, and injuries all dropped significantly in Miami following the adoption of a restrictive pursuit policy that (1) strictly forbade pursuits under certain conditions; (2) required that officers consider certain specified factors before initiating a pursuit (weather, risk to bystanders, seriousness of the offense); (3) required completion of a written report detailing the incident; and (4) required supervisory review of that incident report.[65]

Additionally, during the 1990s the Los Angeles Sheriff's Department (LASD) was criticized because of an increasing number of lawsuits alleging excessive force and racial discrimination in the deployment of police dogs. As a result, the LASD adopted a more restrictive policy that limited use of canines against unarmed suspects, especially auto theft suspects. Moreover, handlers were required to announce or warn before releasing their dog, and dogs were trained to "find and bark" rather than "find and bite." Following adoption of the new policy, canine deployments declined by 25 percent.[66] Last, in response to growing awareness of the dangers associated with foot pursuits, the International Association of Chiefs of Police developed a model policy that strictly confines officers' discretion by prohibiting foot pursuits under a wide range of circumstances, such as when the danger to the officer outweighs the necessity of immediate apprehension; when the officer is alone (unless exigent circumstances exist); when the suspect runs into structures, confined spaces, or isolated areas; and when the suspect's identity is known and apprehension at a later time is likely.[67]

The adoption of clearly articulated policies governing police stops of citizens, with specific prohibitions of racial profiling, is absolutely crucial for controlling unlawful, unjust police behavior. The body of research that highlights police departments' success in managing officer discretion across a wide range of police actions provides an important backdrop for consideration of SQF practices. The latter piece of the Walker and Archbold framework—the supervisory review and accountability component—is especially critical for stop and frisk because the practice generally does not reach the level of being classified as a critical incident.[68] For example, over the past several years in New York City, nearly 90 percent of SQF encounters have resulted in no formal action—no arrest, no citation, and no contraband found.[69] The "invisible" nature of such stops presents a unique challenge for effective discretionary control and guidance. That said, it is well established that officers' behavior changes when they know that violations of policy will have consequences. In plain terms, officers seek to avoid behavior that will get them into administrative trouble. This has been demonstrated across a range of officer field behaviors, particularly with use of deadly force[70] and automobile pursuits,[71] and it applies equally well to stop and frisk.

Two examples related to race/ethnicity help demonstrate the relevance of administrative rule making for SQF practices. First, as mentioned above, the Glendale (Arizona) Police Department developed clear administrative rules regarding immigration enforcement following the passage of SB 1070, including an Immigration Enforcement Field Card (see figure 5.1). The field card provides officers with guidance on a range of important issues, including relevant factors for determining reasonable suspicion and whether an immigration investigation is "practicable," valid forms of identification, and procedures for immigration questioning and arrest. Importantly, officers' immigration enforcement activities are closely monitored by supervisors. Second, Fridell and colleagues developed a model policy for the use of race or ethnicity in police work:

> Except as provided below, officers shall not consider race/ethnicity in establishing either reasonable suspicion or probable cause. Similarly, except as provided below, officers shall not consider race/ethnicity in deciding to initiate even those nonconsensual encounters that do not amount to legal detentions or to request consent to search. Officers may take into account the reported race or ethnicity of a specific suspect or suspects

Immigration Enforcement Field Card

REASONABLE SUSPICION

Officer is aware of specific, articulable facts which, when considered with objective and reasonable inferences, form a basis for particularized suspicion. Two elements: (1st) the assessment must be based upon the totality of the circumstances (2nd), that assessment must create a reasonable suspicion that the particular person is unlawfully present in the United States.

In determining whether reasonable suspicion of unlawful presence exists, officers should consider all relevant factors, including, among others:

(1) Lack of or false identification (if otherwise required by law)

(2) Possession of foreign identification

(3) Flight and/or preparation for flight; engaging in evasive maneuvers, in vehicle, on foot, etc.

(4) Voluntary statements made by the person regarding their citizenship or lawful presence. Note that if the person is in custody for purposes of Miranda, s/he may not be questioned about immigration status until after the reading and waiver of Miranda rights.

(5) Foreign vehicle registration

(6) Counter-surveillance or lookout activity

(7) In company of other unlawfully present aliens

(8) Location, including for example: a place where unlawfully present aliens are known to congregate looking for work or a location known for human smuggling or known smuggling routes.

(9) Traveling in tandem

(10) Vehicle is overcrowded or rides heavily

(11) Passengers in vehicle attempt to hide or avoid detection

(12) Prior information about the person

(13) Inability to provide their residential address

(14) Claim of not knowing others in same vehicle or at same location

(15) Providing inconsistent or illogical information

(16) Dress. Note: Dress has been recognized by the courts as a valid factor, but in practice is very difficult to articulate.

(17) Demeanor—for example, unusual or unexplained nervousness, erratic behavior, refusal to make eye contact

(18) Significant difficulty speaking English

PRESUMPTIVE (VALID) IDENTIFICATION

(For Detainee's NOT Arrestee's)

If the detainee presents one of the following types of identification, it is presumed that the detainee is lawfully present in the U.S. No further investigation into the person's status is necessary, unless there are additional facts that cast doubt on the person's lawful presence.

1. A valid Arizona driver license,
2. A valid Arizona non-operating identification license,
3. A valid tribal enrollment card or other form of tribal identification, or
4. If the entity requires proof of legal presence in the U.S. before any issuance, any valid U.S. federal, state, or local government issued identification. **

** NOTE: All State Drivers Licenses are acceptable, except Washington, New Mexico, Illinois and Utah. US Passports and some Military ID's are acceptable, see ID reference guide for further. (As of 7/10)

PRACTICABLE?

In determining whether it is practicable, officers should consider things such as work load, criticality of incident and of other present duties, available personnel on scene, location, available back-up, ability to contact ICE/CBP/287(g) and availability of ICE/CBP/287(g).

HINDER INVESTIGATION?

Officer should consider when or whether to investigate immigration status in light of the need for suspect, victim and witness cooperation in an investigation (this consideration is not necessarily limited to the investigation for which you have detained the person). Example – complex investigations of money laundering, human trafficking and drug smuggling may require significant cooperation of those involved.

NEW ARIZONA IMMIGRATION STATUTES

ARS 11-1051 Cooperation and assistance in enforcement of immigration laws

ARS 13-1509 Willful failure to complete or carry an alien registration document

ARS 13-2928 Unlawful stopping to hire and pick up passengers for work

ARS 13-2929 Unlawful transporting, moving, concealing, harboring or shielding of unlawful aliens

If at any time, in the sound judgment of an officer, the officer believes that the deviation from the G.O. is appropriate, the officer should contact a Supervisor.

MDC Enforcement Codes

Four enforcement codes exist for classifying immigration related contact:

I-1 Not Practicable

I-2 Hinder or Obstruct Investigation

I-3 No Reasonable Suspicion

I-4 Arrest and Processed by Detention

** Information contained in the documentation of category I-1 and I-2 will include as much of the following as possible:

1. Name
2. Date of birth
3. Physical description (hair, eyes, height, weight)
4. Home address and phone number
5. Work and/or school information if available
6. Date and time of contact
7. Circumstances of contact
8. Summary of efforts made (including date, time, name, and ID if ICE is contacted) Vehicle information (minimum of license plate, state, vehicle description)
9. Vehicle information (minimum of license plate, state, vehicle description)
10. Any other pertinent information

ARRESTS

All arrested persons shall have their immigration status verified by ICE/CBP/287(g) prior to the arrestee being released. Presentation by the arrestee of presumptive identification and/or agency identification processes does not meet this requirement

All arrested persons shall be asked the following questions, with the answers documented in the departmental report:

1. **What is your country of citizenship?**
   - If other than the United States, the next question should be asked, but only after Miranda warnings have been given (if a juvenile, use Juvenile Miranda Form).
   - Officers must comply with agency policies regarding consular notification for persons who self identify as being foreign citizens.

2. **Are you in the United States legally?**

3. **Do you have any registration documents or other proof of lawful presence?**

136

based on trustworthy, locally relevant information that links a person or persons of a specific race/ethnicity to a particular unlawful incident(s). Race/ethnicity can never be used as the sole basis for probable cause or reasonable suspicion.[72]

The body of research on administrative rule making provides strong evidence that a policy like the one above, if made available to officers and enforced by the department leadership, will effectively control police officer behavior related to stop and frisk.

Supervision, Accountability, and Commitment from the Top of the Organization

Department policies and rules, by themselves, are sometimes not enough to control police conduct.[73] The organizational leadership must clearly demonstrate support for those rules. If the informal norms of the department support racially biased strategies (including SQF practices), and those who engage in it go unpunished, administrative policies become meaningless. The informal norms of the department are greatly determined by the leadership of the organization. Chiefs of police who demand accountability, who punish officers for their transgressions, and who hold supervisors accountable for their subordinates' misbehavior will send a clear message to their line officers regarding what will (and will not) be tolerated. Darryl Gates in Los Angeles, Frank Rizzo in Philadelphia, and Harold Breier in Milwaukee demonstrate how attitudes of the chief can send a message to line staff that abusive and racially biased conduct is acceptable.[74] Similarly, unwavering support from the chief's office, even in the face of widespread criticism, can lead officers to justify and rationalize questionable practices. That was likely the case in New York, as both Mayor Michael Bloomberg and Police Commissioner Raymond

FIGURE 5.1 (left). Glendale (Arizona) Police Department Immigration Enforcement Field Card. Source: Glendale (Arizona) Police Department.

Kelly were adamant in their support of SQF, as illustrated by the quotes below:

> Mayor Bloomberg: "There is just no question that Stop-Question-Frisk has saved countless lives."[75]

> Mayor Bloomberg: "Every day, Commissioner Kelly and I wake up determined to keep New Yorkers safe and save lives. And our crime strategies and tools, including stop, question, frisk, have made New York City the safest big city in America."[76]

> Mayor Bloomberg: "Today, we have the lowest percentage of teenagers carrying guns of any major city across our country, and the possibility of being stopped by—acts as a vital deterrent—which is a critically important byproduct of stop, question, frisk."[77]

> Commissioner Kelly: "Last year, we saw continued, outstanding work from our police officers. . . . We ended 2011 with the lowest murder total in half a century and the lowest rate of auto theft in modern memory."[78]

> Commissioner Kelly: "No question about it, violent crime will go up [if SQF is abandoned by the NYPD]."[79]

Alternatively, police chiefs can change the informal norms of a department, as former Commissioner Patrick Murphy did for the NYPD following the corruption scandal in the early 1970s. "Murphy used his three and a half years in office to create an environment that loudly and clearly condemned abusive police conduct, those who engaged in it, and—equally important—those who tolerate it."[80] Twenty years later, the Mollen Commission concluded in its investigation of misconduct in the NYPD that "commitment to integrity cannot be an abstract value. . . . It must be reflected not only in the words, but in the deeds of the Police Commissioner."[81]

The words and deeds of the chief are equally important for preventing racially biased SQF practices and promoting lawful standards for officers' behavior during stops of citizens. We can return again to the immigration debate that occurred in Arizona a few years ago. Following passage of SB 1070, several police chiefs publicly challenged the new law. Then Chief Jack Harris of the Phoenix Police Department stated in his declaration before the U.S. District Court for the District of Arizona, "Deterring, investigating and solving serious and violent crimes are the department's top priorities, and it would be impossible for us to do our job without the collaboration and support of community members, including those who may be in the country unlawfully."[82] George Gascon, former chief of the Mesa Police Department (and current district attorney of San Francisco), similarly noted that the law

> will put officers in the impossible position of trying to enforce the law without racially profiling. . . . Most professional law enforcement leaders around [the] country are fairly united in their concerns about the impact that making immigration enforcement the primary function of local policing would have on resources, our ability to fight crime and our ability to work with various communities that may have significant representation of immigrants whether here with or without authority.[83]

Perhaps the best example of the impact of the chief (and city leaders) comes from New York City. The number of stop and frisks conducted by officers peaked in 2011 at 685,724, and though the number declined slightly in 2012, the NYPD still conducted more than half a million stops (532,911). The following year, 2013, was defined by the federal judge's ruling that the NYPD's SQF program was discriminatory, and by a mayoral election that served as a referendum on the SQF program (i.e., there were candidates both in favor and against the SQF program, and Mayor de Blasio, a major critic of SQF, won the election). The number of stops dropped precipitously during 2013 (191,558), and with a new police commissioner in place, the numbers during the first three quarters of 2014 continued to plummet (38,456).[84] Just as Commissioner Kelly was adamant about the use of SQF, his successor, Commissioner Bratton, was equally clear that changes were needed, as illustrated by comments from his first press conference:

> We will all work hard to identify why so many in this city do not feel good about this department. . . . My commitment and the commitment of the NYPD that I am privileged to lead will be to work with you and to ensure that at all times, policing in this city is done constitutionally, respectfully and compassionately.[85]

Also, in an extensive interview with ABC News three months into his tenure, Commissioner Bratton commented on the previous regime's use of SQF: "When asked point-blank . . . if he thought Bloomberg and Kelly went too far, Bratton said: 'In terms of stop, question and frisk, certainly.'"[86] Statements such as these from the chief send a clear message to officers regarding what is expected of them on the street. La Vigne and colleagues identified several core roles for the chief in managing a stop and frisk program:

- Communicate clear expectations within the department, and reinforce a culture of ethical and respectful behavior.
- Recruit officers who are service-oriented, representative of the communities they serve, and diverse in terms of their backgrounds and perspectives.
- Communicate with and solicit input from both internal and external stakeholders.
- Build accountability through measures such as documenting police interactions with citizens, analyzing data, and holding officers responsible for their actions.
- Train officers in the proper procedures for conducting stops and frisks and provide opportunities for continuing education.
- Assign officers to patrol the same neighborhoods to build relationships with the community.[87]

Supervision

Supervision of police officers is a critical department task that serves as a foundational element in the agency's effort to control officer field behavior, including SQF practices. Weisburd and colleagues reported that nearly 90 percent of police officers surveyed agreed that effective supervision prevents misconduct such as racially biased policing.[88] As Fyfe noted, "*Everything* that supervisors do or tolerate, every interpretation of broad departmental philosophy, every application of specific rules and policies is a training lesson that has at least as much impact on officers' performance as what they may have learned in their rookie days."[89] There are many good discussions of how to ensure effective supervision.[90] Key principles include proper span of control (eight to ten officers per sergeant), proper training (good supervision can and should be taught), and holding supervisors accountable for the behavior of their subordinates. The International Association of Chiefs of Police stated that "many officers face temptations everyday. . . . [M]anagement has the capacity and control to reinforce high integrity, detect corruption, and limit opportunities for wrong doing."[91] These words apply to *Terry* stops as well as they do for other forms of police field behavior. Simply put, if officers believe that they will be caught and punished for their racially biased, unjust behavior, they will be less likely to engage in those activities.[92]

External Oversight

The auditor model of oversight holds great promise as a reform and accountability mechanism. Under this model, one individual (or office) with some degree of legal and/or policing expertise serves as a full-time independent auditor. Auditors are typically permanent positions created by local or state law, and in the vast majority of cases, they have much greater authority than the more traditional citizen oversight board. As Walker and Archbold describe it,

> Police auditors have two special capabilities that enhance their ability to
> promote organizational change. First, as full-time government officials
> they have the authority to probe deeply into departmental policies and
> procedures with an eye toward correcting them and reducing future mis-
> conduct. . . . Second, as permanent agencies they can follow up on issues
> and determine whether or not prior recommendations for change have
> been implemented.[93]

Specific functions of the auditor include a range of activities such as
auditing the complaint process (how citizen complaints are received and
investigated), auditing police operations (use of the Taser), policy review
(use of canines—"find and bite" versus "find and bark"), community
outreach (serving as a liaison between police and citizens), and contributing to transparency (publishing reports that detail the activities of the
auditor).[94]

There are more than a dozen police auditors in the United States;
the most active and well established include the San Jose independent
police auditor, the Denver Office of the Independent Monitor, the special counsel to the Los Angeles Sheriff's Department, and the Boise ombudsman. A few examples may help to illustrate the importance of the
auditor model for controlling police discretion across a range of field
behaviors, including SQF practices. In 2003 the special counsel for the
LASD conducted a thorough review of the department's early intervention system, the Personnel Performance Index (PPI), and issued a report that detailed numerous deficiencies with the system.[95] In 2006 the
Boise ombudsman examined the Boise Police Department's handling
of encounters with the homeless. The ombudsman interviewed police
personnel, homeless providers, and homeless citizens, and examined
police reports detailing law enforcement actions taken against homeless
citizens. The report issued by the ombudsman included a number of
policy and practice recommendations, including the creation of a Crisis
Intervention Team (CIT):

Because of the number of homeless persons who suffer from mental illness, the Boise Police Department should institute a CIT program, or its equivalent. This would permit officers to better identify situations involving mental health issues and to respond to those situations by linking people to resources.[96]

In New York City, the Civilian Complaint Review Board (CCRB) performs some auditing functions, though its primary responsibility involves receiving and investigating specific citizen complaints against NYPD officers. In the wake of the federal court's ruling that the NYPD's SQF program was discriminatory, the New York City Council passed Local Law 70, which authorized the creation of the Office of Inspector General (OIG). The OIG functions as an independent auditor (it is part of the city's Department of Investigation) with the following mission:

> OIG-NYPD examines the NYPD's practices in a comprehensive and thorough way, identifying areas of concern and proposing reforms that add to the ongoing efforts to build a stronger relationship between New Yorkers and their police force. A cornerstone of OIG-NYPD's work is transparency; in addition to furnishing reports to the Mayor, the City Council and the Police Commissioner, OIG-NYPD posts reports on this website for the public to download and access.[97]

In January 2015 the OIG issued its first report, an examination of the use of chokeholds by NYPD officers. Though chokeholds are prohibited by the NYPD, the OIG identified and examined ten incidents where chokeholds were used (from 2009 to 2014), and the report describes each of those incidents, as well as their review and disposition by both the CCRB and the department.[98] Notably, the report does not cover the Eric Garner case. On July 17, 2014, NYPD officers conducted a stop and frisk of Garner, whom they suspected of selling untaxed cigarettes. During the officers' attempt to arrest Garner, one of the officers applied a chokehold.

Garner died shortly after the arrest, and in July 2015, the City of New York settled the impending lawsuit for $5.9 million. The OIG report highlights a number of problem areas, including the police commissioner's consistent rejection of CCRB recommendations on discipline for the officers who used chokeholds, inconsistency in the tracking and investigation of such cases, and potential training deficiencies.[99] Given its mission, the OIG will clearly monitor the NYPD's use of SQF going forward. This external review mechanism will provide an important check on officers' discretion in initiating stop and frisks of the citizens of New York.

Conclusion

By drawing on the larger body of research on police discretion, we have identified several lessons that departments can apply to prevent their officers from engaging in racially biased or otherwise improper and illegal behavior during *Terry* stops of citizens. These lessons must, of course, be considered in the context of the larger undercurrent of racial injustice that has defined police practices over the last 175 years. With that context as a backdrop, these lessons are as follows:

- Careful recruitment and selection includes both "screening out" and "screening in" processes. Muir's professional policeman, Mike Marshall, offers an excellent model for hiring officers who will both avoid racially biased behavior and bring a sense of empathy and compassion to policing.[100]
- Fyfe's recommendations for violence reduction training offer a solid foundation for training to prevent unjust and illegal stop and frisks.[101] This can be achieved with training that is realistic (adult learning, role-plays, instruction by legal experts, and coverage of implicit bias and the suspicion heuristic) and continuous; tailored to the department and the community (e.g., Glendale PD's response to SB 1070); and focused on the means (or process), not just the ends (i.e., avoiding the split-second syndrome).
- Administrative rules that are clear and routinely enforced will effectively control officer behavior on the street, and will shape the informal norms of the department.

- Accountability begins in the chief's office and flows down through the organization to the first-level supervision of line officers.
- External oversight through an independent auditor provides a critically important check on police officer discretionary decision making.

These lessons are clear and straightforward, with obvious implications for policy and practice. Just as important, they are supported by empirical research, and they offer a road map for effective control and guidance of officer discretion during stop and frisk activities.

6

The Future of Stop and Frisk

Policing, like all professions, learns from experience. It follows, then, that as modern police executives search for more effective strategies of policing, they will be guided by the lessons of police history.
—George Kelling and Mark Moore, 1988[1]

Stop and frisk was not "invented" in the 1990s in New York City as part of the NYPD's broken windows style of policing. The strategy has a long legal and historical tradition dating back long before the *Terry v. Ohio* decision in 1968. Yet the experiences in New York have been profoundly complex. Disentangling the potential crime-control benefits of SQF and fully understanding the consequences of SFQ for the residents of New York neighborhoods where the strategy has been concentrated have been some of the primary goals of this book. Moreover, although the dialogue over SQF, its crime-control impact, and its consequences centers on New York City, the strategy is commonly used by police departments across the United States—in some cases, with the same controversy and concerns over racial profiling that emerged in New York. As we have stressed, a police officer's decision to stop a citizen based on reasonable suspicion is an exercise in discretion. As a consequence, there is a large body of robust empirical research that we can draw on to effectively guide (and control) officer decision making in stop and frisk encounters. The lessons outlined in the previous chapter provide a clear road map forward for both departments and their officers to ensure that discretion during stop and frisk activities is exercised in a fair, just, and constitutional manner.

It is also important to recognize that the historical backdrop for stop and frisk has changed considerably over the last several decades. The last forty years have arguably been the most innovative in the history of policing. Since the mid-1970s, a host of new strategies have emerged on the law enforcement landscape, beginning with problem-oriented policing (POP) and community-oriented policing (COP), to more recently, hot spots policing, focused deterrence/pulling levers (e.g., targeted offender strategies), intelligence-led policing, Smart Policing, and even predictive policing. The innovation in strategies has been matched by the development of new technologies such as geographic information systems (GIS), crime analysis and advanced analytics, CompStat, DNA and forensics, license plate readers, less-lethal alternatives (pepper spray, Taser), drug and alcohol field testing, body-worn cameras, and gunshot detection systems. The tremendous innovation in how police go about their daily business (strategies) and the tools they use to conduct that business (technologies) will clearly define the policing profession in the twenty-first century. The proper role for SQF practices in twenty-first-century policing, in the wake of this tremendous innovation, warrants serious consideration and is the focus of this final chapter.

The epigraph at the beginning of the chapter from Kelling and Moore highlights the importance of history for policing, as it provides valuable lessons regarding the next best steps moving forward. Interestingly, Kelling and Moore made those statements back in 1988, just as the wave of innovation was beginning (COP and POP had emerged, but little else of the innovation describe above). They go on to offer a historical framework that "presents an interpretation of police history that may help police executives considering alternative future strategies of policing."[2] Their framework divides policing into three eras—political, reform, and community/problem-solving—and they describe each era in terms of seven interrelated categories: source of legitimacy/authority; police primary function or role; organizational design; relationship to the external environment; management of the demand for police services; tactics and technologies employed to achieve their objectives; and the measures of police success.

Though by no means perfect, this framework provides both a useful characterization of police history and a means for considering the next era of policing—what we call *twenty-first-century policing*. Clearly, much has changed since the late 1980s, but the Kelling and Moore framework provides a useful tool for organizing our thoughts on the key features of twenty-first-century policing, as well as the role of stop and frisk in this new era. Not coincidentally, at the time we write this book there is a Presidential Task Force on 21st Century Policing, which has held hearings throughout the first several months of 2015. The task force, created in the wake of the shooting of Michael Brown in Ferguson, Missouri (and several other racially charged police incidents, including the chokehold death of Eric Garner by New York City police officers), is seeking to identify evidence-based and best practices that should shape policing in the years to come, with a specific emphasis on community collaboration and public trust. The existence of the President's Task Force and the growing number of highly publicized police killings of citizens in 2014 and 2015 are stark reminders of the undercurrent of racial injustice in American policing. The prominence of this undercurrent, at a time when police have made significant advances in other areas, is both disheartening and sobering. As we consider the role of SQF in twenty-first-century policing, we recognize the persistent tensions that have plagued American policing for decades and produced the current crisis in police relations with minority citizens.

Kelling and Moore's Historical Framework

In their classic essay, Kelling and Moore categorized approximately 150 years of professional policing in the United States into three specific eras—political, reform and community/problem-solving—each of which was "distinguished by the apparent dominance of a particular strategy of policing."[3] The three eras were characterized in terms of seven organizational categories, as shown in table 6.1. Each of the eras warrants some discussion.[4]

TABLE 6.1 Kelling and Moore's Three Eras of Policing

Dimensions	Political (1840s–1900s)	Reform (1920s–1970)	Community/ problem-solving (1970s–1980s)
Legitimacy/source of authority	Primarily local/ political	Law and professionalism (reject politics)	Law still; but also community support
Function	Crime control, order maintenance, broad service	Crime control	Crime control, order maintenance, problem solving, conflict resolution
Organizational design	Decentralized/ geographical	Bureaucracy: centralized, specialized hierarchy	Decentralized
Relationship to environment	Close and personal	Professionally remote ("just the facts"); disconnected	Partnership; community involvement
Demand	Local politicians/face-to-face with citizens	Calls for service	De-emphasize 911; citizen consultation (customer preference)
Tactics and technology	Foot patrol; individual power and authority	Reactive, preventive patrol (car); rapid response	Foot patrol; problem solving
Key outcome	Political satisfaction	Crime control, measured by "activity"	Quality of life; citizen satisfaction; crime

Source: Kelling and Moore, "Evolving Strategy of Policing."

Political Era

The political era (1840s–1900s) began with the development of the first professional police departments in the United States in quickly expanding northeastern urban centers such as Philadelphia, New York, and Boston. Unlike the London Metropolitan Police Department, where officers were representatives of the crown, police departments in the United States were tied to local, ward-level politics. Officers served at the pleasure of a local politician, and in fact, patrol positions were typically given out (or bought) because of connections to a local ward leader. Departments had no selection criteria, pre-service standards, or training—their authority derived directly from local politics. The function of the police during the political era was very broad and determined by both politicians and citizens. Though crime control was a clear responsibility, officers spent much of their time engaged in order maintenance and service-related responsibilities, from managing conflicts between citizens on the street to staffing soup kitchens. Police departments were highly decentralized. Each specific precinct functioned as its own department, with little regular or direct contact with headquarters. Similarly, officers were very isolated from their colleagues and supervisors once on the job, given the lack of communication and transportation at the time (though call boxes were invented in the 1890s). Since all patrol was done by foot, police were well integrated into the fabric of the neighborhood where they worked. Police officers found out about crime because they either observed it themselves or were flagged down on the street by a witness. "Street justice" was a common method for handling problems, given officers' lack of pre-service standards and training, poor supervision, and the isolated nature of patrol work. The primary outcome measure was, of course, political satisfaction (and to a lesser extent, citizen satisfaction).

Reform Era

The first fifty years of professional policing represented an inauspicious start, characterized by no hiring standards, no training, corruption, brutality, intimate involvement in politics, and virtually no professionalism. Early external efforts to reform the police (and city politics more generally) in the 1880s (i.e., the Progressives reform effort) failed, but by the turn of the twentieth century, a reform agenda had begun to take hold within policing itself. The professionalism movement was led by August Vollmer, O. W. Wilson, and other reform-minded chiefs who sought to isolate police from politics, increase hiring standards and training, and improve the performance of officers on the street. As table 6.1 indicates, the police reformers sought to ground the authority of the police in the law and professionalism, rather than local politics. They also sought to strip away all of the service-related functions from the police, and to limit their function to crime control. In fact, the reform era (1920s–1970) was characterized by officers who were deemed to be professional crime fighters, remote and disconnected from citizens (e.g., Joe Friday's oft-quoted "Just the facts, ma'am" [from the television series *Dragnet*]). Citizens were viewed as simply a source of information about crime.

The leaders of the reform movement applied bureaucratic principles to the organization and management of the police, most notably centralization of authority to headquarters, strict organizational hierarchy with a rigid chain of command, and specialization of expertise (e.g., the formulation of special units that dealt with very specific types of crimes—robbery, gangs, juvenile, vice, etc.). Moreover, the emergence of three technological advances—the telephone, the automobile, and the two-way radio—facilitated the development of a reactive, preventive patrol strategy whereby officers drove around their geographic beats in marked vehicles waiting for calls for service from citizens in need. When a call came in, officers responded rapidly and dealt with the problem in a triage-like or superficial manner so that they could return to preventive patrol as quickly as possible (without really solving the problem that led to the call in the first place). The nature of this formulaic response, coupled with the professionally remote relationship to citizens, served to distance police from the citizens they served, particularly citizens in minority communities. Not surprisingly, the primary outcome measures during the reform era focused on crime, "activity" (arrests, tickets, etc.), and rapid response—what Skolnick and Fyfe called the "numbers game."[5]

Community Problem-Solving Era

The professional model developed by Vollmer and other police leaders represented a clear improvement over the state of affairs in the political era, but by the 1960s a number of developments signaled that the professional model was in trouble. First, from 1960 to 1970 the national crime rate more than doubled. The reform era was premised on the notion that the police were professional crime fighters, and when the police were unable to respond effectively to a soaring crime rate, serious questions began to emerge about the manner in which they conducted their day-to-day business (e.g., reactive, preventive patrol; rapid response with a triage-like handling of incidents). Additionally, the 1960s were a tumultuous time when police were under the national spotlight as a result of the Due Process revolution (e.g., the watershed rulings from the U.S. Supreme Court that placed new restrictions on the police with regard to rights of the accused—right to legal counsel, *Miranda* rights, search and seizure, etc., as explained in chapter 3), their role in managing civil rights and antiwar demonstrations, and their actions that sparked a number of race riots throughout the decade. Interestingly, the Supreme Court also handed down the ruling in *Terry v. Ohio* (1968) during this decade (as well as the *Sibron* and *Peters* cases), which gave police a new investigative tool with a lower burden of proof (reasonable suspicion). Notably, many of the problems that faced police were tied directly to their inability to connect with citizens, particularly minority citizens.[6]

As the professional model was coming under fire, a number of police departments opened themselves up to researchers, and scholars began studying the police and their role. Scholars like James Q. Wilson, Jerome Skolnick, William Westley, Egon Bittner, William Muir, Herman Goldstein, and Peter Manning began to question the core elements of the professional model of policing. This emerging body of research led to what Kelling and Moore called the "community problem-solving era"—the last column in table 6.1 (1970s–1980s).[7] In this era, the law still served as the source of police authority, but community support emerged as an important alternative source. In effect, the police were to be responsive to community needs. Crime control, of course, remained a central function of the police, but the development of community- and problem-oriented approaches required that police address a larger array of problems, including order-maintenance issues and disorder problems. The central thrust of problem-oriented policing requires that officers go through a problem-solving process that includes identification of a problem (through repeated calls for service from the same location;

through talking to citizens, etc.), investigation of the causes of the problem, and then development of responses to address the problem.

In this era, the police moved back to a decentralized organizational model, in which responding to 911 calls was de-emphasized. Instead, police were to proactively engage with citizens to identify specific problems, and they were to include citizens in their activities as co-producers of public safety. Additionally, seminal research in the 1970s had seriously undermined the perceived effectiveness of the reactive, preventive patrol model (e.g., Kansas City Preventive Patrol study), and suggested that foot patrol, in conjunction with a problem-solving model, was a more effective way to engage with citizens, deal with crime and disorder problems (with *Terry* stops as one of many mechanisms for doing so), and reduce fear of crime. In terms of outcome measures, police performance continued to be measured using the "numbers game," but quality of life and citizen satisfaction also emerged as additional performance indicators.[8]

Critiques of the Kelling and Moore Framework

Despite its popularity, the Kelling and Moore framework has been heavily criticized for the manner in which it paints a broad-brush, White, Anglo-Saxon picture of police history. Police scholars Williams and Murphy articulated a "minority view" of policing that is vastly different from the Kelling and Moore view across all three of their eras, as they argue that the police role in upholding legal order (traditionally defined by control of minorities and the lower class) has set the tone for police-minority relations over the last 150 years.[9] For example, in their analysis of the political era, Williams and Murphy trace the origins of professional policing in the United States to slave patrols in the South, and note that Kelling and Moore completely ignore anti-Black sentiment in northern cities.[10] Moreover, the political era was defined by political influence: those who had power and influence controlled the police. Black communities were completely left out of this equation.

Williams and Murphy point to more of the same during the reform era, as the shift away from political influence had little impact on Black residents, and the efforts to professionalize police largely excluded Blacks as potential police officers. Quite simply, at a time when Vollmer was revolutionizing police standards and practices, communities throughout the United States continued to segregate Blacks from Whites under the U.S. Supreme Court–approved "separate but equal" doctrine.[11] Finally, in the community problem-solving era, Black communities were gutted as "White flight" and quiet riots (unemployment, poverty, social disorganization) left those communities with little in the way of resources or infrastructure to generate the requisite empowerment and cohesiveness that defines successful community policing.[12]

The New Era: Twenty-First-Century Policing

Kelling and Moore published the document that outlined this framework in 1988,[13] and clearly, much has changed in the last twenty-five years. We believe that policing has entered a new era—*twenty-first-century policing*—and a result, we have added a new column to the Kelling and Moore historical framework (see table 6.2). Many of the principles from the community problem-solving era also define the twenty-first-century policing era, as both community- and problem-oriented policing remain popular and empirically supported strategies.[14] For example, the law and the community continue to be the primary sources of police authority, and the police function remains broad enough to include crime, disorder, and quality of life issues. In the post-9/11 era, most departments (especially big-city agencies) have incorporated counterterrorism into their mission. Departments still tend to be organizationally decentralized, but the twenty-first-century police department is much more focused and data-driven. Departments engage in strategic planning, research, and evaluation. The police relationship to the external environment is defined by collaboration with the community and a host of other stakeholders, including external researchers.[15]

TABLE 6.2 The New Era of Policing

Dimensions	Political (1840s–1900s)	Reform (1920s–1970)	Community/problem-solving (1970s–1980s)	21st-century policing (1990s–current)
Legitimacy/source of authority	Primarily local/political	Law and professionalism (reject politics)	Law still; but also community support	Law and community support
Function	Crime control, order maintenance, broad service	Crime control	Crime control, order maintenance, problem solving, conflict resolution	Crime, disorder, quality of life issues, terrorism
Organizational design	Decentralized/geographical	Bureaucracy: centralized, specialized hierarchy	Decentralized	Decentralized, flexible
Relationship to environment	Close and personal	Professionally remote ("just the facts"); disconnected	Partnership; community involvement	Collaboration with community and other stakeholders
Demand	Local politicians/face-to-face with citizens	Calls for service	De-emphasize 911; citizen consultation (customer preference)	Proactive; data-driven crime analysis and GIS; focus on problem places and people
Tactics and technology	Foot patrol; individual power and authority	Reactive, preventive patrol (car); rapid response	Foot patrol; problem solving	*Terry* stops, COP/ POP; hot spots/ targeted offenders; analytics, body-worn cameras and other technology
Key outcome	Political satisfaction	Crime control, measured by "activity"	Quality of life; citizen satisfaction; crime	Procedural justice and legitimacy; crime reduction

Though the demand for police service is still driven by community needs, the twenty-first-century police department is much more pro-active about identifying problems. Advanced crime analysis, crime mapping (geographic information systems, or GIS), and intelligence gathering serve to identify problem areas and problem people, and routine examination of daily and weekly trends assess whether existing problems have been addressed and whether new problems have emerged (e.g., weekly CompStat meetings; partnerships with independent researchers). Departments also increasingly rely on a body of empirical evidence from researchers and organizations that document effective and promising practices, from Crimesolutions.gov[16] and the George Mason Policing Matrix[17] to the Smart Policing Initiative[18] and the Center for Problem-Oriented Policing.[19] For example, the Smart Policing Initiative website states,

> The Smart Policing Initiative (SPI) . . . supports law enforcement agencies in building evidence-based, data-driven law enforcement tactics and strategies that are effective, efficient, and economical, . . . a strategic approach that brings more "science" into police operations by leveraging innovative applications of analysis and technology. . . . The goal of the SPI is to improve policing performance and effectiveness while containing costs.[20]

Technology continues to play a foundational role in twenty-first-century policing, as the 1990s and 2000s have been defined by enormous technological advancement. Examples include GIS, crime analysis and advanced analytics, CompStat, DNA and forensics, license plate readers, less-lethal alternatives (pepper spray, Taser), drug and alcohol field testing, body-worn cameras, and gunshot detection systems. Police strategies and tactics have also continued to develop over time, with increased emphasis on the places and people that create the most crime problems (e.g., hot spots and targeted offender approaches), as well as the continued emphasis on community- and problem-oriented policing. And for many police departments, *Terry* stops remain a core strategy for combatting crime.

In terms of outcomes, police performance is still measured by crime levels, as well as citizen satisfaction, but the terms "procedural justice" and "legitimacy" have now entered the police lexicon. Law professor Tom Tyler defines legitimacy as "a psychological property of an authority, institution, or social arrangement that leads those connected to it to believe that it is appropriate, proper, and just."[21] Tyler argues that legitimacy generates deference to authority through self-regulation, as people follow the rules "even when the risk of getting caught is low or nonexistent."[22] In other words, people follow the law (and obey the police) because they believe it is the right thing to do, not because they fear the consequences that may occur if they get caught breaking the law. The value of legitimacy for police lies in how it shapes citizens' attitudes and behavior. Prior research has consistently connected enhanced police legitimacy to important outcomes for the police—most notably, citizen compliance with police commands during an encounter, cooperation with police authority (reporting crimes, providing information about crimes, etc.), and obedience to the law.[23] Tyler and Fagan concluded that

> [t]he value of a legitimacy based approach rests on the finding that appeals to legitimacy shape people's behavior. The findings outlined here show that they can. They demonstrate that people are more willing to cooperate with the police when they view the police as legitimate social authorities. If people view the police as more legitimate, they are more likely to report crimes in their neighborhood.[24]

Under Tyler's normative framework, the most viable method for generating police legitimacy is procedural justice. Procedural justice is typically defined as the way police treat citizens and the fairness of the decisions that police make.[25] Prior research has identified four key components of procedural justice: citizen participation (being given the opportunity to state one's case), fairness and neutrality, dignity and respect, and trustworthy motives.[26] Importantly, research has highlighted the importance of procedural justice as a mechanism for generating enhanced police legitimacy.[27] As criminologist Lorraine Mazerolle and colleagues concluded,

> Perceptions of procedural justice in the specific context not only influence specific attitudes about police, but also more general beliefs about the police. . . . [O]ur findings show that the more "procedurally just" the

police strive to make even a short encounter, the more likely citizens are to perceive the police as legitimate. Put simply: A little bit of being nice goes a long way.[28]

In plain terms, how police treat people matters a great deal. It matters during informal encounters. It matters during stop and frisk encounters. It matters during arrest encounters. Treating citizens with dignity, respect, and fairness is the cornerstone of procedurally just policing.

The Persistent Undercurrent of Racial Injustice in Twenty-First-Century Policing

A number of events during the summer of 2014 and spring of 2015 have demonstrated the persistence of the most difficult problem plaguing police during the last seventy years: tense, antagonistic relations with minority communities. These events also highlight the larger undercurrent of racial injustice that has permeated American policing since its origins in the mid-1800s. The shooting of Michael Brown in Ferguson, Missouri, in August 2014, and the civil disorder that followed, laid bare the fact that many police departments have failed to build trust and legitimacy with residents in minority communities. Other examples that highlight continued race relations problems include the racial profiling cases against the Maricopa County (Arizona) Sheriff's Office and the New York City Police Department, and the deaths of Black citizens at the hands of the police, including Eric Garner (New York), Tamir Rice (Cleveland), Tony Robinson (Madison), Walter Scott (North Charleston), and Freddie Gray (Baltimore). The continuing race-relations problems of police can be linked to their role as enforcers of a legal order that has traditionally been defined by racism.[29] In effect, as police progressed through the political, reform, and community problem-solving eras, the minority community was left behind. Events in 2014 and 2015 suggest that the same is occurring in the new era of twenty-first-century policing.

The events in 2014 led to the creation of the President's Task Force on 21st Century Policing in December of that year. The task force, composed of police leaders, scholars, attorneys, and civil rights advocates handpicked by the White House, was charged with the following mission:

> The Task Force seeks to identify best practices and make recommendations to the President on how policing practices can promote effective crime reduction while building public trust and examine, among other issues, how to foster strong, collaborative relationships between local law enforcement and the communities they protect.[30]

During the first few months of 2015, the task force heard testimony from more than two dozen experts across a range of general topics, including trust and legitimacy, policy and oversight, technology (most notably, body-worn cameras) and social media, community-oriented policing, training and education, officer safety and wellness, and the future of community-oriented policing. The task force issued a final report to President Obama in May 2015 based on the testimony. The opening statement of the final report clearly identifies the foundation of twenty-first-century policing: "Trust between law enforcement agencies and the people they protect and serve is essential in a democracy. It is key to the stability of our communities, the integrity of our criminal justice system, and the safe and effective delivery of policing services."[31]

The final report outlines nearly sixty specific recommendations and action items that should be taken to build trust between police and citizens, ranging from broad-based reviews of the entire criminal justice system and community-based initiatives that address poverty, education, health, and safety, to very concrete recommendations involving the racial/ethnic diversification of police departments, the promotion of positive contacts between citizens and police, and the consideration of collateral consequences resulting from crime-control strategies. The takeaway message from the summer of 2014 and spring of 2015, the creation of the President's Task Force, and the recommendations of that task force to the White House, is straightforward and troubling: Despite the substantial progress made during the community problem-solving and twenty-first-century policing eras, there are many jurisdictions across the country where the relationship between police and citizens, particularly minority citizens, is defined by mistrust, anger, and tension. The racial injustice undercurrent in American policing remains disturbingly strong.

Charting a Course for Stop and Frisk in Twenty-First-Century Policing

We believe that the President's Task Force report provides a road map for better policing in the United States. Clearly, procedural justice, police legitimacy, and community trust in police will continue to serve as the foundation of twenty-first-century policing. Innovation in strategies, tactics, and technology will also continue to play a central role. A key question for our purposes here is the identification of a proper role for stop, question, and frisk in collaboration with the various strategies that police departments will employ as part of twenty-first-century policing. Importantly, the use of SQF must occur in a way so that the strategy does not contribute to racial injustice.[32]

Problem-Oriented Policing

In 1979 Herman Goldstein argued that the police had gotten caught up in a "means over ends" syndrome, where their focus was directed toward maintaining internal process measures, such as response times and administrative efficiency, rather than dealing with the problems they were being called upon to handle.[33] More specifically, the police should focus their efforts on discrete types of problems (e.g., homicide, disorder, drunk driving) and develop customized responses to each type of problem. This would require the police to define problems with greater specificity, engage in research to understand the problems, and explore alternative responses to the identified problems. Police scholars John Eck and William Spelman enabled agencies across the country to more easily adopt problem-oriented policing (POP) by articulating its basic concepts through an easy-to-remember acronym—SARA: scanning (problem identification), analysis (investigation of the causes of the problem), response (comprehensive strategies that attack the causes of the problem), and assessment (evaluate the impact of the response).[34]

Problem-oriented policing has taken on a variety of forms over the past thirty years, with police agencies often focusing on particular people, places, and events that generate crime, disorder, or other problem behavior. Prior evaluations have consistently supported the effectiveness of POP strategies in reducing crime and disorder such as firearm-related homicides, street-level drug dealing, and violent and property crime.[35] Weisburd and colleagues identified more than 5,500 studies of problem-oriented policing; they conducted a meta-analysis of ten methodologically rigorous studies (i.e., those that utilized an experimental or quasi-experimental design), concluding that POP had "a small but meaningful impact" on crime and disorder.[36] The researchers lamented the fact that most POP projects have not used methodologically rigorous research designs.[37] Other scholars have noted that, in practice, agencies often engage in "shallow problem solving," which does not reflect Goldstein's original vision.[38]

A number of scholars have responded to these concerns by employing more sophisticated research designs as well as researcher-practitioner partnerships to ensure sufficient implementation of the SARA model, especially the analysis and assessment phases. For example, as part of its Smart Policing Initiative, the Glendale (Arizona) Police Department partnered with criminologists from Arizona State University to devise a problem-oriented approach to address convenience store crime. The project began with advanced POP/SARA training (twenty classroom hours), followed by in-depth, continuous problem analysis (led by the ASU researchers and crime analysts), comprehensive response development (suppression, stakeholder engagement, prevention), and advanced assessment (process and impact evaluations). The evaluation demonstrated that calls for service at target convenience stores declined by 42 percent, while calls at other convenience stores in the city remained flat or increased.[39]

SQF and Problem-Oriented Policing

Problem-oriented policing will continue to be a central focus of twenty-first-century policing, and stop, question, and frisk should play an important role in the deployment of POP. As officers begin the scanning process, they should draw on a host of data to identify potential problems, and the official reports generated through SQF are a valuable source of information that should be tapped. How often are individuals being stopped? What are they being stopped for? Where are they being stopped? A content analysis of stop and frisk reports can also be part of the problem analysis phase. Should SQF be considered part of a response plan in POP? The answer to this question is simple: it depends on the problem. The SARA model is designed to be intuitive and fluid, with strong connections between each phase. In other words, a response in the POP model should be specifically designed to target the underlying causes of the problem that are identified in the analysis phase. POP projects tend to be focused on problem places (hot spots), problem people (prolific offenders), or problem people in problem places (prolific offenders in targeted hot spots). Though responses that are consistent with Goldstein's original vision should be comprehensive (not just enforcement-based), stop and frisk can play a vital role in effective POP responses. Police departments should be acutely aware of the potential for widespread use of SQF to create or exacerbate racial tensions, and use of the strategy should be measured, not systemic.

For example, in 2007 the Boston Police Department developed problem-oriented policing teams (called safe street teams, or SSTs) and deployed those teams to identified crime hot spots.[40] The specially

trained POP teams utilized nearly four hundred specific POP strategies, which included situational/environmental interventions (focused
on changing environmental features conducive to crime), community outreach/social service interventions (community engagement in
crime prevention), and enforcement interventions (formal law enforcement activities design to address crime, including *Terry* stops).[41] The
work of the safe street teams reflected the spirit of Goldstein's vision,
as enforcement interventions, such as SQF, were the least commonly
used strategy. In each of the thirteen identified hot spots, the POP team
implemented, on average, 15 situational/environmental interventions,
9.4 community outreach/social service interventions, and 6.1 enforcement interventions. The Boston SST program (part of its Smart Policing Initiative) reduced violent crime by nearly 20 percent, while at the
same time officers effectively engaged with the residents and business
owners in those neighborhoods. Stop and frisk was an enforcement tool
that was employed as part of a larger comprehensive response to crime
and violence.

Community-Oriented Policing

Community-oriented policing (COP) is grounded in the philosophical
argument that the best way for police to address disorder, community
decay, and crime is to build a collaborative relationship with the residents of the community. This collaborative relationship will provide
police with greater access to information and, in turn, will make the
police more responsive to community needs.[42] In effect, the police and
community are co-producers of public safety. This strategy emerged in
the 1970s and is reflected in the third era of Kelling and Moore's historical framework. The COP strategy has continued as part of the policing
dialogue into the twenty-first century, in large part because of Title I of
the 1994 Violent Crime Control and Law Enforcement Act (the Public Safety Partnership and Community Policing Act). Title I created the
Office of Community Oriented Policing Services (the COPS Office), and

FIGURE 6.1 President Obama's Community Policing Plan

authorized it to spend $9 billion on grants to state and local law enforcement agencies to facilitate the implementation of community policing.[43]

Additionally, in September 2014 the U.S. Department of Justice announced the creation of a National Initiative for Building Community Trust and Justice, designed to "enhance community trust and help repair and strengthen the relationship between law enforcement and the communities they serve. The National Initiative will explore, advance, assess, and disseminate information about strategies intended to enhance procedural justice, reduce implicit bias, and support racial reconciliation."[44] And of course, community-oriented policing is central to the recent work of the White House in the wake of the events during the summer of 2014 and the spring of 2015. Figure 6.1 shows the president's three-part plan to strengthen COP, including the Body-Worn Camera Partnership Program and the President's Task Force on 21st Century Policing.[45]

There is no set list of programs or elements that are to be employed when adopting community policing, in large part because COP is intended to be a cultural change in a department rather than a programmatic change.[46] However, there are some common characteristics from department to department. Cordner notes that there are four major dimensions of community policing:

- Philosophical dimension: citizen input, broad police function, and personal service.
- Strategic dimension: reoriented operations (less car patrol; disorder focus); geographic focus (permanent beat assignments); prevention focus.
- Tactical dimension: positive interactions; partnerships; problem solving.
- Organizational dimension: structure (decentralized, de-specialized); management (strategic planning; appreciation for creativity); information (broader performance measures; use of crime analysis).[47]

The core elements of COP have also recently been compared to counterinsurgency strategies employed by the military in Afghanistan and Iraq.[48] More generally, there is a clear shift away from the "cops as soldiers in a war" mentality, and the term "counterinsurgency" is problematic because of its overt militaristic connotations.[49] Nevertheless, the parallels between COP and counterinsurgency are noteworthy, as demonstrated by a *60 Minutes* segment on May 5, 2013, that highlighted how in both strategies, officers engage with the residents of a community; gain their trust and confidence; explain their actions, especially crime-control activities; and focus on developing positive relationships so citizens will provide police with valuable information about the criminal activity in the neighborhood.

Evaluations of COP have produced mixed results. Most studies demonstrate that it is difficult to implement on a full scale.[50] One study reviewed sixty COP evaluations and found some modest positive effects on crime and disorder as well as fear of crime.[51] Moreover, this study found that both citizens and officers generally embraced COP (especially if the officers were volunteers for the program). The most comprehensive implementation of COP to date, called the Chicago Alternative Policing Strategy (CAPS) Program, produced similar, somewhat mixed results: COP comes with a high degree of difficulty in terms of implementation; it was not fully embraced by the community; but it did lead to less crime, less fear of crime, less gang activity, and more positive attitudes toward the police.[52] A consistent theme in research on COP is that the strategy tends to work most effectively in communities that have, at the very least, modest reserves of cohesiveness and collective efficacy.[53] In effect, community-oriented policing requires active participation by the community, and not just a handful of activists or leaders, but a significant portion of residents and business owners who are intimately involved in the community.[54] Williams and Murphy noted that minority communities experienced "quiet riots" during the 1960s and 1970s that stripped those areas of the necessary social and material infrastructure necessary to engage in COP.[55] Additionally, the undercurrent of racial injustice often runs deep and strong in those same communities, leaving many residents with anger, resentment, and distrust of police, which can undermine a COP strategy before it even starts. The implementation of COP in such communities comes with a much higher degree of difficulty.

SQF and Community-Oriented Policing

Community-oriented policing will continue to make a resurgence during the twenty-first-century policing era, driven in large part by the COPS Office, the White House, and the National Initiative for Building Community Trust and Justice. What role can SQF play in community-oriented policing? Criminologist Gary Cordner's description of the four dimensions of COP offers a framework for considering the proper role of SQF in community-oriented policing.[56] For example, the philosophical and strategic dimensions are characterized by strong citizen input and permanent beat assignments that allow officers to develop relationships and become integrated into the fabric of their assigned neighborhoods. Officers can use SQF as a tool that is targeted at specific individuals based on information gathered from community members (e.g., consistent with "counterinsurgency" principles, and not employed in a programmatic, department-wide manner). Constitutional standards still apply, of course, but under a COP approach the reasonable suspicion required for a stop and frisk can frequently be generated through third-party intelligence gathering (or that information can at least serve as a starting point). In terms of the tactical dimension of COP, Cordner highlighted problem solving and a focus on positive interactions between police and citizens.[57] The overlap here between COP and POP brings into play the previous discussion of how SQF can be integrated into problem-oriented policing. The intelligence-gathering function mentioned above can be part of a broader positive interaction program that emphasizes informal citizen encounters that can serve to build community trust in police. And with regard to the organizational dimension, Cordner highlighted the importance of gathering information.[58] As described here, SQF is both a product of information gathering from citizens as well as a source of additional information on potential crime in a neighborhood, based on the information gathered during the *Terry* stops.

Hot Spots and Targeted Offender Strategies

Two other popular twenty-first-century policing strategies involve the identification and targeting of specific places and people that are disproportionately responsible for crime, often referred to as hot spots and targeted offender policing.

Hot spots policing has a strong theoretical foundation grounded in the crime and place research, situational crime prevention, and routine activities theory, which states that crime occurs when a motivated offender and suitable target come together in time and place absent a capable guardian.[59] The general principle is that crime tends to cluster disproportionately in a few areas, in many cases very small micro places such as specific houses, bars, and street corners. A number of studies have supported this principle. One study found that 3 percent of the addresses in the city of Minneapolis were responsible for 50 percent of the calls for service to police.[60] Hot spots policing seeks to better direct limited police resources to those areas where crime is most prevalent, and to reduce crime at those locations by increasing guardianship, increasing risk of detection, and reducing crime opportunities. Hot spots policing has received strong empirical support. In the Minneapolis hot spots experiment, Sherman and Weisburd randomized 110 hot spots to either receive supplemental preventive patrol (two to three times the normal amount of patrol) or serve as control areas.[61] After an eight-month study period, they reported significant declines in crime calls and observed disorder in the treatment hot spots. Criminologist Anthony Braga conducted a systematic review of hot spots studies; among the nine studies he identified, seven documented significant crime reductions.[62] The National Academy of Sciences report concluded,

> Studies that focused police resources on crime hot spots provide the strongest collective evidence on police effectiveness that is now available. On the basis of a series of randomized experimental studies, we conclude that the practice described as hot spots policing is effective at reducing crime and disorder and can achieve these reductions without significant displacement of crime control. Indeed, the research evidence suggests that the diffusion of crime control benefits to areas surrounding treated hot spots is stronger than any displacement outcome.[63]

A more recent meta-analysis found similarly positive crime-control benefits for hot spots studies (with evidence of diffusion of benefits), but the authors also noted that the crime reductions were greatest when officers engaged in problem-oriented policing in the hot spots, as opposed to simple police patrol.[64]

Relatedly, a number of law enforcement agencies have sought to target the most active criminal offenders in identified crime hot spots. In some cases, the most prolific offenders are identified for law enforcement intervention (arrest and prosecution). As part of its Smart Policing Initiative, the Los Angeles Police Department developed Operation LASER:

> The basic premise is to target violent repeat offenders and gang members who commit crimes in the specific target areas with "laser-like precision," analogous to laser surgery, where a trained medical doctor uses modern

technology to remove tumors or improve eyesight. First, the area is care-fully diagnosed—who are the offenders and where and when are they involved in criminal activity? Plans are then developed to remove offend-ers from an area, while minimizing the disruption and harm to the larger community. Extraction of offenders takes place in a "non-invasive" man-ner (no task forces or saturation patrol activities) and the result produces less disruption of neighborhoods by police.[65]

In other cases, the intervention is much more sophisticated, such as the "pulling levers" framework (also referred to as focused deterrence). Developed in Boston in the 1990s to address gang violence, the pull-ing levers strategy applies the basic POP framework: a crime problem is identified; a multi-agency stakeholder group is convened that includes law enforcement, prosecution (federal and local), community leaders, and social service representatives; key offenders are identified; and a response is designed with multiple interventions for different types of offenders.[66] For example, the most active, violent offenders (called "A listers") are targeted for arrest and prosecution. The second group of offenders, those who are not as violent or who are on the periphery of the criminal group ("B listers"), are targeted for a "call-in." The call-in is a formal meeting of relevant stakeholders and offenders, where "B listers" are given a very specific focused deterrence message that puts them on notice (law enforcement knows you are committing crime; if you continue, we will arrest you); conveys the impact of their behavior on the community; and offers services to help them break their cycle of criminal behavior. The pulling levers approach has been applied in a number of jurisdictions across the country through U.S. Department of Justice–funded programs such as Strategic Approaches to Community Safety and Project Safe Neighborhoods, and the results suggest that the approach can significantly reduce crime and violence.[67]

Questions remain regarding what officers should do in identified hot spots. The Philadelphia Police Department and researchers at Temple University recently compared the crime reduction effects of foot patrol,

POP, and offender-focused strategies in identified hot spots. Eighty-one hot spots were selected, with twenty-seven assigned to each strategy. Within each strategy, twenty hot spots were randomly assigned to get the strategy and seven hot spots served as controls.[68] The police interventions lasted from four to seven months, and the results showed that only the offender-focused strategies produced significant crime declines: 22 percent decrease in violent crime; 31 percent decrease in violent street felonies.[69]

SQF, Hot Spots, and Hot People

Hot spots policing is an established and empirically supported twenty-first-century policing strategy. The research demonstrates that officers can do any number of things in crime hot spots, from simple preventive patrol, to COP and POP, to laser-like targeting of specific offenders. SQF can and should be a valued tool in hot spots and targeted offender approaches. If officers are assigned to do community- or problem-oriented policing in hot spots, there are a number of ways to effectively include SQF in those strategies. The danger with hot spots policing approaches, particularly those that rely heavily on SQF, is that many of the targeted areas will likely be low-income, minority neighborhoods. In fact, one study recently characterized the NYPD's use of SQF as a form of hot spots policing that may have effectively led to reduced crime in the city, albeit with significant negative consequences for citizens who live and work in those hot spots.[70] The more recent hot spots projects in Los Angeles and Philadelphia offer a viable framework for including SQF in hot spots policing. In Los Angeles, the Criminal Intelligence Detail developed more than a hundred "chronic offender bulletins" that offered detailed information on wanted offenders who were known to frequent the identified hot spots. The offender bulletins, which were updated on a regular basis, provided officers with an important resource to focus their attention on specific offenders rather than applying an NYPD-like expansive approach that has a larger community impact.

Ratcliffe and colleagues effectively articulated the proper role of SQF in twenty-first-century targeted place/offender strategies:

> A carefully implemented OF [offender-focused] strategy can be less intrusive for law abiding citizens. By focusing on specific people who are suspected or known to be involved in illegal and/or violent activity, police can avoid broad-based increases in pedestrian and automobile stops which disproportionately affect those living in impoverished, minority neighborhoods. The fact that there were no significant differences in the numbers of pedestrian or car stops or narcotics incidents lends support to the interpretation that OF enables police officers to be more judicious with their field investigations. Second, an add-on benefit of stopping the "right" people instead of a wide cross-section of people is that such a strategy makes it more likely that the community will perceive police actions as procedurally just.[71]

Stop and frisk can play an important role in place-based and targeted offender strategies. But that role should be defined carefully, monitored closely, and assessed regularly for collateral consequences.

Broken Windows/Order-Maintenance Policing

James Q. Wilson and George Kelling published their seminal article "Broken Windows: The Police and Neighborhood Safety" in the *Atlantic Monthly* in 1982.[72] Wilson and Kelling make a crucial link between disorder and crime, and describe how this link impacts the social fabric of a neighborhood. Their argument centers on the proverbial broken window, which if left unrepaired, sends a message that no one cares about the appearance of the property. In practical terms, the broken window is a metaphor for disorder and indicates that there is a breakdown in the informal social controls that govern behavior in the neighborhood. No one cares, so no one fixes the window. The unrepaired broken window will soon draw other signs of disorder, which can spark a downward spiral of deterioration. The spread of disorder in the area is facilitated by the fear it creates. Residents begin to avoid spending time outside; they become unconcerned about who is standing on street corners; they become less likely to get involved in community activities; and they become less likely to call the police. The decline in the sense of the community and the increasing level of disorder make the area vulnerable to criminal activity and predatory behavior.[73]

Wilson and Kelling argued that because of this link between disorder, social cohesion, and crime, police should focus their efforts on disorder and quality of life issues in neighborhoods, and they should engage with the community in their efforts. As police reduce the level of disorder, residents' fear will decrease and the informal social controls will begin to take hold again. Finally, the absence of disorder and the strengthened social cohesion will prevent the spread of serious crime into the area. In many ways, broken windows serves as the foundation for community-oriented policing. But it is also clearly the theoretical backdrop for order-maintenance (or broken windows) policing. The best example of order-maintenance policing comes from New York City, and its implementation coincided with large drops in crime in New York that have persisted well into the twenty-first century. The role of the NYPD generally, and order-maintenance policing specifically, in the crime decline has been hotly contested (see chapter 4).

Many scholars have equated order-maintenance policing with "zero tolerance" policing, though Kelling and other proponents strongly oppose the connection.[74] Zero tolerance is distinctive from broken windows in several ways. First, there is no partnership between the community and the police in zero tolerance policing.[75] From the zero tolerance perspective, the community is likely unable to possess the strong institutions and social cohesiveness to effectively partner with police in crime-control efforts.[76] Under a pure broken windows approach, the citizens are involved and, in fact, the efforts by police are designed to increase their community engagement. Second, in the zero tolerance model there is no emphasis on identifying the underlying conditions of problems or engaging in any sort of problem-solving process. It simply involves a law enforcement response to low-level offenders such as fare beaters, prostitutes, vagrants, loiterers, and aggressive panhandlers. Under broken windows, physical and social disorder is targeted by police because it is the underlying condition. Last, zero tolerance does not involve any sort of innovation like the previously described strategies (POP, COP, hot spots, targeted offenders). It simply involves a back-to-the-basics approach that focuses on low-level crime and disorder.[77] A pure version of broken windows or order-maintenance policing would involve problem solving by officers as well as aspects of community-oriented policing.

In sum, there are clear conceptual distinctions between broken windows/order-maintenance policing and zero tolerance policing. But there is also evidence to suggest that those conceptual distinctions can disappear in practice. For example, many scholars have argued that the NYPD approach in the 1990s and 2000s devolved into zero tolerance policing.[78] In 1999, for example, the NYPD created Operation Condor, which used up to a thousand officers per day to flood drug-infested areas of the city and to target low-level drug transactions with aggressive tactics. Criminologists Amanda Geller and Jeffrey Fagan reported that in 2006 alone there were 32,000 arrests for marijuana possession, a 500 percent increase from the previous decade.[79] Another study linked the zero tolerance tactics, especially stop and frisk, to indicators of police problem behavior (e.g., citizen complaints and civil suits) and to tension between police and minority neighborhoods.[80] Similar claims have been made about a strategy employed by the Los Angeles Police Department in the skid row section of Los Angeles.[81] The Safer Cities Initiative was designed as a broken windows–based approach that would employ saturation patrol, problem solving, and linkages to services for homeless. In practice, the initiative was dominated by a strategy that mirrored zero tolerance:

> The officers worked eastward through the skid row section, breaking up homeless encampments, issuing citations and making arrests for viola-

tions of the law. The plan was to clear out specific street areas, maintain a visible police presence for at least a week, and then move onto other parts of downtown.[82]

More generally, police scholars have highlighted concerns with zero tolerance tactics, including a negative impact on police-community relations; a potential to increase crime in the long run (as arrest records for targeted individuals hinder their ability to find and maintain employment); and the disproportionate impact on poor and minority communities.[83]

SQF and Broken Windows/Order-Maintenance Policing

Given the current focus on building community trust and police legitimacy, and the persistent undercurrent of racial injustice, it is likely that order-maintenance/broken windows policing will play a diminishing role in twenty-first-century policing. And zero tolerance will have no place at all. For law enforcement agencies that employ broken windows policing, it is unclear how SQF can be effectively incorporated into the strategy. The NYPD's experience over the last twenty years has created an implicit linkage in the minds of many between SQF and "hyperaggressive crime-control tactics."[84] Extensive use of stop and frisk, even if done within constitutionally required standards, may have deleterious consequences for police relations with citizens, particularly in minority communities. The perceptions of racial injustice in some minority communities is simply too pervasive to tolerate programmatic use of SQF. There are limits to what a community will tolerate with regard to aggressive use of stop and frisk, and the line between broken windows policing and zero tolerance policing can quickly become blurred. Moreover, several scholars have also questioned the disorder-crime connection, which is at the very core of broken windows theory.[85]

This is not to say that police should ignore disorder or low-level offenses. Rather, the focus on such offenses should be derived through other twenty-first-century policing strategies that garner community input and support, such as POP, COP, and even hot spots policing. If the use of SQF in conjunction with a focus on low-level crime and disorder is developed through community engagement, problem solving, and crime analysis, the strategy will be insulated from the vulnerabilities of broken windows/order-maintenance policing—particularly the susceptibility to devolve into zero tolerance policing.

A Brief Note on Technology: Stop and Frisk, Body-Worn Cameras, and Big Data

New and emerging technologies may interface with the use of *Terry* stops in complex ways. First, consider the rapidly expanding use of police officer body-worn cameras. Officer body-worn cameras (BWCs) are relatively small devices that record interactions between community members (e.g., the public, suspects, and victims) and officers, from the officer's point of view. The video and audio recordings can be used by the police to document statements, observations, behaviors, and other evidence. The technology creates a permanent video record of formal police activities as officers engage with citizens during traffic stops, arrests, searches, interrogations, and critical incidents such as officer-involved shootings.[86] Though interest and experimentation with police officer body-worn cameras dates as far back as 2005, interest in the technology has skyrocketed since the summer of 2014, with the deaths of Michael Brown in Ferguson and Eric Garner in New York. Though there are few good estimates available, data from a Bureau of Justice Statistics (BJS) survey in 2013 found that nearly one-third of police departments in the United States (approximately 6,000) were using BWCs.[87] Experts estimate that the number of BWC adopters will continue to grow exponentially.[88]

On December 1, 2014, President Obama announced a three-year, $263 million plan to strengthen community policing through enhanced training, additional resources, and increased partnerships between the U.S.

Department of Justice and local law enforcement. As part of that plan, the White House Body Worn Camera Partnership Program seeks to establish, build, and sustain trust between communities and their local and state law enforcement agencies through the deployment of body-worn cameras. The plan includes a proposed $75 million investment that would provide a 50 percent match to state and local agencies for the purchase of up to 50,000 cameras and requisite video storage. In May 2015 the Bureau of Justice Assistance of the U.S. Department of Justice rolled out a National Body-Worn Camera Toolkit to serve as an information warehouse that will guide police departments in their efforts to properly plan and implement body-worn camera programs.[89] In September 2015 the U.S. Department of Justice announced grant awards for body-worn cameras to seventy-three law enforcement agencies totaling $19.3 million.

Among agencies adopting body-worn cameras, most have built into their administrative policy the requirement that supervisors review officer video under certain circumstances. Nearly all agencies require supervisors to review available video in response to a specific complaint or if there is a critical incident such as a use of force, officer or suspect injury, or pursuit (automobile or foot). The vast majority of *Terry* stops would not fall into these review criteria. However, given the problems associated with overuse and misuse of SQF and the collateral consequences of the strategy, body-worn cameras provide a unique opportunity for police leaders to routinely monitor officer behavior during stop and frisk activities. Much like official data collection procedures employed by agencies to monitor racial profiling (e.g., data collection and public issuance of statistical reports), BWC video provides an accountability and transparency mechanism for police agencies to, first of all, ensure that their officers are engaged in proper and just use of stop and frisk; and second, demonstrate and share with the public the information from those reviews.

There are a number of ways that agencies could design their body-worn camera reviews of SQF practices. The review could be targeted only at specific officers who have been identified as potentially problematic, either through complaints, an early intervention system, or supervisor nomination. The review could also be implemented through a periodic random process where, for example, each month some number of randomly selected officers' recent SQF activity is reviewed by a supervisor. This could also be a responsibility of an independent auditor. Or a department could decide to review all SQF activity that is captured by a body-worn camera. Decisions on the review process would have to be made locally between the department leadership, union representatives, and other relevant stakeholders. That said, federal oversight into local law enforcement is likely to increase during the twenty-first-century policing era through both the traditional Special Litigation Section of the Civil Rights Division, U.S. Department of Justice,[90] and the more recent collaborative reform process through the COPS Office.[91] In the near future it is likely that both federal mechanisms will include body-worn cameras as a required element of the standard accountability remedy package. Police departments can be proactive by embracing the use of body-worn cameras for stop and frisk review in order to short-circuit problems before they occur, and to demonstrate accountability and transparency to their communities (especially if they allow for external, independent review of BWC video).

The second technological development that will likely shape the use of stop and frisk is "big data"—that is, vast troves of information that can be used by police such as databases that capture criminal and driving history, biometric data, employment and housing records, spending habits, and a wide range of other individually specific behaviors or attributes. Professor Andrew Ferguson has recently suggested that the use of big data by police has implications for the Fourth Amendment and the articulation of reasonable suspicion to justify stop and frisk.[92] Ferguson argues that, until now, reasonable suspicion has been generated through "small data": behavior that the officer witnesses (e.g., furtive movements) or limited information the officer has about the individual being observed (e.g., known offender on probation). But what if a police officer is able to achieve the reasonable suspicion threshold by drawing on aggregate big data sources that are accessible in the field?

Suppose police are investigating a series of robberies in a particular neighborhood. Arrest photos from a computerized database are uploaded in patrol cars. Facial recognition software scans people on the street. Suddenly there is a match—police recognize a known robber in the targeted neighborhood. The suspect's personal information scrolls across the patrol car's computer screen—prior robbery arrests, prior robbery convictions, and a list of criminal associates also involved in robberies. The officer then searches additional sources of third-party data, including the suspect's GPS location information for the last six hours or license plate records which tie the suspect to pawn shop trades close in time to prior robberies. The police now have particularized, individualized suspicion about a man who is not doing anything overtly criminal. . . . This new reality simultaneously undermines the protection that reasonable suspicion provides against police stops and potentially transforms reasonable suspicion into a means of justifying those same stops.[93]

Earlier we highlighted the problem of conflating a highly discretionary police activity with a very low burden of proof, and Ferguson's questions about the potential role of big data and predictive analytics in policing only enhance these concerns. Recall the events that transpired on October 31, 1963, when Officer McFadden observed Terry and Chilton on a street in Cleveland (*Terry v. Ohio*, 1968). McFadden did not know either man, and he could not specifically say what drew his attention to them. As he observed their behavior for at least ten minutes, he became increasingly suspicious, leading him to detain and frisk the men (and another who had joined them). Now imagine how differently that case may have played out if it happened in 2015, not 1963, and McFadden is the officer described in Ferguson's scenario above. At what point does McFadden have articulable reasonable suspicion to initiate the stop? The officer's use of big data—arrestee photos, facial recognition, GPS, and license plate records—would have occurred in a minute or two, well before Terry and Chilton's "small data" behavior would have generated enough suspicion to justify the stop and frisk.

This is an intriguing and in many ways worrisome hypothetical that highlights the increasingly important role of technology in policing, and the challenges that technology will pose for maintaining a balance between crime-control efforts of police and the protection of citizens' civil liberties. This balance becomes even more precarious in distressed communities where there is a long history of tension and antagonism between police and citizens (the aforementioned undercurrent of racial injustice). Quite simply, residents in poor, mostly minority communities may resent the deployment of technology and big data in their neighborhoods. Research has not sufficiently explored citizens' views about police body-worn cameras, for example, leaving open the possibility that there could be a backfire effect with the technology. That is, BWCs are designed to enhance transparency and legitimacy, but in communities where reserves of police legitimacy are low and the racial injustice undercurrent is strong, residents may view BWCs as an unwarranted intrusion into their daily lives. Under such circumstances, BWCs could actually further damage police-minority community relations. Police leaders should be conscious of this potential backfire effect, and should engage with residents as they develop their BWC programs.

Conclusion

We began this book with two quotes that represent an almost fifty-year journey for the stop, question, and frisk strategy. The first quote comes from the majority decision in *Terry v. Ohio* (1968), in which Chief Justice Earl Warren lays out the rationale for creating a new constitutional theory supporting a practice that allows police to stop, question, and frisk (and search in some cases) citizens based on a lower burden of proof than probable cause. The rationale is based on officer safety and effective crime control. The second quote, from the federal court in the litigation against the NYPD's use of stop and frisk, demonstrates how horribly wrong things had gone in one police department's use of this strategy. The majority of this book focuses on what has transpired during the five decades between *Terry v. Ohio* and *Floyd v. City of New York*, as well as what role SQF should play in the new era of twenty-first-century policing. There are several major lessons from this five-decade journey, and these lessons represent our primary conclusions on the impact, consequences, and proper role of stop and frisk in American policing.

Stop and Frisk Is a Constitutionally Accepted Practice

Though the NYPD experience has influenced the judgment of many observers, SQF is a constitutionally accepted practice with a long legal history. This is a fact. Stop and frisk should not be used interchangeably with the term "racial profiling." The origins of SQF can be traced back to English common law. The contemporary legal framework was set forth in *Terry v. Ohio*, but SQF in twenty-first-century policing is the culmination of a series of important court rulings that have shaped and expanded the authority granted to police in the original *Terry* case in 1968. A complete understanding of SQF, its implementation, impact, and consequences requires consideration of the full legal history and tradition—not just the *Terry* case.

The Historical Undercurrent of Racial Injustice Is Still Strong

The core controversy surrounding SQF programs involves police and race, but this controversy is part of a larger race relations problem that must be considered as we contemplate the future of SQF.[94] Scholars have claimed that police reform over the first 150 years ignored minority communities,[95] and that assertion remains true in the twenty-first century. The minority view of policing is not defined by evidence-based practices, data-driven decision making, or randomized controlled trials that rigorously test police tactics. The minority view of policing is more likely defined by unconstitutional stop and frisks, disproportionate use of force, and a seemingly contradictory combination of overly aggressive policing in some communities and abandonment in others. The prominence of this racial injustice backdrop is reflected in the police killings of Michael Brown, Eric Garner, Walter Scott, and Freddie Gray (among others). The backdrop is even centrally featured in the final report of the President's Task Force on 21st Century Policing, which recommends that "[l]aw enforcement agencies should acknowledge the role of policing in past and present injustice and discrimination and how it is a hurdle to the promotion of community trust."[96] Any discussion of the role of SQF in twenty-first-century policing must acknowledge the long history of racial injustice in policing.

Widespread SQF Programs Do Not Produce Notable Crime-Control Benefits

There is little consensus on the crime-control effects of SQF in New York or elsewhere. Clearly, New York experienced a significant crime decline that coincided with numerous changes in the NYPD under William Bratton's leadership—one of which was increased use of SQF. But crime declined in many other places that did not employ aggressive use of SQF, CompStat, and broken windows policing (or zero tolerance policing, depending on one's perspective). The authors believe that SQF played some role in the New York City crime decline, but that role cannot possibly be disentangled from the effects of other NYPD activities or other local, state, national, or even global-level factors that may have also contributed to the decline. Moreover, available evidence indicates that the crime-control effects were likely modest.[97] Given the resources required to manage a large-scale SQF program like the one implemented by the NYPD, and the collateral consequences that may be generated, the return on investment for a widespread, deterrence-based SQF program is very likely to be poor.

Widespread SQF Programs Generate Collateral Consequences

Regardless of its crime-control effect, the NYPD's overuse and misuse of SQF violated the constitutional rights of thousands of New Yorkers. The unconstitutional SQF program produced severe collateral consequences: it negatively affected the emotional and physical well-being of thousands of mostly minority New Yorkers through violation of their constitutional rights; caused significant damage to the NYPD's relationship with minority residents in neighborhoods throughout the city; and as a result, seriously impaired the NYPD's ability to effectively fight crime in those neighborhoods. Unfortunately, the experiences in New York were witnessed in other jurisdictions that also overused and misused SQF. Law professor Tracey Meares has noted that the *Terry* stop was intended as an individualized crime investigation tactic that police could employ in response to suspect behaviors that generated reasonable suspicion of criminal activity.[98] The NYPD SQF program was expanded far beyond these original intentions into a pervasive, department-wide surveillance program that sought to generate deterrence through fear of being stopped. A program designed in this manner is at great risk of producing unconstitutional behavior on the part of the police.[99]

Moreover, the deployment of an NYPD-like SQF program in communities where the racial injustice undercurrent is strong will undoubtedly exacerbate tensions between police and minority citizens, and will quickly erode the limited reserves of police legitimacy. When police-minority community relations reach this level, they represent a powder keg that will explode in the wake of a controversial arrest, use of force, or citizen death. The deaths of Michael Brown in Ferguson and Freddie Gray in Baltimore demonstrate this tragic point. Last, the President's Task Force on 21st Century Policing highlighted the potential for collateral consequences in two of its recommendations, concluding that police "should consider the potential damage to public trust when implementing crime fighting strategies," and that evaluations of the "effectiveness of crime fighting strategies should specifically look at the potential for collateral damage of any given strategy on community trust and legitimacy."[100]

Previous Efforts at Discretion Control Offer Important Lessons for Stop and Frisk

Stop and frisk is, in its most basic form, an exercise in discretion. There is a long history of police abuses of discretion, especially in encounters with minority citizens. That history has led to a large body of literature on effective police discretion control, and the lessons from that research provide a road map for successful control and guidance of officer discretion during stop and frisk. Those lessons are grounded in careful recruit selection (screening out [and in] processes); training (by legal experts and including a focus on implicit bias [and the suspicion heuristic[101]]); administrative policy; supervision, accountability, and commitment from the chief; and external oversight through an auditor. Yet the potential impact of SQF on race relations is perhaps greater than other areas where discretion control has been successful, such as consent searches, police shootings, use of K-9s, and automobile pursuits. Such critical incidents are rare in their occurrence, compared to SQF, which can become a daily part of minority citizens' lives.[102] We agree with Bellin that a large-scale SQF program, even if devised with noble intentions, will inevitably drift into "unconstitutional waters" if the program is not rigorously and continually monitored.[103] The auditor model of police oversight provides opportunities to routinely regulate an SQF program, as an auditor can periodically investigate organizational processes that include training, policy, supervision, data collection (e.g., ensure that officers are completing appropriate reports to document stops), and accountability. An auditor can also assess the legality of specific stops, either in certain neighborhoods or by certain police units, and he or she can engage with citizens to assess the potential for collateral consequences (e.g., act as a liaison between citizens and the police).

Body-worn cameras (BWCs) are becoming a routine part of policing in the twenty-first century. BWCs offer a unique opportunity for police departments to track, monitor, and control officer decision making during stop and frisk activities through systematic (or at least periodic) review of officers' BWC footage. BWC review can be performed by first line supervisors, by training units, by internal affairs units, or by external auditors. The technology also represents an opportunity for police departments to demonstrate accountability and transparency to their communities. Other new and emerging technologies, such as big data, will also shape SQF in the next several years.

Stop and Frisk Has a Proper Role in Twenty-First-Century Policing

We have entered a new era of policing defined by a host of promising and effective strategies—community- and problem-oriented policing, hot spots, and targeted offender strategies, and a wide range of technological advances from DNA and crime analysis to license plate readers and body-worn cameras. Moreover, procedural justice and legitimacy have emerged as critically important outcomes for police that, especially in the wake of the events of the summer of 2014 and spring of 2015, will define the measurement of professional, humane policing in the twenty-first century. SQF has a proper place in twenty-first-century policing, though its use and impact vary depending on the strategy that is employed. SQF, if used justly and selectively (and not as a widespread deterrence-based program where SQF activity itself becomes a performance measure), can be successfully applied with community-oriented policing, problem-oriented policing, hot spots policing, and focused deterrence/pulling levers policing. As agencies couple stop and frisk with evidence-based strategies, they must still be mindful of the potential for collateral consequences, particularly in communities where the undercurrent of racial injustice remains strong. Deploying a constitutionally permissible, effective stop and frisk program requires intensive training, clear administrative policy, and continuous monitoring, preferably by both internal management and external stakeholders. In short, the management of an effective stop and frisk program involves a high degree of difficulty, and the consequences of failure are potentially severe.

As a final parting thought, the authors draw on one of the primary recommendations in the final report of the President's Task Force on 21st Century Policing:

> Law enforcement culture should embrace a guardian mindset to build public trust and legitimacy. Toward that end, police and sheriffs' departments should adopt procedural justice as the guiding principle for internal and external policies and practices to guide their interactions with the citizens they serve.[104]

Procedural justice involves treating people with dignity and respect; giving individuals "voice" during encounters (an opportunity to tell their side of the story); being neutral and transparent in decision making; and conveying trustworthy motives.[105] Stop, question, and frisk activities should be examined critically in terms of legal standards (was there articulable reasonable suspicion?) and in terms of procedural justice standards. During a stop and frisk, was the citizen treated with dignity and respect? Was the citizen given an opportunity to tell his or her side of the story? Was the officer neutral and transparent? Did the officer convey trustworthy motives? Police departments that benchmark their SQF practices along these standards, while applying the lessons described above, will achieve police legitimacy in the eyes of their citizens and will emerge as leadership organizations in twenty-first-century policing.

Epilogue

During the time that this book was in production, the federal monitor appointed to oversee the settlement in *Floyd* issued a report analyzing NYPD stop and frisk activities for a portion of 2015. The report found a number of problems with the stops, including officers' failure to document the reasons for stops, supervisors' failure to question the missing information, and shortcomings in officer training. There are several important points that provide context for interpretation of the monitor findings.

First, it is extraordinarily difficult to reform police departments that have been engaged in widespread unconstitutional policing. Under the authority of 42 U.S.C. § 14141, the U.S. Department of Justice has initiated actions against nearly forty law enforcement agencies for a "pattern or practice" of unconstitutional policing, resulting in more than two dozen consent decrees. The consent decree, which outlines the remedies an agency must implement, are typically designed to last five years, though federal oversight often lasts much longer. For example, the Los Angeles Police Department was under consent decree for nine years. The Detroit Police Department was under consent decree for nearly fourteen years. And some agencies, such as the Cleveland Division of Police, have been under consent decree twice. Police reform is a complex, multi-year process with a high level of difficulty. It involves organizational change in a profession characterized by resistance to change, and the remedies target functions that go to the very core of policing: supervision, training, policy, and accountability.

Second, the NYPD relied on stop and frisk as the dominant crime-control strategy for twenty years. Stop and frisk is deeply embedded in the department, and few patrol officers have any memory of the department before the stop and frisk program emerged. Yet, in 2015, the NYPD conducted approximately 24,000 stops—an enormous decline from the 685,000 stops conducted in 2011. Moreover, our own analysis of the data reveals that although every NYPD precinct experienced a significant decline in the total number of stops, that decrease was particularly notable in communities that had previously been affected by racially disproportional rates of stop and frisk activities. Indeed, the ten precincts with large minority populations showed that the racial/ethnic concentration of stops had dropped by nearly 10 percent overall in those precincts, with some precincts experiencing declines of 50 percent or more.

Third, even though the number of stops had fallen dramatically, the percentage of stops resulting in arrest had more than doubled. And although the percentage of stops where weapons and contraband were seized remained low, those percentages had doubled or tripled compared to the 2011 rates. These data suggest that the NYPD is transitioning to more effective practices. In other words, stops appear to be more efficient and accurate.

Fourth, the NYPD has initiated new policies (such as the tear-off receipt) and new training. Thus far, it appears the department has altered its day-to-day practices. Importantly, the reforms in the NYPD's stop and frisk program coincided with continued declines in crime and violence in New York, especially homicides, which declined by 35 percent from 2011 to 2014. The downward trends in both property crimes and violent crimes—especially the decrease in homicides—directly contradict any claim that reduced use of stop and frisk caused an increase in violence in New York. In short, there is no evidence to suggest that reforms to stop and frisk compromised the NYPD's ability to fight crime effectively.

Finally, and dishearteningly, racial disparities in those subjected to stop and frisk persisted. Minorities remained overrepresented among those stopped, frisked, searched, and arrested by the NYPD. Thus, as the monitor's report suggests, there is still much work to be done, but we should not overlook the progress that has been made during the last two years. The structure for effective police reform in New York is in place. The federal monitor reviews NYPD activities, analyzes data, and issues public reports with recommendations for change. The public nature of the reports places tremendous pressure on the NYPD to follow that road map and address those deficiencies.

Although this epilogue focuses on the NYPD, the post-*Floyd* story in New York City underscores our recommendations in chapter 6 about the role of stop and frisk in twenty-first-century policing. The recent monitor's report highlights deficiencies in supervision, policy, and training, but it also provides a plan for continued reform. There is reason to be hopeful—both in New York and elsewhere.

NOTES

CHAPTER 1. TWO TALES OF STOP AND FRISK

1 *Terry v. Ohio*, 392 U.S. 1 (1968).

2 *Floyd v. City of New York*, 959 F. Supp. 2d 540, 562 (2013).

3 In this book we use the terms "stop, question, and frisk," "SQF," "stop and frisk," and "*Terry* stop" interchangeably.

4 *Floyd v. City of New York*, 959 F. Supp. 2d 540 (2013).

5 Johnson et al., "International Implications of Quality-of-Life Policing."

6 White, "New York City Police Department."

7 Wintemute, "Guns and Gun Violence."

8 See, e.g., Kelling and Bratton, "Declining Crime Rates"; Zimring, *City That Became Safe*; and *Justice Quarterly* 31, no. 1 (2014).

9 Spitzer, *New York City Police Department's "Stop and Frisk" Practices*.

10 Fagan et al., "Street Stops and Broken Windows Revisited," 310.

11 *Daniels v. City of New York*, 138 F. Supp. 2d 562 (S.D.N.Y. 2001).

12 Jones-Brown et al., *Stop, Question, and Frisk Policing Practices*.

13 *Floyd v. City of New York*, Complaint.

14 Jones-Brown et al., *Stop, Question, and Frisk Policing Practices*, 20.

15 12 Civ. 2274 (S.D.N.Y. March 28, 212); see also 538 Fed. Appx. 101 (2d Cir. 2013); 736 F.3d 118 (2d Cir. 2013); 736 F.3d 231 (2d Cir. 2013); 743 F. 3d 362 (2d Cir. 2014).

16 10 Civ. 0699 (S.D.N.Y. June 24, 2010); see also 812 F. Supp. 2d 333 (S.D.N.Y. 2011); 902 F. Supp. 2d 405 (S.D.N.Y. 2012); 959 F. Supp. 2d 324 (S.D.N.Y. 2013).

17 Fratello et al., *Coming of Age with Stop and Frisk*.

18 Center for Constitutional Rights, *Stop and Frisk*, 1.

19 Jones-Brown et al., *Stop, Question, and Frisk Policing Practices*.

20 Ibid. In 2003 there were 627 guns recovered out of a total of 160,851 stops. In 2008 there were 824 guns recovered out of a total of 540,320 stops.

21 Ibid.

22 *Bailey v. City of Philadelphia*, Consent Decree.

23 Ofer and Rosmarin, *Stop and Frisk*, 5.

24 Brennan and Lieberman, "Florida City's 'Stop and Frisk.'"

25 *Terry* stops of pedestrians have been the central issue in New York, Philadelphia, and Newark, as well as other jurisdictions. Stops of citizens in automobiles is a related issue that has also drawn much controversy, particularly with regard to racial profiling (e.g., see Rice and White, *Race, Ethnicity, and Policing.*). *Stop and Frisk*

focuses on exclusively pedestrian stops by police, although some of the law governing these stops is also drawn from automobile stops. Clearly, SQF of citizens on the
street is primarily a tactic used by police in densely populated, typically large urban
areas such as New York. The strategy is much less popular in rural and sprawling
suburban areas where pedestrian traffic is light. As a consequence, many of the
jurisdictions that have experienced problems with *Terry* stops can be found in the
Northeast, or in densely populated sections of cities in other parts of the country.

26 Hawkins and Curwood, *Pleas of the Crown*, 129.

27 Warner, "Uniform Arrest Act," 317.

28 *Brown v. Texas*, 443 U.S. 47 (1979); *United States v. Mendenhall*, 446 U.S. 544
(1980); *Michigan v. Long*, 463 U.S. 1032 (1983).

29 *Alabama v. White*, 496 U.S. 325 (1990).

30 *Whren v. United States*, 517 U.S. 806 (1996).

31 *Here & Now*, "Bill Bratton."

32 See Jablonski, "Cleveland Councilman Zack Reed."

33 *Michigan Daily*, "Dismiss Stop and Frisk."

34 Walker and Archbold, in *The New World of Police Accountability*, offer a similar
accountability framework summarized as "PTSR": policy, training, supervision,
and review.

35 Tyler, *Why People Obey the Law*.

36 Mazerolle et al., "Shaping Citizen Perceptions of Police Legitimacy."

37 Kelling and Moore, "Evolving Strategy of Policing."

38 Williams and Murphy, "Evolving Strategy of Police: A Minority View."

39 Fyfe, "Police Use of Deadly Force."

40 Skolnick and Fyfe, *Above the Law*.

41 Research has consistently demonstrated that use of force by police is rare,
occurring in less than 2 percent of all police-citizen encounters. White, *Current
Issues and Controversies in Policing*.

42 See list at http://www.justice.gov/crt/
special-litigation-section-cases-and-matters0#police.

43 *Sibron v. New York*, 392 U.S. 40 (1968).

44 *Peters v. New York*, 392 U.S. 40 (1968).

45 *Michigan Department of State Police v. Sitz*, 496 U.S. 444 (1990).

46 *Justice Quarterly* 31, no. 1 (2014).

47 Kelling and Moore, "From Political Reform to Community."

48 E.g., Ferguson, Missouri; President's Task Force on 21st Century Policing;
Baltimore, Maryland.

CHAPTER 2. THE HISTORICAL CONTEXT

1 Feld, "Race, Politics, and Juvenile Justice," 1453; see also Brezina, *Industrial
Revolution in America*; Hirschman and Mogford, "Immigration and the
American Industrial Revolution"; Hobsbawm, *Industry and Empire*; Ward,

"Population Growth, Migration, and Urbanization"; and Weightman, *Industrial Revolutionaries.*

2 Ferdico, Fradella, and Totten, *Criminal Procedure*, 5; see also Monkkonen, *Police in Urban America*; and Walker, *Popular Justice.*

3 Kamisar, "Equal Justice in the Gatehouses"; Neely, "Warren Court."

4 Graham, *Due Process Revolution*; Sullivan and Massaro, *Arc of Due Process.*

5 Barrett-Lain, "Countermajoritarian Hero or Zero?," 1372.

6 *Terry v. Ohio*, 392 U.S. 1 (1968).

7 Ferdico, Fradella, and Totten, *Criminal Procedure*, 307.

8 U.S. CONST. amend. IV.

9 Sundby, "Return to Fourth Amendment Basics," 384.

10 Lasson, *History and Development of the Fourth Amendment*; Fraenkel, "Concerning Searches and Seizures."

11 Davies, "Recovering the Original Fourth Amendment," 558.

12 Ibid.

13 Ibid.; see also Taylor, *Two Studies in Constitutional Interpretation.*

14 Davies, "Recovering the Original Fourth Amendment," 574, quoting Amar, "Bill of Rights as a Constitution"; Amar, "Fourth Amendment First Principles."

15 Davies, "Recovering the Original Fourth Amendment," 577.

16 Ibid., 577–78.

17 See Arcila, "Death of Suspicion."

18 *Wong Sun v. United States*, 371 U.S. 471, 479–80 (1963).

19 Neubauer and Fradella, *America's Courts*, 34.

20 Ibid.

21 *United States v. Cortez*, 449 U.S. 411, 417–18 (1981).

22 Neubauer and Fradella, *America's Courts*, 34–35.

23 Ibid., 35.

24 See Fradella, "From Insanity to Beyond Diminished Capacity."

25 See *In re Winship*, 397 U.S. 358 (1970).

26 *Victor v. Nebraska*, 511 U.S. 1, 18 (1994).

27 Neubauer and Fradella, *America's Courts*, 35.

28 *United States v. Arvizu*, 534 U.S. 266 (2002).

29 *Adams v. Williams*, 407 U.S. 143 (1972).

30 *Alabama v. White*, 496 U.S. 325 (1990); *Navarette v. California*, 134 S. Ct. 1683 (2014).

31 *United States v. Hensley*, 469 U.S. 221 (1985).

32 See *United States v. Jones*, 132 S. Ct. 945 (2012).

33 See *Katz v. United States*, 389 U.S. 347 (1967).

34 *United States v. Jacobsen*, 466 U.S. 109, 113 (1984).

35 *United States v. Mendenhall*, 446 U.S. 544 (1980).

36 Ferdico, Fradella, and Totten, *Criminal Procedure*, 367.

37 *Kentucky v. King*, 131 S. Ct. 1849, 1858 (2011); see also *Schneckloth v. Bustamonte*, 412 U.S. 218 (1973); *United States v. Drayton*, 536 U.S. 194 (2002).

38 See *Schneckloth v. Bustamonte*, 412 U.S. 218 (1973); *Ohio v. Robinette*, 519 U.S. 33 (1996). A person's submission to a false or mistaken assertion of authority by a police officer does not constitute a voluntary consent. *Bumper v. North Carolina*, 391 U.S. 543 (1968); *Johnson v. United States*, 333 U.S. 10 (1948).

39 See, e.g., ACLU of Illinois, "Press Release"; Harris, *Profiles in Injustice*; Farrell and McDevitt, *Rhode Island Traffic Stop Statistics*; Persico and Todd, "Hit Rates for Racial Bias in Motor Vehicle Searches"; and Smith et al., *North Carolina Highway Traffic Study*; see also *State v. Carty*, 790 A.2d 903 (N.J. 2002); Rudovsky, "Law Enforcement by Stereotypes and Serendipity"; and Ward, "Consenting to a Search and Seizure in Poor and Minority Neighborhoods." Note, however, that some recent studies suggest that the racial disparities in consent searches have been drastically reduced in recent years, probably as a result of external scrutiny on police in the exercise of their discretion. See Warren and Tomaskovic-Devey, "Racial Profiling and Searches"; and Ridgeway, *Cincinnati Police Department Traffic Stops*.

40 Warren and Tomaskovic-Devey, "Racial Profiling and Searches."

41 *Entick v. Carrington*, 19 Howell's State Trials 1029, 95 Eng. Rep. 807, 817–18 (1765).

42 *Olmstead v. United States*, 277 U.S. 438 (1928).

43 Ibid., 455.

44 Ibid., 464.

45 *Goldman v. United States*, 316 U.S. 129 (1942).

46 *Silverman v. United States*, 365 U.S. 505 (1961).

47 *Katz v. United States*, 389 U.S. 347 (1967).

48 *United States v. Jones*, 132 S. Ct. 945 (2012).

49 Ibid., 949.

50 Ibid., 948–49.

51 *Katz v. United States*, 389 U.S. 347, 351–52 (1967).

52 Ibid., 353.

53 Ibid., 361, *Harlan, J., concurring*.

54 *Payton v. New York*, 445 U.S. 573 (1980).

55 *Kyllo v. United States*, 533 U.S. 27 (2001).

56 *United States v. Dunn*, 480 U.S. 294 (1987).

57 *Oliver v. United States*, 466 U.S. 170 (1984).

58 *California v. Greenwood*, 486 U.S. 35 (1988).

59 *Smith v. Maryland*, 442 U.S. 735 (1979).

60 *United States v. Miller*, 425 U.S. 435 (1976).

61 *United States v. White*, 401 U.S. 745 (1971).

62 *United States v. Arnold*, 523 F.3d 941 (9th Cir. 2008).

63 Fradella et al., "Quantifying *Katz*."

64 Ibid., 372.

65 *Ornelas v. United States*, 517 U.S. 690, 695–96 (1996).

66 *Carroll v. United States*, 267 U.S. 132, 162 (1925).

67 *Illinois v. Gates*, 462 U.S. 213, 238 (1983).

68 *Brinegar v. United States*, 338 U.S. 160, 175–76 (1949) (internal quotations omitted).

69 For example, in databases such as the Automated Fingerprint Identification System, the National DNA Database, the National Missing Persons Database, and the National Unidentified Persons Database; or through information shared with police (or between police officers or agencies), such as citizen complaints, case files, broadcasts over police radios, and conversations between investigators. Owen et al., *Foundations of Criminal Justice*, 222–23.

70 For example, information obtained through an officer's senses, such as seeing a crime committed or witnessing possession of real/physical evidence of a crime, hearing gunfire, smelling marijuana, or touching an object that reveals its nature as contraband; or information interpreted in light of an officer's experience, such as observing flight by a suspect upon seeing police; observing furtive gestures by a suspect; receiving false, implausible, or evasive answers from a suspect; a person's presence at a crime scene or in a high-crime area; a suspect's association with other known criminals; a suspect's past criminal conduct. Ibid.

71 For example, from firsthand accounts, such as from eyewitnesses, co-conspirators, or eavesdroppers; or from secondhand accounts obtained from credible sources who possessed firsthand knowledge of the crime. Ibid.

72 *Illinois v. Gates*, 462 U.S. 213 (1983).

73 *Terry v. Ohio*, 392 U.S. 1, 19 (1968).

74 *Go-Bart Importing Co. v. United States*, 282 U.S. 344, 357 (1931).

75 *New Jersey v. T.L.O.*, 469 U.S. 325, 340–41 (1985).

76 *Terry v. Ohio*, 392 U.S. 1, 18 (1968).

77 See Clancy, "Fourth Amendment's Concept of Reasonableness."

78 Lee, "Reasonableness with Teeth"; Maclin, "Central Meaning of the Fourth Amendment."

79 *Commonwealth v. Tarver*, 345 N.E.2d 671 (Mass. 1975); *In re Will County Grand Jury*, 604 N.E.2d 929 (Ill. 1992).

80 *Maryland v. King*, 133 S. Ct. 1958 (2013); *Rise v. Oregon*, 59 F.3d 1556 (9th Cir. 1995).

81 *Cupp v. Murphy*, 412 U.S. 291 (1973).

82 *Missouri v. McNeely*, 133 S. Ct. 1552 (2013); *Schmerber v. California*, 384 U.S. 757 (1966).

83 *Bell v. Wolfish*, 441 U.S. 520 (1979); *Florence v. Burlington Board of Chosen Freeholders*, 132 S. Ct. 1510 (2012).

84 *Evans v. Stephens*, 407 F.3d 1272, 1281 (11th Cir. 2005).

85 *Rochin v. California*, 342 U.S. 165 (1952).

86 *Winston v. Lee*, 470 U.S. 753 (1985).

87 *Tennessee v. Garner*, 471 U.S. 1 (1985); *Graham v. Connor*, 490 U.S. 386 (1989); *Scott v. Harris*, 550 U.S. 372 (2007); *Plumhoff v. Rickard*, 134 S. Ct. 2012 (2014).

88 Arcila, "Death of Suspicion," 1278; see also Amar, "Fourth Amendment First Principles."

89 Ronayne, "Right to Investigate."

90 Ibid.

91 Hale, *History of the Pleas of the Crown*, 96; see also *Lawrence v. Hedger*, 3 Taunt. 14, 128 Eng. Rep. 6 (C.P. 1810).

92 Hawkins and Curwood, *Pleas of the Crown*, 129.

93 Hale, *History of the Pleas of the Crown*, 89; see also *Queen v. Tooley*, 2 Ld. Raym. 1296, 92 Eng. Rep. 349 (K.B. 1709). The Metropolitan Police Act of 1839 extended the authority of English law enforcement "to search vessels and carriages on reasonable suspicion that they were being used to convey stolen goods, and also to search persons who may be reasonably suspected of such possession" (Ronayne, "Right to Investigate," 214; see also Williams, "Police Detention and Arrest"). As chapter 3 in this volume should make clear, the authority of police to engage in SQF is limited to a brief "frisk" for weapons. Searches of places or people under circumstances authorized in England under the Metropolitan Police Act of 1839 would not be valid in the United States because the Fourth Amendment to the U.S. Constitution requires probable cause for police to conduct a search. Ronayne, "Right to Investigate," 214.

94 Williams, "Police Detention and Arrest," 413.

95 Ibid.

96 Ibid.

97 Warner, "Uniform Arrest Act."

98 Ferdico, Fradella, and Totten, *Criminal Procedure*, 308.

99 Warner, "Uniform Arrest Act," 317.

100 Ibid.

101 The other seven were "the force permissible in making an arrest"; "the right to resist an illegal arrest"; "arrest without a warrant"; "summons instead of arrest"; "release of persons arrested"; "permissible delay in bringing before magistrate"; and "identification of witnesses" Ibid.

102 Ibid., 320.

103 Ibid.

104 Ibid., 324.

105 Ibid.

106 Ibid., 326.

107 Ibid., 327.

108 *Gisske v. Sanders*, 9 Cal. App. 13 (1908).

109 Warner, "Uniform Arrest Act."

110 N.H. Laws 1941, c. 982, *codified as amended in* N.H. REV. STAT. ANN. §§ 594:1–594:23 (1955).

111 4S Laws of Del. ch. 304, 1951, *codified as amended in* DEL. CODE ANN. tit. 11, §§ 1901–1912 (1953).

112 Ronayne, "Right to Investigate," 215.

113 *Sibron v. New York*, 392 U.S. 40, 61 (1968).

114 See Act of Mar. 2, 1964, ch. 86, sec. 2, § 180-a, 1964 N.Y. Laws 111 (codified at N.Y. CODE CRIM. PROC. § 180-a).

115 367 U.S. 643 (1961).

116 See, e.g., Brief for NAACP Legal Def. and Educ. Fund, Inc. Supporting Appellant, Terry, 392 U.S. 1 (Nos. 63, 74, 67); LaFave, "Detention for Investigation by the Police."

117 As quoted in National Center on Police and Community Relations, *National Survey of Police and Community Relations*, 18; see also Segal, "'All of the Mysticism of Police Expertise.'"

118 *People v. Rivera*, 201 N.E.2d 32 (N.Y. 1964).

119 392 U.S. 40 (1968).

120 Ronayne, "Right to Investigate," 215–19.

121 *People v. Simon*, 290 P.2d 531 (Cal. 1955).

122 *People v. Henneman*, 10 N.E.2d 649 (Ill. 1937).

CHAPTER 3. THE CONTEMPORARY LEGAL CONTEXT

1 See Boger and Wegner, *Race, Poverty, and American Cities*; Kusmer and Trotter, *African American Urban History*.

2 Kerner Commission, *Final Report*, 1.

3 Ibid., 157.

4 Livingston, "Police Discretion," 571.

5 *Terry v. Ohio*, 392 U.S. 1 (1968).

6 *Sibron v. New York*, 392 U.S. 40 (1968).

7 *Peters v. New York*, 392 U.S. 40 (1968).

8 *Terry v. Ohio*, 392 U.S. 1, 4–8 (1968).

9 Ferdico, Fradella, and Totten, *Criminal Procedure*, 209.

10 *Terry v. Ohio*, 392 U.S. 1, 20 (1968).

11 Ibid., 20–21.

12 Ibid., 21.

13 Ibid., 22.

14 Ibid., 22–23.

15 Ibid., 23–24.

16 Ibid., 26.

17 Ibid., 29–30.

18 *Sibron v. New York*, 392 U.S. 40, 44–45 (1968).

19 N. Y. CODE CRIM. PROC. § 180-a (1964).

20 *Sibron v. New York*, 392 U.S. 40, 59 (1968).

21 Ibid., 60–61, quoting *Cooper v. California*, 386 U.S. 58, 61 (1967).

22 *Sibron v. New York*, 392 U.S. 40, 60 (1968), n. 20 (internal case citations omitted). For a detailed discussion of the New York stop and frisk statute, see Harvard Law Review Association, "Criminal Law: New York Authorizes Police to 'Stop and Frisk'"; Kalhan, "Stop and Frisk"; Kuh, "Reflections on New York's 'Stop-and-Frisk' Law"; Ronayne, "Right to Investigate"; and Segal, "'All of the Mysticism of Police Expertise.'"

23 *Sibron v. New York*, 392 U.S. 40, 62 (1968).

24 Ibid., 64.

25 Ibid.

26 Ibid., 65–66.

27 *Peters v. New York*, 392 U.S. 40, 48–49 (1968).

28 Ibid., 66.

29 Barrett, "Deciding the Stop-and-Frisk Cases."

30 *Sibron v. New York*, 392 U.S. 40, 80 (1968), *Black, J., dissenting.*

31 *Terry v. Ohio*, 392 U.S. 1, 35–39 (1968).

32 Barrett, "Deciding the Stop-and-Frisk Cases."

33 Ibid.

34 Ibid., 797.

35 Ibid., 798.

36 Ibid., 816–17.

37 Ibid., 813.

38 *Terry v. Ohio*, 392 U.S. 1, 31 (1968), *Harlan, J., concurring.*

39 Ibid., 33, *Harlan, J., concurring.*

40 Barrett, "Deciding the Stop-and-Frisk Cases," 835.

41 Lerner, "Reasonable Suspicion and Mere Hunches," 424–25.

42 Rosenthal, "Pragmatism, Originalism, Race," 300; see also Katz, "*Terry v. Ohio* at Thirty-Five"; Maclin, "Central Meaning of the Fourth Amendment"; and McAffee, "Setting Us Up for Disaster."

43 *Minnesota v. Dickerson*, 508 U.S. 366, 380 (1993), *Scalia, J., concurring.*

44 Ibid., 381; emphasis in original.

45 See Rosenthal, "Pragmatism, Originalism, Race."

46 See Amar, "Fourth Amendment First Principles."

47 Rosenthal, "Pragmatism, Originalism, Race," 333.

48 *Dunaway v. New York*, 442 U.S. 200, 208–10 (1979).

49 Lerner, "Reasonable Suspicion and Mere Hunches," 432.

50 Blumstein and Wallman, "The Crime Drop and Beyond"; Rosenthal, "Pragmatism, Originalism, Race"; cf. Fagan, Davies, and Holland, "Paradox of the Drug Elimination Program"; Johnson, Golub, and Dunlap, "Rise and Decline of Hard Drugs"; and Kelling and Sousa, *Do Police Matter?* For alternative explanations, see Harcourt and Ludwig, "Broken Windows: New Evidence"; Rosenfeld, Fornango, and Rengifo, "Impact of Order-Maintenance Policing"; Rosenfeld and Fornango, "Impact of Police Stops"; and Smith and Purtell, "Empirical Assessment of NYPD's 'Operation Impact.'"

51 Jones-Brown et al., *Stop, Question, and Frisk Policing Practices.*

52 Center for Constitutional Rights, *Racial Disparity in NYPD Stops-and-Frisks.*

53 See Gelman, Fagan, and Kiss, "Analysis of the New York City Police Department's 'Stop and Frisk' Policy"; Goel, Rao, and Shroff, "Precinct or Prejudice?"; Morrow, "Examining the Potential for Racial/Ethnic Disparities"; and Thompson, "Stopping the Usual Suspects."

54 Bellin, "Inverse Relationship," 1513.

55 Ibid., 1513–14.

56 *Floyd v. City of New York*, 959 F. Supp. 2d 540, 558 (2013).

57 See New York Civil Liberties Union, "Stop-and-Frisk Data."

58 See *Floyd v. City of New York*, 959 F. Supp. 2d 540, 606 (2013); Bloomberg, "Michael Bloomberg"; see also Bowling, "Rise and Fall of New York Murder," 546; Taylor, "Stop-and-Frisk Policy 'Saves Lives,'" A14.

59 *Floyd v. City of New York*, 959 F. Supp. 2d 540, 559, 572–83 (2013).

60 As quoted in Bellin, "Inverse Relationship," 1538.

61 Jones-Brown et al., *Stop, Question, and Frisk Policing Practices*.

62 *Floyd v. City of New York*, 959 F. Supp. 2d 540, 561 (2013); see also Bellin, "Inverse Relationship," 1541–48.

63 See, e.g., Alexander, *New Jim Crow*; Capers, "Rethinking the Fourth Amendment"; and Katz, "*Terry v. Ohio* at Thirty-Five."

64 Harris, "Frisking Every Suspect," 44; see also Tonry, *Punishing Race*.

65 Richardson and Goff, "Self-Defense and the Suspicion Heuristic," 296.

66 Devine et al., "Prejudice with and without Compunction."

67 Lane, Kang, and Banaji, "Implicit Social Cognition and Law"; Nosek, "Implicit-Explicit Relations"; Nosek, Banaji, and Greenwald, "Harvesting Implicit Group Attitudes."

68 Greenwald and Banaji, "Implicit Social Cognition."

69 Cameron, Payne, and Knobe, "Do Theories of Implicit Race Bias Change Moral Judgments?," 274, citing Fazio et al., "Variability in Automatic Activation."

70 See Wilson, Lindsey, and Schooler, "Model of Dual Attitudes."

71 Cameron, Payne, and Knobe, "Do Theories of Implicit Race Bias Change Moral Judgments?," 273. Internal citations to the following sources were omitted from the quotation: Blair, Judd, and Chapleau, "Influence of Afrocentric Facial Features in Criminal Sentencing"; Correll et al., "Police Officer's Dilemma"; Dovidio, Kawakami, and Gaertner, "Implicit and Explicit Prejudice"; Eberhardt et al., "Looking Deathworthy"; Jost et al., "Existence of Implicit Bias"; McConnell and Leibold, "Relations among the Implicit Association Test"; Payne, "Prejudice and Perception"; and Payne and Cameron, "Divided Minds, Divided Morals."

72 Banaji and Greenwald, *Blindspot*.

73 Richardson and Goff, "Self-Defense and the Suspicion Heuristic," 317; see also Bargh, "Cognitive Monster."

74 Lee, "Making Race Salient"; Richardson and Goff, "Self-Defense and the Suspicion Heuristic."

75 Eberhardt et al., "Seeing Black."

76 Correll et al., "Across the Thin Blue Line."

77 Plant and Peruche, "Consequences of Race for Police Officers' Responses"; Peruche and Plant, "Correlates of Law Enforcement Officers' Automatic and Controlled Race-Based Responses"; Correll et al., "Influence of Stereotypes on Decisions to Shoot."

78 *Ornelas v. United States*, 517 U.S. 690, 700 (1996).

79 Katz, who was white, was not charged. He was held as a "suspicious person" and released after two days. Barrett, "Appendix B," 1465.

80 Ibid.

81 Ibid., 1449.

82 Jones-Brown and Maule, "Racially Biased Policing."

83 Katz, "*Terry v. Ohio* at Thirty-Five," 429–30; see also Barrett, "Appendix B."

84 Jones-Brown and Fradella, "From *Simpson* to *Zimmerman*."

85 McAffee, "Setting Us Up for Disaster," 609.

86 Maclin, "*Terry v. Ohio*'s Fourth Amendment Legacy," 1277.

87 *Brown v. Texas*, 443 U.S. 47, 49 (1979).

88 Ibid., 49.

89 Ibid., 52.

90 *Ybarra v. Illinois*, 444 U.S. 85, 94 (1979).

91 *United States v. Cortez*, 449 U.S. 411, 417 (1981).

92 Harris, "Factors for Reasonable Suspicion," 666.

93 *United States v. Mendenhall*, 446 U.S. 544 (1980).

94 Ibid., 554–55.

95 *Florida v. Royer*, 460 U.S. 491 (1983).

96 Ibid., 501–2 (internal quotations omitted); see also *United States v. Sokolow*, 490 U.S. 1 (1989).

97 *I.N.S. v. Delgado*, 466 U.S. 210 (1984).

98 Ibid., 220–21.

99 *Florida v. Bostick*, 501 U.S. 429, 435 (1991).

100 Ibid., 436; see also *United States v. Drayton*, 536 U.S. 194 (2002).

101 See *Arizona v. Johnson*, 551 U.S. 323 (2009); *Brendlin v. California*, 551 U.S. 249 (2007).

102 *California v. Hodari D.*, 499 U.S. 621 (1991).

103 *Michigan v. Long*, 463 U.S. 1032 (1983).

104 *Minnesota v. Dickerson*, 508 U.S. 366 (1993).

105 Ibid., 379.

106 *Alabama v. White*, 496 U.S. 325 (1990).

107 *Michigan Department of State Police v. Sitz*, 496 U.S. 444 (1990).

108 Ibid., 448–49.

109 Ibid., 461–62, Stewart, J., dissenting.

110 Ferdico, Fradella, and Totten, *Criminal Procedure*.

111 *Illinois v. Wardlow*, 528 U.S. 119 (2000); see also *Hoover v. Walsh*, 682 F.3d 481 (6th Cir. 2012); *United States v. Dunning*, 666 F.3d 1158 (8th Cir. 2012); and *United States v. Jordan*, 232 F.3d 447 (5th Cir. 2000).

112 *State v. Lund*, 573 A.2d 1376 (N.J. 1990); *State v. Schlosser*, 774 P.2d 1132 (Utah 1989); *Spence v. State*, 525 So. 2d 442 (Fla. Dist. Ct. App. 1988); *People v. Mills*, 450 N.E.2d 935 (Ill. Ct. App. 1983); *People v. Superior Court of Yolo County*, 478 P.2d 449 (Cal. 1970).

113 *Pennsylvania v. Mimms*, 434 U.S. 106 (1977).

114 *United States v. Cruz*, 909 F.2d 422 (11th Cir. 1989); *United States v. Sprinkle*, 106 F.3d 613 (4th Cir. 1997).

115 *United States v. Fisher*, 364 F.3d 970 (8th Cir. 2004); *United States v. Hensley*, 469 U.S. 221 (1985).

116 *Illinois v. Wardlow*, 528 U.S. 119, 124 (2000).

117 See also *Maryland v. Buie*, 494 U.S. 325 (1990).

118 See Katz, "*Terry v. Ohio* at Thirty-Five."

119 See, e.g., Alpert, MacDonald, and Dunham, "Police Suspicion and Discretionary Decision Making"; Fagan, "Crime and Neighborhood Change"; Ferguson and Bernache, "'High-Crime Area' Question"; and Loury, *Anatomy of Racial Inequality*.

120 Fagan et al., "Street Stops and Broken Windows Revisited."

121 Cf., e.g., Brandl, Chamlin, and Frank, "Aggregation Bias"; Chamlin, "Determinants of Police Expenditures in Chicago"; Greenberg, Kessler, and Loftin, "Social Inequality and Crime Control"; Kane, "Ecology of Police Misconduct"; Liska, Lawrence, and Benson, "Perspectives on the Legal Order"; Nalla, Lynch, and Leiber, "Determinants of Police Growth in Phoenix."

122 Quillian and Pager, "Black Neighbors, Higher Crime?"

123 Morrow, "Examining the Potential for Racial/Ethnic Disparities."

124 Skolnick, *Justice without Trial*; see also Hunt, "Police Accounts of Normal Force"; Kappeler, Sluder, and Alpert, *Forces of Deviance*; and Van Maanen, "The Asshole."

125 Skolnick and Fyfe, *Above the Law*; Van Maanen, "The Asshole."

126 Katz, "*Terry v. Ohio* at Thirty-Five," 480; see also Capers, "Rethinking the Fourth Amendment"; Cole, *No Equal Justice*; Harris, "Factors for Reasonable Suspicion"; Maclin, "*Terry v. Ohio*'s Fourth Amendment Legacy"; McAffee, "Setting Us Up for Disaster"; and Thompson, "Stopping the Usual Suspects."

127 Ferguson and Bernache, "'High-Crime Area' Question," 1592, n. 21.

128 McAffee, "Setting Us Up for Disaster," 618; see also Cole, *No Equal Justice*.

129 *Whren v. United States*, 517 U.S. 806 (1996).

130 Ibid., 813; see also *Arkansas v. Sullivan*, 532 U.S. 769 (2001).

131 Thompson, "Stopping the Usual Suspects," 982.

132 See Allport, *Nature of Prejudice*; and Duncan, "Differential Social Perception and Attribution of Intergroup Violence."

133 Eberhardt et al., "Seeing Black"; Plant and Peruche, "Consequences of Race for Police Officers' Responses"; Skolnick and Fyfe, *Above the Law*; Welsh, "Black Criminal Stereotypes and Racial Profiling."

134 *Hiibel v. Sixth Judicial Dist. Ct. of Nev., Humboldt County*, 542 U.S. 177 (2004).

CHAPTER 4. CRIME-CONTROL BENEFITS AND COLLATERAL CONSEQUENCES

1 *Terry v. Ohio*, 392 U.S. 1 (1968).

2 Sullivan and Ulmer, "Examination of the Constitutional Issues."

3 Zimring, *Great American Crime Decline*; Zimring, *City That Became Safe*.

4   Kelly, "New York Police Commissioner Ray Kelly."

5   Bloomberg, "Michael Bloomberg."

6   Fagan et al., "Street Stops and Broken Windows Revisited."

7   White, "New York City Police Department," 8.

8   For a full discussion on the NYPD prior to 1994, see White, "New York City Police Department"; and Lardner and Repetto, *NYPD*.

9   Blumstein and Rosenfeld, "Explaining Recent Trends in U.S. Homicide Rates"; Cook and Laub, "Unprecedented Epidemic"; Cork, "Examining Space-Time Interaction in City-Level Homicide Data"; Grogger and Willis, "Emergence of Crack Cocaine."

10 Fryer et al., "Measuring Crack Cocaine and Its Impact," 1652.

11 Ibid.

12 Johnson et al., "International Implications of Quality-of-Life Policing," 18.

13 Kelling and Coles, *Fixing Broken Windows*, 117–18.

14 Joanes, "Does the New York City Police Department Deserve Credit?"

15 Wilson and Kelling, "Broken Windows."

16 Ibid.

17 Livingston, "Police Discretion."

18 Fagan and Davies, "Street Stops and Broken Windows," 468.

19 Waldeck, "Cops, Community Policing, and the Social Norms Approach to Crime Control."

20 New York City Police Department, *Reclaiming the Public Spaces of New York*.

21 New York City Police Department, *Getting Guns off the Streets of New York*.

22 Smith and Bratton, "Performance Management in New York City."

23 Davis and Mateu-Gelabert, *Respectful and Effective Policing*, 1.

24 Wintemute, "Guns and Gun Violence."

25 Geller and Fagan, "Pot as Pretext." Part of this increase is associated with Operation Condor, which began in 1999 as an aggressive narcotics enforcement program. Condor used up to a thousand officers per day to flood drug-infested areas of the city and target low-level drug transactions (Geller and Fagan, "Pot as Pretext"). The program came under intense scrutiny because of its aggressive tactics, and because of the controversial shooting of Patrick Dorismond in 2000.

26 Bellin, "Inverse Relationship."

27 New York City Police Department, *Getting Guns off the Streets of New York*.

28 See also Kocieniewski, "Success of Elite Police Unit Exacts a Toll."

29 Ibid.

30 Bellin, "Inverse Relationship."

31 Skolnick and Fyfe, *Above the Law*.

32 Fagan and Davies, "Street Stops and Broken Windows."

33 Hammer and Champy, *Reengineering the Corporation*.

34 Willis, Mastrofski, and Weisburd, "Making Sense of COMPSTAT."

35 CompStat was adopted at the same time as the OMP policing strategy and SQF. A full discussion of CompStat is outside the scope of this chapter. For more detail on CompStat in New York, readers should refer to McDonald, *Managing Police Operations*; and White, "New York City Police Department."

36 Golden and Almo, *Reducing Gun Violence*.

37 Ibid.

38 MacDonald, Fagan, and Geller, "Effects of Local Police Surges," 15–16.

39 Ridgeway, *Analysis of Racial Disparities*; Smith and Purtell, "Does Stop and Frisk Stop Crime?"

40 Skolnick and Fyfe, *Above the Law*.

41 Zimring, *City That Became Safe*.

42 Ibid., 5.

43 Ibid.

44 Ibid.

45 Barron, "Police Officer Suicide"; Rayman, "NYPD Tapes."

46 Lauritsen and Schaum, "Violent Victimization among Males." See also Xie, "Area Differences and Time Trends in Crime Reporting."

47 Zimring, *City That Became Safe*.

48 Fagan, Zimring, and Kim, "Declining Homicide in New York"; Rosenfeld, Fornango, and Baumer, "Did Ceasefire, Compstat, and Exile Reduce Homicide?"

49 Baumer and Wolff, "Evaluating Contemporary Crime Drop(s)."

50 Ibid., 10, 13; see also McDowall and Loftin, "Do U.S. City Crime Rates Follow a National Trend?"

51 Gelman, Fagan, and Kiss, "Analysis of the New York City Police Department's 'Stop and Frisk' Policy."

52 Schneiderman, *Report on Arrests*.

53 Jones-Brown et al., *Stop, Question, and Frisk Policing Practices*.

54 *Floyd v. City of New York*, 959 F. Supp. 2d 540 (2013).

55 Jones-Brown et al., *Stop, Question, and Frisk Policing Practices*.

56 Ibid.

57 Beccaria, *On Crimes and Punishment*; Bentham, *Principles of Morals and Legislation*. See also, e.g., Andenaes, *Punishment and Deterrence*; and Nagin and Pogarsky, "Integrating Celerity, Impulsivity, and Extralegal Sanction Threats."

58 Stafford and Warr, "Reconceptualization of General and Specific Deterrence."

59 Ibid.

60 Pratt et al., "Empirical Status of Deterrence Theory."

61 Jones-Brown et al., *Stop, Question, and Frisk Policing Practices*; Fagan et al., "Street Stops and Broken Windows Revisited."

62 Baker and Goldstein, "2 Opinions on Stop-and-Frisk Report."

63 Rosenfeld and Fornango, "Impact of Police Stops," 102.

64 Corman and Mocan, "Carrots, Sticks, and Broken Windows." See also Davis and Mateu-Gelabert, *Respectful and Effective Policing*.

65 Kelling and Sousa, *Do Police Matter?* Harcourt and Ludwig replicated Kelling and Sousa's study, but employed additional community controls. In their revised analysis, the significant misdemeanor arrest effect disappeared. Harcourt and Ludwig, "Broken Windows: New Evidence."

66 Smith and Purtell, "Empirical Assessment of NYPD's 'Operation Impact.'"

67 CDC Youth Online, http://perma.cc/NV7C-ZFNW; New York City Department of Health and Mental Hygiene, http://perma.cc/ZV2J-R2TQ.

68 New York City Department of Health and Mental Hygiene, *Firearm Deaths and Injuries in New York City*.

69 Zimring, *City That Became Safe*.

70 Ibid., 131–32.

71 Rosenfeld, Fornango, and Rengifo, "Impact of Order-Maintenance Policing." See also Cerdá et al., "Misdemeanor Policing"; and Cerdá et al., "Investigating the Effect of Social Changes."

72 Messner et al., "Policing, Drugs, and the Homicide Decline." In "Declining Homicide in New York," Fagan, Zimring, and Kim also reported that the sharp drop in firearm-related homicides paralleled rigor on behalf of the NYPD. Their results, however, are based on descriptive statistics, meaning that they are unable to "parse causal responsibility between law enforcement, social trends, and regression for the city's gun homicide record" (1320). Thus, their conclusions are largely speculative.

73 Baumer and Wolff, "Evaluating Contemporary Crime Drop(s)," 31. Xie considered the crime-control impact of policing in New York from an entirely different lens—by examining the effect on victim reporting of crime. Xie used data from the National Crime Victimization Survey (NCVS) to assess whether crime reporting in New York has followed a similar pattern to reporting in other jurisdictions. The results showed that, overall, New York experienced a decline in reporting of violent crime while other similar, large jurisdictions actually experienced increases in violent crime victim reporting. Alternatively, reporting of property crime in New York has remained relatively flat. Xie concluded that the reported drop in certain types of crime in New York may have been artificially inflated by declines in victim reporting, and that variations in crime reporting across jurisdictions likely confounded the comparison of crime drops among major cities. Xie, "Area Differences and Time Trends in Crime Reporting."

74 Eligon, "Taking on Police Tactic."

75 Harris, "Across the Hudson," 863.

76 Smith and Purtell, "Does Stop and Frisk Stop Crime?"

77 Rosenfeld and Fornango suggested that the use of a single SQF measure (total stops) failed to capture the potential variable impact of stops resulting in arrest versus stops that produced no formal activity (often referred to as "innocent" stops). The overall measure also is not nuanced enough to capture whether impacts on crime may differ among stops of citizens of different race/ethnicities. Other criticisms focus on technical aspects of the Smith and Purtell analysis. Rosenfeld

and Fornango note that Smith and Purtell's "estimates are not conditioned by the effects of other precinct characteristics on crime rates and perhaps also SQF, such as economic deprivation, race and ethnic heterogeneity, and residential stability, which prior research has found to be highly correlated with crime rates. . . . Failure to control for such conditions can result in omitted variable bias." Moreover, Smith and Purtell did not account for spatial dependence, the extent to which crime rates in a given precinct are influenced by crime rates in adjacent precincts, nor did they "incorporate period fixed effects, which adjust the estimates of SQF effects for unobserved time-varying sources of heterogeneity in crime rates." Along those same lines, Rosenfeld and Fornango also questioned the use of a one-month spatial lag for SQF on crime, suggesting that a more traditional approach would also include lagged crime rates to account for the effect of prior crime rates on both SQF and current crime. Rosenfeld and Fornango, "Impact of Police Stops."

78 Rosenfeld and Fornango, "Impact of Police Stops," 104.

79 Ibid., 116.

80 Ibid., 117–18.

81 MacDonald, Fagan, and Geller, "Effects of Local Police Surges," 32.

82 Weisburd, Telep, and Lawton, "Could Innovations in Policing Have Contributed?"

83 Ibid., 146.

84 Ibid.

85 Bellin, "Inverse Relationship."

86 Ibid., 1538.

87 Ibid., 1549.

88 Boydstun and Sherry, *San Diego Community Profile.*

89 Sherman and Rogan, "Effects of Gun Seizures on Gun Violence."

90 Cohen and Ludwig, "Policing Gun Crimes."

91 Ratcliffe et al., "Philadelphia Foot Patrol Experiment."

92 Ibid., 823.

93 Smith and Purtell, "Does Stop and Frisk Stop Crime?"; Rosenfeld and Fornango, "Impact of Police Stops."

94 Weisburd, Telep, and Lawton, "Could Innovations in Policing Have Contributed?," 148.

95 Spitzer, *New York City Police Department's "Stop and Frisk" Practices.*

96 On February 4, 1999, four officers in the Street Crime Unit conducted a stop and frisk of Amadou Diallo, an African immigrant whom the officers stated matched the description of a rapist. When Diallo pulled out his wallet, the officers mistook the wallet for a gun and opened fire. The officers fired forty-one shots at Diallo, striking him nineteen times. The officers were charged with second-degree murder, but all four were acquitted at trial.

97 Spitzer, *New York City Police Department's "Stop and Frisk" Practices.*

98 Fagan et al., "Street Stops and Broken Windows Revisited," 310.

99 Ridgeway, *Analysis of Racial Disparities.*

100 Ibid., xi.

101 Ibid., xiv.

102 Gelman, Fagan, and Kiss, "Analysis of the New York City Police Department's 'Stop and Frisk' Policy." See also Fagan and Davies, "Street Stops and Broken Windows."

103 Jones-Brown et al., *Stop, Question, and Frisk Policing Practices.*

104 In 2003 there were 627 guns recovered out of a total of 160,851 stops. In 2008, there were 824 guns recovered out of a total of 540,320 stops.

105 Fagan et al., "Street Stops and Broken Windows Revisited," 337.

106 *Floyd v. City of New York*, 959 F. Supp. 2d 668, 606 (2013).

107 Fermino, "Mayor Bloomberg on Stop-and-Frisk."

108 Rayman, "New NYPD Tapes Introduced in Stop and Frisk Trial."

109 Nislow, "Are Americans Ready to Buy into Racial Profiling?"

110 Bornstein, "Antiterrorist Policing in New York City after 9/11."

111 *USA Today*, "NYPD Confirms CIA Advisory Role."

112 *Daniels v. City of New York*, Complaint.

113 *CityLaw*, "Current Development."

114 Ibid.

115 Kalhan, "Stop and Frisk."

116 *Daniels v. City of New York*, Stipulation of Settlement.

117 *Floyd v. City of New York*, Complaint and Demand for Jury Trial.

118 *Floyd v. City of New York*, Report of Jeffrey Fagan, Ph.D.; *Floyd v. City of New York*, Second Supplemental Report of Jeffrey Fagan, Ph.D.

119 Center for Constitutional Rights, *Racial Disparity in NYPD Stops-and-Frisks.*

120 Ibid.

121 *Floyd v. City of New York*, Report of Jeffrey Fagan, Ph.D.; *Floyd v. City of New York*, Second Supplemental Report of Jeffrey Fagan, Ph.D.

122 *Floyd v. City of New York*, 959 F. Supp. 2d 540 (2013).

123 *Floyd v. City of New York*, 959 F. Supp. 2d 668 (2013).

124 Ibid., 676.

125 Ibid., 686.

126 Ibid., 685.

127 Ofer and Rosmarin, *Stop and Frisk.*

128 Ibid.

129 American Civil Liberties Union of Illinois, *Stop and Frisk in Chicago*, 2.

130 Ibid.

131 *Bailey v. City of Philadelphia*, Complaint.

132 *Bailey v. City of Philadelphia*, Consent Decree.

133 *Bailey v. City of Philadelphia*, Plaintiffs' Third Report, 4.

134 *Bailey v. City of Philadelphia*, Plaintiffs' Fifth Report.

135 Brennan and Lieberman, "Florida City's 'Stop and Frisk.'"

136 Knight, "Ed Lee Drops Stop-Frisk Plan amid Uproar."

137 Volk, "Cleveland Councilmen Reed and Johnson."

138 Lee, "Councilman Zack Reed's Stop and Frisk Plan."

139 Williams and Murphy, "Evolving Strategy of Police: A Minority View," 28.

140 Center for Constitutional Rights, *Racial Disparity in NYPD Stops-and-Frisks*.

141 Jones-Brown et al., *Stop, Question, and Frisk Policing Practices*.

142 Morrow, "Examining the Potential for Racial/Ethnic Disparities."

143 Ibid.

144 Ibid.

145 Solis, Portillos, and Brunson, "Latino Youths' Experiences."

146 La Vigne et al., *Stop and Frisk*, 18.

147 Fratello et al., *Coming of Age with Stop and Frisk*.

148 Ibid., 2.

149 Wilkinson, Beaty, and Lurry, "Youth Violence—Crime or Self-Help?"

150 Solis, Portillos, and Brunson, "Latino Youths' Experiences," 46.

151 Hynynen, *Community Perceptions of Brownsville*; Rengifo and Slocum, "Community Responses to 'Stop-and-Frisk'"; Stoudt, Fine, and Fox, "Growing Up Policed."

152 Center for Constitutional Rights, *Stop and Frisk*, 1.

153 *Ligon v. City of New York*, 538 Fed. Appx. 101 (2d Cir. 2013).

154 Ibid., 102–3.

155 *Ligon v. City of New York*, 736 F.3d 118 (2d Cir. 2013).

156 *Ligon v. City of New York*, 736 F.3d 166 (2d Cir. 2013).

157 *Floyd v. City of New York*, Opposition of Sergeants Benevolent Association, 2–3.

158 *Floyd v. City of New York*, 302 F.R.D. 69 (S.D.N.Y. 2014).

159 Russo, Dienst, and Siff, "De Blasio Picks Bill Bratton."

160 Paybarah, "Bill Bratton."

161 *Floyd v. City of New York*, 770 F.3d 1051 (2d Cir. 2014).

162 *Floyd v. City of New York*, 2015 U.S. Dist. LEXIS 34453 (S.D.N.Y. March 19, 2015).

163 Bellin, "Inverse Relationship."

164 *Terry v. Ohio*, 392 U.S. 1 (1968).

165 Bellin, "Inverse Relationship," 1519–20.

166 La Vigne et al., *Stop and Frisk*.

167 Attendees also expressed serious concern about the conflation of stop decisions and frisk decisions, which should be assessed independently through two separate processes.

168 Tyler, "Legitimacy and Legitimation"; Eck and Rosenbaum, "New Police Order."

169 President's Commission on Law Enforcement and Administration of Justice, *Task Force Report*, 1.

CHAPTER 5. BEYOND A FEW BAD APPLES

1 Skolnick and Fyfe, *Above the Law*, 187.

2 An earlier version of this chapter was presented at the Roundtable on Current Debates, Research Agendas and Strategies to Address Racial Disparities in Police-Initiated Stops in the UK and USA, John Jay College of Criminal Justice, New York, August 10–11, 2011.

3 Skolnick, *Justice without Trial*; Skolnick and Fyfe, *Above the Law*.

4 President's Commission on Law Enforcement and Administration of Justice, *Task Force Report*.

5 Skolnick and Fyfe, *Above the Law*; Fyfe and Kane, *Bad Cops*.

6 Kane and White, *Jammed Up*.

7 Cohen and Chaiken, *Police Background Characteristics and Performance*.

8 Mollen Commission, *Anatomy of Failure, a Path for Success*.

9 Kane and White, "Bad Cops," 765.

10 Harris, "Onset of Police Misconduct."

11 White and Kane, "Pathways to Career-Ending Police Misconduct."

12 See also Harris, *Pathways of Police Misconduct*.

13 Mollen Commission, *Anatomy of Failure, a Path for Success*.

14 Grant and Grant, "Officer Selection and the Prevention of Abuse of Force."

15 Ibid.

16 Kane and White, "Bad Cops," 765. Protective factors against misconduct that emerged in Kane and White's study include college education, older age at appointment, married at appointment, and a recommendation to hire from the department's background investigator.

17 See Grant and Grant, "Officer Selection and the Prevention of Abuse of Force."

18 Eterno, "Cadets and Policing."

19 Harris, "Onset of Police Misconduct"; Kane and White, "Bad Cops."

20 Shjarback and White, "Departmental Professionalism and Its Impact."

21 Miller, *Cops and Bobbies*.

22 President's Commission on Law Enforcement and Administration of Justice, *Task Force Report*; Bittner, "Police on Skid Row"; Goldstein, "Improving Policing"; Goldstein, *Problem-Oriented Policing*; Skogan and Frydl, *Fairness and Effectiveness in Policing*.

23 Muir, *Police: Streetcorner Politicians*, 50. Muir's emphasis on coercion reflected a growing recognition of the centrality of force to the police role. Bittner (*Functions of the Police in Modern Society*, 40), for example, stated that the capacity to threaten or use physical force is a core function of the police: "Whatever the substance of the task at hand, whether it involves protection against an undesired imposition, caring for those who cannot care for themselves, attempting to solve a crime, helping to save a life, abating a nuisance, or settling an explosive dispute, police intervention means above all making use of the capacity and authority to overpower resistance."

24 Muir, *Police: Streetcorner Politicians*, 65, 67.

25 Ibid., 66.

26 Ibid., 79–80.

27 Bittner, "Police on Skid Row."

28 President's Task Force on 21st Century Policing, *Final Report*.

29 Fyfe, "Training to Reduce Police-Civilian Violence," 164.

30 Ibid.

31 Ibid., 167.

32 Bayley and Bittner, "Learning the Skills of Policing," 55.

33 Brookfield, *Understanding and Facilitating Adult Learning*; Caffarella, "Self-Directed Learning"; Merriam and Caffarella, *Learning in Adulthood*.

34 Birzer, "Theory of Andragogy Applied to Police Training."

35 Ibid., 34–35. Proponents of the andragogical approach for police training argue that it (1) draws on trainees' past experiences; (2) treats trainees as adults; (3) adapts to the needs of participants; and (4) fosters critical thinking and creativity. See Birzer and Tannehill, "More Effective Training Approach."

36 Fyfe, "Training to Reduce Police-Civilian Violence," 171.

37 Commission for Accreditation of Law Enforcement Agencies, "Law Enforcement Program: The Standards."

38 Skolnick and Fyfe, *Above the Law*.

39 E.g., Skogan and Frydl, *Fairness and Effectiveness in Policing*.

40 Haberfeld, *Critical Issues in Training*.

41 Association of Chief Police Officers, "Statement of Mission and Values."

42 SB 1070 was signed into law by Arizona Governor Jan Brewer on April 23, 2010, and was set to go into effect July 29, 2010. Seven different lawsuits were filed challenging the law, including one by the U.S. Department of Justice. In July 2010, federal district court judge Susan Bolton issued an injunction prohibiting four major components of the law from going into effect. The major thrust of her injunction was that immigration is the responsibility of the federal government, not individual states. On April 11, 2011, the 9th Circuit Court of Appeals upheld Bolton's injunction. In April 2012 the U.S. Supreme Court heard oral arguments on the SB 1070 case, and on June 25, 2012, the Court issued a ruling that struck down all but one of the provisions of the law (ABC 15 Arizona, "Timeline").

43 Glendale Police Department, *SB1070 Instructor Points*.

44 Fyfe, "Training to Reduce Police-Civilian Violence," 173.

45 Ibid.

46 Palmiotto, "Overview of Police Training," 15.

47 Fyfe, "Training to Reduce Police-Civilian Violence," 174.

48 Bayley, "Tactical Choices of Police Patrol Officers"; Binder and Scharf, "Violent Police-Citizen Encounter." Binder and Scharf characterized five important decision phases in police-citizen encounters: anticipation, entry and initial confrontation, dialogue and information exchange, final frame decision, and aftermath.

49 Fyfe, "Split-Second Syndrome and Other Determinants of Police Violence."

50 Fyfe, "Training to Reduce Police-Civilian Violence," 174.

51 In "Training to Reduce Police-Civilian Violence," Fyfe described several other principles for violence reduction training that are less relevant for SQF practices. According to Fyfe, violence-reduction training must not make matters worse by

creating a sense of paranoia among officers (dealing with the traditional overemphasis on danger). In addition, violence-reduction training must address the role of police officers during their non-working hours (e.g., off-duty conduct).

52 Muir, *Police: Streetcorner Politicians.*

53 Fyfe, "Training to Reduce Police-Civilian Violence," 163–64. Notably, Fyfe ("Police/Citizen Violence Reduction Project") put these principles in practice as part of the Metro-Dade Police/Citizen Violence Reduction Project, which culminated in the development of a five-day role-play training program. Results from the project indicate substantial reductions in use of force, officer injuries, and citizen complaints after the training program was implemented. See also Klinger, "Can Police Training Affect the Use of Force on the Streets?"

54 Fyfe, "Training to Reduce Police-Civilian Violence," 163–64.

55 Kappeler, Sluder, and Alpert, *Forces of Deviance.*

56 Commission for Accreditation of Law Enforcement Agencies, "Law Enforcement Accreditation."

57 Walker and Archbold, *New World of Police Accountability.* Walker and Archbold drew heavily from the work of Davis, *Police Discretion.*

58 Walker and Archbold, *New World of Police Accountability.*

59 Ibid., 71.

60 Fyfe, "Police Use of Deadly Force"; Gain, *Discharge of Firearms Policy*; Geller and Scott, *Deadly Force.*

61 Fyfe, "Administrative Interventions on Police Shooting Discretion."

62 White, "Controlling Police Decisions to Use Deadly Force."

63 Walker, *Taming the System,* 32.

64 Walker and Archbold, *New World of Police Accountability*; White, *Current Issues and Controversies in Policing.*

65 Alpert, *Police Pursuit.* See also Alpert and Dunham, *Police Pursuit Driving.*

66 Bobb, *13th Semiannual Report.*

67 Walker and Archbold, *New World of Police Accountability.*

68 Ibid.

69 Jones-Brown et al., *Stop, Question, and Frisk Policing Practices.*

70 Fyfe, "Police Use of Deadly Force."

71 Alpert, *Police Pursuit.*

72 Fridell et al., *Racially Biased Policing,* 52.

73 For discussions of the limitations of administrative rule making, see Skolnick and Fyfe, *Above the Law*; and White, *Current Issues and Controversies in Policing.*

74 Skolnick and Fyfe, *Above the Law.*

75 Capehart, "'Stop and Frisk,' Bloomberg and Me."

76 PBS, "New Yorkers Weigh Safety and Harassment."

77 Ibid.

78 Walker, "Ray Kelly Defends NYPD."

79 Terkel, "Ray Kelly on Stop and Frisk."

80 Skolnick and Fyfe, *Above the Law*, 179–80.

81 Mollen Commission, *Anatomy of Failure, a Path for Success*, 112.

82 *Tucson Sentinel*, "Declaration of Jack Harris on SB 1070."

83 Rau, "Arizona Immigration Bill."

84 New York Civil Liberties Union, "Stop-and-Frisk Data."

85 Destefano, "Bratton: NYPD, Communities Need Mutual Respect."

86 Hechtman, "Bratton Raps Kelly and Bloomberg."

87 La Vigne et al., *Stop and Frisk*, 3.

88 Weisburd et al., *Police Attitudes toward Abuse of Authority*.

89 Fyfe, "Training to Reduce Police-Civilian Violence," 164.

90 See, e.g., Kappeler, Sluder, and Alpert, *Forces of Deviance*; Skolnick and Fyfe, *Above the Law*; and White, *Current Issues and Controversies in Policing*.

91 International Association of Chiefs of Police, *Building Integrity and Reducing Drug Corruption*, 53.

92 Klockars et al., *Measurement of Police Integrity*.

93 Walker and Archbold, *New World of Police Accountability*, 179.

94 Ibid.

95 Bobb, *14th Semiannual Report*.

96 Murphy, *Ombudsman's Special Report*, 46.

97 NYPD Inspector General, "About NYPD Inspector General."

98 Eure, *Examination of Substantiated Chokehold Cases*.

99 Ibid.

100 Muir, *Police: Streetcorner Politicians*.

101 Fyfe, "Training to Reduce Police-Civilian Violence."

CHAPTER 6. THE FUTURE OF STOP AND FRISK

1 Kelling and Moore, "Evolving Strategy of Policing," 2.

2 Ibid.

3 Ibid., 3.

4 The historical discussion in this section is necessarily brief. For more detail, see Kelling and Moore, "Evolving Strategy of Policing"; Monkkonen, "History of Urban Police"; and Lane, "Urban Police and Crime in Nineteenth-Century America."

5 Skolnick and Fyfe, *Above the Law*.

6 See, e.g., National Advisory Commission on Civil Disorder, *Report of the National Advisory Commission on Civil Disorder*; President's Commission on Law Enforcement and Administration of Justice, *Task Force Report*.

7 Kelling and Moore, "Evolving Strategy of Policing."

8 The Kelling and Moore historical framework was criticized by some scholars as being imprecise and incomplete. For example, in "The Evolving Strategy of Police: A Minority View," Williams and Murphy argued that the framework completely disregarded the experience of African Americans and ignored the role of police in

marginalizing minority communities. Strecher ("Revising the Histories and Futures of Policing") argued that the three eras in the framework were artificial and inexact. Nevertheless, the authors believe that it is a useful framework for reviewing police history, and for considering the development of strategies—including *Terry* stops—that will define twenty-first-century policing.

9 Williams and Murphy, "Evolving Strategy of Police: A Minority View."

10 Ibid.

11 *Plessy v. Ferguson*, 163 U.S. 537 (1896).

12 Williams and Murphy, "Evolving Strategy of Police: A Minority View."

13 Kelling and Moore, "Evolving Strategy of Policing."

14 Braga and Weisburd, "Problem-Oriented Policing."

15 See, e.g., the Bureau of Justice Assistance's Smart Policing Initiative, http://www. smartpolicinginitiative.com/.

16 Crimesolutions.gov.

17 CEBCP.org.

18 Smartpolicinginitiative.com.

19 Popcenter.org.

20 Smartpolicinginitiative.com.

21 Tyler, *Why People Obey the Law*, 375.

22 Tyler, "Legitimacy and Legitimation," 271.

23 Hinds, "Youth, Police Legitimacy and Informal Contact"; Hinds and Murphy, "Public Satisfaction with Police"; Tyler, *Why People Obey the Law*; Tyler and Huo, *Trust in the Law*.

24 Tyler and Fagan, "Legitimacy and Cooperation," 263.

25 Reisig and Lloyd, "Procedural Justice"; Sunshine and Tyler, "Role of Procedural Justice and Legitimacy."

26 Goodman-Delahunty, "Four Ingredients"; Tyler and Huo, *Trust in the Law*.

27 Casper, Tyler, and Fisher, "Procedural Justice in Felony Cases"; Hinds and Murphy, "Public Satisfaction with Police"; Leventhal, "What Should Be Done with Equity Theory?"; Lind, "Psychology of Courtroom Procedure"; Lind and Tyler, *Social Psychology of Procedural Justice*; McEwan and Maiman, "Mediation in Small Claims Court"; Tyler, Rasinski, and Spodick, "Influence of Voice."

28 Mazerolle et al., "Shaping Citizen Perceptions of Police Legitimacy," 55.

29 Williams and Murphy, "Evolving Strategy of Police: A Minority View."

30 President's Task Force on 21st Century Policing, *Final Report*.

31 Ibid., 1.

32 The descriptions of the strategies in this section are necessarily brief. Moreover, because of space constraints the authors focus on the most popular strategies. This is by no means an all-inclusive list of twenty-first-century policing strategies. For additional information on the strategies, see the references provided in each section. For an excellent general review of the strategies, see Weisburd and Braga, *Police Innovation*. In addition, an edited volume that examines SQF in the United

Kingdom was published in 2015: Delsol and Shiner, *Stop and Search: The Anatomy of a Police Power*.

33 Goldstein, "Improving Policing."

34 Eck and Spelman, *Problem-Solving*.

35 Green-Mazerolle et al., "Problem-Oriented Policing in Public Housing"; Kennedy, *Juvenile Gun Violence*; Reitzel, Piquero, and Piquero, "Problem-Oriented Policing"; Sherman, "Repeat Calls for Service"; Weisburd and Eck, "What Can Police Do?"; White et al., "Police Role in Preventing Homicide"; White and Katz, "Policing Convenience Store Crime."

36 Weisburd et al., "Is Problem-Oriented Policing Effective?," 153.

37 Ibid.

38 Braga and Weisburd, "Problem-Oriented Policing," 146.

39 White and Katz, "Policing Convenience Store Crime."

40 Braga, Hureau, and Papachristos, "Ex-Post-Facto Evaluation Framework."

41 Braga and Schnell, "Evaluating Place-Based Policing Strategies."

42 Walker and Katz, *Police in America*.

43 Roth, Roehl, and Johnson, "Trends in Community Policing."

44 National Initiative for Building Community Trust and Justice, website.

45 Hudson, "Building Trust between Communities and Local Police."

46 Skogan, "Promise of Community Policing."

47 Cordner, "Community Policing," 402–14.

48 *60 Minutes*, "Counterinsurgency Cops."

49 Skolnick and Fyfe, *Above the Law*.

50 Mastrofski, "Community Policing."

51 Cordner, "Community Policing."

52 Skogan and Hartnett, *Community Policing, Chicago Style*. Scholars have identified a number of challenges with implementing COP: the communities that need COP the most are the most difficult to engage; there is often resistance from line officers who value a more crime control–focused role; it requires decentralization and significant line officer discretion (including free time away from responding to calls for service); there are few examples of successful organizational change; and evidence of its impact on crime is mixed. Mastrofski, "Community Policing"; Skogan, "Promise of Community Policing."

53 Skogan and Frydl, *Fairness and Effectiveness in Policing*.

54 Meares, "Praying for Community Policing."

55 Williams and Murphy, "Evolving Strategy of Police: A Minority View."

56 Cordner, "Community Policing."

57 Ibid.

58 Ibid.

59 Cohen and Felson, "Social Change and Crime Rate Trends"; Weisburd and Braga, *Police Innovation*.

60 Sherman, Gartin, and Buerger, "Hot Spots of Predatory Crime."

61 Sherman and Weisburd, "General Deterrent Effects of Police Patrol."

62 Braga, "Effects of Hot Spots Policing."

63 Skogan and Frydl, *Fairness and Effectiveness in Policing*, 250.

64 Braga, Papachristos, and Hureau, "Effects of Hot Spots Policing."

65 LASER was implemented in five hot spots in the Newton Division. Following program implementation, Uchida et al. (*Los Angeles, California Smart Policing Initiative*) found that Part I violent crimes in the Newton Division dropped by an average of 5.4 crimes per month, and homicides dropped by 22.6 percent per month.

66 Kennedy, "Old Wine in New Bottles."

67 Ibid.

68 Ratcliffe et al., *Philadelphia, Pennsylvania Smart Policing Initiative*.

69 For a discussion of the increased level of difficulty and implementation challenges with POP and foot patrol, see ibid.

70 Weisburd, Telep, and Lawton, "Could Innovations in Policing Have Contributed?"

71 Ratcliffe et al., *Philadelphia, Pennsylvania Smart Policing Initiative*, 8.

72 Wilson and Kelling, "Broken Windows."

73 Ibid.

74 Bratton, *Turnaround*.

75 Dixon, "Beyond Zero Tolerance."

76 Walker and Katz, *Police in America*.

77 Ibid.

78 Geller and Fagan, "Pot as Pretext"; Jones-Brown et al., *Stop, Question, and Frisk Policing Practices*.

79 Geller and Fagan, "Pot as Pretext."

80 Greene, "Zero Tolerance."

81 White, "Jim Longstreet."

82 Berk and MacDonald, "Policing the Homeless," 817.

83 Walker and Katz, *Police in America*.

84 Greene, "Zero Tolerance," 185.

85 Harcourt, *Illusion of Order*; Sampson and Raudenbush, "Systematic Social Observation of Public Spaces."

86 White, *Police Officer Body-Worn Cameras*.

87 Bureau of Justice Statistics, *Local Police Departments, 2013*.

88 Capps, "Police Body Cameras."

89 See description at https://www.bja.gov/bwc/.

90 U.S. Department of Justice, "Conduct of Law Enforcement Agencies."

91 Community Oriented Policing Services, "Collaborative Reform Initiative for Technical Assistance."

92 Ferguson, "Big Data and Predictive Reasonable Suspicion."

93 Ibid., 329.

94 Alexander, *New Jim Crow*; Rios, *Punished*.

95 Williams and Murphy, "Evolving Strategy of Police: A Minority View."

96 President's Task Force on 21st Century Policing, *Final Report*, 10.

97 MacDonald, Fagan, and Geller, "Effects of Local Police Surges."

98 Meares, "Programming Errors."

99 Bellin, "Inverse Relationship."

100 President's Task Force on 21st Century Policing, *Final Report*, 15.

101 Richardson and Goff, "Self-Defense and the Suspicion Heuristic."

102 Stoudt, Fine, and Fox, "Growing Up Policed."

103 Bellin, "Inverse Relationship."

104 President's Task Force on 21st Century Policing, *Final Report*, 9.

105 Mazerolle et al., *Legitimacy in Policing*.

REFERENCES

ABC 15 Arizona. "Timeline: Story of Controversial SB 1070." June 25, 2012. http://www.abc15.com/news/state/timeline-story-of-controversial-sb-1070.

Adams v. Williams, 407 U.S. 143 (1972).

Alabama v. White, 496 U.S. 325 (1990).

Alexander, Michelle. *The New Jim Crow: Mass Incarceration in the Age of Colorblindness*. New York: New Press, 2011.

Allport, Gordon W. *The Nature of Prejudice*. Reading, MA: Addison-Wesley, 1954.

Alpert, Geoffrey P. *Police Pursuit: Policies and Training*. Washington, DC: U.S. Department of Justice, Office of Justice Programs, National Institute of Justice, 1997.

Alpert, Geoffrey P., and Roger G. Dunham. *Police Pursuit Driving: Controlling Responses to Emergency Situations*. New York: Greenwood, 1990.

Alpert, Geoffrey P., John M. MacDonald, and Roger G. Dunham. "Police Suspicion and Discretionary Decision Making during Citizen Stops." *Criminology* 43, no. 2 (2005): 407–34.

Amar, Akhil Reed. "The Bill of Rights as a Constitution." *Yale Law Journal* 100 (1991): 1131–1210.

———. "Fourth Amendment First Principles." *Harvard Law Review* 107 (1994): 757–819.

American Civil Liberties Union of Illinois. "Press Release: ACLU of Illinois Files Complaint with U.S. Department of Justice Requesting Investigation of Persistent Racial Bias in Illinois State Police Consent Searches." June 7, 2011. http://www.aclu.org/racial-justice/aclu-illinois-files-complaint-us-department-justice-requesting-investigation.

———. *Stop and Frisk in Chicago*. Chicago: ACLU of Illinois, 2015. http://www.aclu-il.org/wp-content/uploads/2015/03/ACLU_StopandFrisk_6.pdf.

Andenaes, Johannes. *Punishment and Deterrence*. Ann Arbor: University of Michigan Press, 1974.

Arcila, Fabio, Jr. "The Death of Suspicion." *William and Mary Law Review* 51 (2010): 1275–341.

Arizona v. Johnson, 551 U.S. 323 (2009).

Arkansas v. Sullivan, 532 U.S. 769 (2001).

Association of Chief Police Officers. "Statement of Mission and Values." 2011. http://www.acpo.police.uk/About/missionandvalues.aspx.

Bailey v. City of Philadelphia, Complaint, 2:10-cv-05952 (E.D. Pa. November 4, 2010). http://www.aclupa.org/download_file/view_inline/669/198/.

Bailey v. City of Philadelphia, Consent Decree, 2:10-cv-05952 (E.D. Pa. June 21, 2011). http://www.aclupa.org/download_file/view_inline/744/198/.

Bailey v. City of Philadelphia, Plaintiffs' Fifth Report to Court and Monitor on Stop and Frisk Practices, 2:10-cv-05952 (E.D. Pa. February 24, 2015). http://www.aclupa.org/download_file/view_inline/2230/198/.

Bailey v. City of Philadelphia, Plaintiffs' Third Report to Court and Monitor on Stop and Frisk Practices, 2:10-cv-05952 (E.D. Pa. March 19, 2013). http://www.aclupa.org/download_file/view_inline/2230/198/.

Baker, Al, and Joseph Goldstein. "2 Opinions on Stop-and-Frisk Report." *New York Times*, May 9, 2012. http://www.nytimes.com/2012/05/10/nyregion/police-stop-and-frisk-tactic-had-lower-gun-recovery-rate-in-2011.html?_r=1&ref=nyregion.

Banaji, Mahzarin R., and Anthony G. Greenwald. *Blindspot: Hidden Biases of Good People*. New York: Delacorte, 2013.

Bargh, John A. "The Cognitive Monster: The Case against the Controllability of Automatic Stereotype Effects." In *Dual Process Theories in Social Psychology*, edited by Shelly Chaiken and Yaacov Trope, 361–82. New York: Guilford, 1999.

Barrett, John Q. "Appendix B: *State of Ohio v. Richard D. Chilton* and *State of Ohio v. John W. Terry*: The Suppression Hearing and Trial Transcripts." *St. John's Law Review* 72, no. 3 (1998): 1387–524.

———. "Deciding the Stop-and-Frisk Cases: A Look inside the Supreme Court's Conference." *St. John's Law Review* 72, no. 3 (2012): 749–844.

Barrett-Lain, Corinna. "Countermajoritarian Hero or Zero? Rethinking the Warren Court's Role in the Criminal Procedure Revolution." *University of Pennsylvania Law Review* 152 (2004): 1361–452.

Barron, Stephen. "Police Officer Suicide within the New South Wales Police Force from 1999 to 2008." *Police Practice and Research: An International Journal* 11, no. 4 (2010): 371–82.

Baumer, Eric P., and Janet L. Lauritsen. "Reporting Crime to the Police, 1973–2005: A Multivariate Analysis of Long-Term Trends in the National Crime Survey (NCS) and National Crime Victimization Survey (NCVS)." *Criminology* 48, no. 1 (2010): 131–85.

Baumer, Eric P., and Kevin T. Wolff. "Evaluating Contemporary Crime Drop(s) in America, New York City, and Many Other Places." *Justice Quarterly* 31, no. 1 (2014): 5–38.

Bayley, David H. "The Tactical Choices of Police Patrol Officers." *Journal of Criminal Justice* 14, no. 4 (1986): 329–48.

Bayley, David H., and Egon Bittner. "Learning the Skills of Policing." *Law and Contemporary Problems* 47, no. 4 (1984): 35–59.

Beccaria, Cesare. *On Crimes and Punishment*. Translated by H. Paolucci. Indianapolis: Bobbs-Merrill, 1963. First published 1764.

Bell v. Wolfish, 441 U.S. 520 (1979).

Bellin, Jeffrey. "The Inverse Relationship between the Constitutionality and Effectiveness of New York City 'Stop and Frisk.'" *Boston University Law Review* 94 (2014): 1495–550.

Bentham, Jeremy. *The Principles of Morals and Legislation*. Amherst, NY: Prometheus, 1988. First published 1843.

Berk, Richard, and John MacDonald. "Policing the Homeless: An Evaluation of Efforts to Reduce Homeless-Related Crime." *Criminology and Public Policy* 9, no. 4 (2010): 813–40.

Binder, Arnold, and Peter Scharf. "The Violent Police-Citizen Encounter." *Annals of the American Academy of Political and Social Science* 452 (1980): 111–21.

Birzer, Michael L. "The Theory of Andragogy Applied to Police Training." *Policing: An International Journal of Police Strategies and Management* 26, no. 1 (2003): 29–42.

Birzer, Michael L., and Ronald Tannehill. "A More Effective Training Approach for Contemporary Policing." *Police Quarterly* 4, no. 2 (2001): 233–52.

Bittner, Egon. *The Functions of the Police in Modern Society*. Rockville, MD: National Institute of Mental Health, 1970.

———. "The Police on Skid Row: A Study of Peace Keeping." *American Sociological Review* 32, no. 5 (1967): 699–715.

Blair, Irene V., Charles M. Judd, and Kristine M. Chapleau. "The Influence of Afrocentric Facial Features in Criminal Sentencing." *Psychological Science* 15 (2004): 674–79.

Bloomberg, Michael R. "Michael Bloomberg: 'Stop and Frisk' Keeps New York Safe." *Washington Post*, August 18, 2013. http://www.washingtonpost.com/opinions/michael-bloomberg-stop-and-frisk-keeps-new-york-safe/2013/08/18/8d4cd8c4–06cf-11e3–9259-e2aafe5a5f84_story.html.

Blumstein, Alfred, and Richard Rosenfeld. "Explaining Recent Trends in U.S. Homicide Rates." *Journal of Criminal Law and Criminology* 88 (1998): 1175–216.

Blumstein, Alfred, and Joel Wallman. "The Crime Drop and Beyond." *Annual Review of Social Science* 2 (2006): 125–46.

Board of Education of Independent School District No. 92 of Pottawatomie County v. Earls, 536 U.S. 822 (2002).

Bobb, Merrick. *13th Semiannual Report*. Los Angeles: Police Assessment Resource Center, 2002.

———. *14th Semiannual Report*. Los Angeles: Police Assessment Resource Center, 2003.

Boger, John Charles, and Judith Welch Wegner, eds. *Race, Poverty, and American Cities*. Chapel Hill: University of North Carolina Press, 1996.

Bond v. United States, 529 U.S. 334 (2000).

Bornstein, Avram. "Antiterrorist Policing in New York City after 9/11: Comparing Perspectives on a Complex Process." *Human Organization* 64 (2005): 52–61.

Bowling, Benjamin. "The Rise and Fall of New York Murder: Zero Tolerance or Crack's Decline?" *British Journal of Criminology* 39 (1999): 531–54.

Boydstun, John E., and Michael E. Sherry. *San Diego Community Profile: Final Report*. Washington, DC: Police Foundation, 1975.

Braga, Anthony A. "The Effects of Hot Spots Policing on Crime." *Annals of the American Academy of Political and Social Science* 578 (2001): 104–25.

Braga, Anthony A., David M. Hureau, and Andrew V. Papachristos. "An Ex-Post-Facto Evaluation Framework for Place-Based Police Interventions." *Evaluation Review* 35, no. 6 (2011): 592–626.

Braga, Anthony A., Andrew V. Papachristos, and David M. Hureau. "The Effects of Hot Spots Policing on Crime: An Updated Systematic Review and Meta-Analysis." *Justice Quarterly* 31, no. 4 (2014): 633–63.

Braga, Anthony A., and Cory Schnell. "Evaluating Place-Based Policing Strategies: Lessons Learned from the Smart Policing Initiative in Boston." *Police Quarterly* 16, no. 3 (2013): 339–57.

Braga, Anthony A., and David Weisburd. *Policing Problem Places: Crime Hot Spots and Effective Prevention*. New York: Oxford University Press, 2010.

———. "Problem-Oriented Policing: The Disconnect between Principles and Practice." In *Police Innovation: Contrasting Perspectives*, edited by David Weisburd and Anthony A. Braga, 133–52. New York: Cambridge University Press, 2006.

Brandl, Steven G., Mitchell B. Chamlin, and James Frank. "Aggregation Bias and the Capacity for Formal Crime Control: The Determinants of Total and Disaggregated Police Force Size in Milwaukee, 1934–1987." *Justice Quarterly* 12, no. 3 (1995): 543–62.

Bratton, William. *Turnaround: How America's Top Cop Reversed the Crime Epidemic*. New York: Random House, 1998.

Brendlin v. California, 551 U.S. 249 (2007).

Brennan, Alice, and Dan Lieberman. "Florida City's 'Stop and Frisk' Nabs Thousands of Kids, Finds Five-Year-Olds 'Suspicious.'" *Fusion*, May 9, 2014. http://fusion.net/story/5568/florida-citys-stop-frisk-nabs-thousands-of-kids-finds-5-year-olds-suspicious/.

Brezina, Corona. *The Industrial Revolution in America: A Primary Source History of American's Transformation into an Industrial Society*. New York: Rosen, 2005.

Brinegar v. United States, 338 U.S. 160 (1949).

Brookfield, Stephen D. *Understanding and Facilitating Adult Learning*. San Francisco: Jossey-Bass, 1986.

Brown v. Texas, 443 U.S. 47 (1979).

Bumper v. North Carolina, 391 U.S. 543 (1968).

Bureau of Justice Statistics. *Local Police Departments, 2013: Equipment and Technology*. Washington, DC: Bureau of Justice Statistics, 2015.

Caffarella, Rosemary S. "Self-Directed Learning." In *An Update on Adult Learning Theory*, edited by Sharan B. Merriam, 25–35. San Francisco: Jossey-Bass, 1993.

California v. Greenwood, 486 U.S. 35 (1988).

California v. Hodari D., 499 U.S. 621 (1991).

Cameron, C. Daryl, B. Keith Payne, and Joshua Knobe. "Do Theories of Implicit Race Bias Change Moral Judgments?" *Social Justice Research* 23 (2010): 272–89.

Capehart, Jonathan. "'Stop and Frisk,' Bloomberg and Me." *Washington Post*, December 30, 2013. http://www.washingtonpost.com/blogs/post-partisan/wp/2013/12/30/stop-and-frisk-bloomberg-and-me/.

Capers, Bennett. "Rethinking the Fourth Amendment: Race, Citizenship, and the Equality Principle." *Harvard Civil Rights-Civil Liberties Law Review* 46 (2011): 1–49.

Capps, Kriston. "Police Body Cameras: Coming Everywhere in Three to Five Years." MSN.com, July 30, 2015. http://www.msn.com/en-gb/news/other/police-body-cameras-coming-everywhere-in-3-to-5-years/ar-AadJrEh.

Carroll v. United States, 267 U.S. 132 (1925).

Casper, Jonathan D., Tom R. Tyler, and Bonnie Fisher. "Procedural Justice in Felony Cases." Law and Society Review 22 (1988): 483–507.

Center for Constitutional Rights. Racial Disparity in NYPD Stops-and-Frisks: The Center for Constitutional Rights Preliminary Report on UF-250 Data from 2005 through June 2008. New York: Center for Constitutional Rights, 2009. https://ccrjustice.org/files/Report-CCR-NYPD-Stop-and-Frisk.pdf.

———. Stop and Frisk: The Human Impact. New York: Center for Constitutional Rights, 2012.

Center for Evidence-Based Crime Policy. "Evidence-Based Policing Matrix." N.d. http://cebcp.org/evidence-based-policing/the-matrix/.

Center for Problem Oriented Policing. Website. http://www.popcenter.org/.

Centers for Disease Control. "Youth Online: High School." 2014. http://perma.cc/NV7C-ZFNW.

Cerdá, Magdalena, Melissa Tracy, Steven F. Messner, David Vlahov, Emily Goldmann, Kenneth Tardiff, and Sandro Galea. "Investigating the Effect of Social Changes on Age-Specific Gun-Related Homicide Rates in New York City during the 1990s." American Journal of Public Health 100, no. 6 (2010): 1107–15.

Cerdá, Magdalena, Melissa Tracy, Steven F. Messner, David Vlahov, Kenneth Tardiff, and Sandro Galea. "Misdemeanor Policing, Physical Disorder, and Gun-Related Homicide: A Spatial Analytic Test of 'Broken-Windows' Theory." Epidemiology 20, no. 4 (2009): 533–41.

Chamlin, Mitchell B. "Determinants of Police Expenditures in Chicago, 1904–1958." Sociological Quarterly 31, no. 3 (1990): 485–94.

Chauhan, Preeti. A Review of the Research on the New York Crime Decline. New York: John Jay College of Criminal Justice, 2011.

CityLaw. "Current Development: City Tort: Wrongful Death: City Settled Diallo Suit." CityLaw 10 (March/April 2004): 43.

Clancy, Thomas K. "The Fourth Amendment's Concept of Reasonableness." Utah Law Review 4 (2004): 977–1044.

Clinton v. Virginia, 377 U.S. 158 (1964).

Cohen, Bernard, and Jan M. Chaiken. Police Background Characteristics and Performance. New York: RAND Institute, 1972.

———. Police Background Characteristics and Performance. Lexington, MA: Lexington Books, 1973.

Cohen, Jacqueline, and Jens Ludwig. "Policing Gun Crimes." In Evaluating Gun Policy: Effects on Crime and Violence, edited by Jens Ludwig and Philip J. Cook, 217–50. Washington, DC: Brookings Institution, 2003.

Cohen, Lawrence E., and Marcus Felson. "Social Change and Crime Rate Trends: A Routine Activity Approach." *American Sociological Review* 44 (1979): 588–605.

Cole, David. *No Equal Justice: Race and Class in the American Criminal Justice System.* New York: New Press, 1999.

Commission for Accreditation of Law Enforcement Agencies (CALEA). "Law Enforcement Accreditation." 2010. http://www.calea.org/content/law-enforcement-accreditation.

———. "Law Enforcement Program: The Standards." 2009. http://www.calea.org/content/law-enforcement-program-standards.

Commonwealth v. Tarver, 345 N.E.2d 671 (Mass. 1975).

Community Oriented Policing Services (COPS). "Collaborative Reform Initiative for Technical Assistance." October 2015. http://www.cops.usdoj.gov/default.asp?Item=2807.

Cook, Philip, and John Laub. "The Unprecedented Epidemic in Youth Violence." In *Crime and Justice: An Annual Review of Research*, edited by Michael Tonry, 26–64. Chicago: University of Chicago Press, 1998.

Cooper v. California, 386 U.S. 58 (1967).

Cordner, Gary. "Community Policing: Elements and Effects." In *Critical Issues in Policing*, 5th ed., edited by Roger G. Dunham and Geoffrey P. Alpert, 148–71. Long Grove, IL: Waveland, 2005.

Cork, Daniel. "Examining Space-Time Interaction in City-Level Homicide Data: Crack Markets and the Diffusion of Guns among Youth." *Journal of Quantitative Criminology* 15, no. 4 (1999): 379–406.

Corman, Hope, and Naci Mocan. "Carrots, Sticks, and Broken Windows." *Journal of Law and Economics* 48, no. 1 (2005): 235–62.

Correll, Joshua, Bernadette Park, Charles M. Judd, and Bernd Wittenbrink. "Across the Thin Blue Line: Police Officers and Racial Bias in the Decision to Shoot." *Journal of Personality and Social Psychology* 92 (2007): 1006–23.

———. "The Influence of Stereotypes on Decisions to Shoot." *European Journal of Social Psychology* 37, no. 6 (2007): 1002–117.

———. "The Police Officer's Dilemma: Using Ethnicity to Disambiguate Potentially Threatening Individuals." *Journal of Personality and Social Psychology* 83 (2002): 1314–29.

CrimeSolutions.gov. Website. http://www.crimesolutions.gov/.

Cupp v. Murphy, 412 U.S. 291 (1973).

Daniels v. City of New York, Complaint, 1:99-cv-01695-SAS (S.D.N.Y. March 8, 1999).

Daniels v. City of New York, Stipulation of Settlement, 1:99-cv-01695-SAS (S.D.N.Y. September 24, 2003). http://ccrjustice.org/files/Daniels_StipulationOfSettlement_12_03_0.pdf.

Davies, Thomas Y. "Recovering the Original Fourth Amendment." *Michigan Law Review* 98 (1999): 547–667.

Davis, Kenneth C. *Police Discretion*. St. Paul, MN: West Publishing, 1975.

Davis, Robert C., and Pedro Mateu-Gelabert. *Respectful and Effective Policing: Two Examples in the South Bronx*. New York: Vera Institute of Justice, 1999. http://www.vera.org/sites/default/files/resources/downloads/respectful_policing.pdf.

Delsol, Rebekah, and Michael Shiner. *Stop and Search: The Anatomy of a Police Power*. Basingstoke, UK: Palgrave MacMillan, 2015.

Destefano, Anthony M. "Bratton: NYPD, Communities Need Mutual Respect." *Newsday*, January 2, 2014.

Devine, Patricia G., Margo J. Monteith, Julia R. Zuwerink, and Andrew J. Elliot. "Prejudice with and without Compunction." *Journal of Personality and Social Psychology* 60, no. 6 (1991): 817–30.

Dixon, David. "Beyond Zero Tolerance." In *Police: Key Readings*, edited by Tim Newburn, 483–507. Portland, OR: Willan, 2005.

Dovidio, John F., Kerry Kawakami, and Samuel L. Gaertner. "Implicit and Explicit Prejudice and Interracial Interaction." *Journal of Personality and Social Psychology* 82 (2002): 62–68.

Dunaway v. New York, 442 U.S. 200 (1979).

Duncan, Birt L. "Differential Social Perception and Attribution of Intergroup Violence: Testing the Lower Limits of Stereotyping of Blacks." *Journal of Personality and Social Psychology* 34, no. 4 (1976): 590–98.

Duncan, Jericka. "Eric Garner Case: Video of Chokehold's Aftermath Raises New Questions." CBSNews.com, December 6, 2014. http://www.cbsnews.com/news/second-tape-of-nypd-chokehold-raises-new-questions-in-eric-garner-case/.

Eberhardt, Jennifer L., Paul G. Davies, Valerie J. Purdie-Vaughns, and Sheri L. Johnson. "Looking Deathworthy: Perceived Stereotypicality of Black Defendants Predicts Capital Sentencing Outcomes." *Psychological Science* 17 (2006): 383–86.

Eberhardt, Jennifer L., Phillip Atiba Goff, Valerie J. Purdie, and Paul G. Davies. "Seeing Black: Race, Crime, and Visual Processing." *Journal of Personality and Social Psychology* 87, no. 6 (2004): 876–93.

Eck, John E., and Dennis Rosenbaum. "The New Police Order: Effectiveness, Equity, and Efficiency in Community Policing." In *The Challenge of Community Policing: Testing the Promises*, edited by Dennis Rosenbaum, 3–23. Thousand Oaks, CA: Sage, 1994.

Eck, John E., and William Spelman. *Problem-Solving: Problem-Oriented Policing in Newport News*. Washington, DC: National Institute of Justice, 1987.

Eligon, John. "Taking on Police Tactic, Critics Hit Racial Divide." *New York Times*, March 22, 2012. http://www.nytimes.com/2012/03/23/nyregion/fighting-stop-and-frisk-tactic-but-hitting-racial-divide.html?_r=0.

Entick v. Carrington, 19 Howell's State Trials 1029, 95 Eng. Rep. 807 (1765).

Eterno, John. "Cadets and Policing: An Analysis of the New York City Police Department's Cadet Corps." Paper presented at the Academy of Criminal Justice Sciences annual meeting, Las Vegas, NV, 1996.

Eure, Philip K. *Examination of Substantiated Chokehold Cases by DIO's Office of the Inspector General for the NYPD Reveals Gaps in Discipline and Communication and Raises Questions about Training of Officers.* New York: City of New York Department of Investigation, Office of Inspector General, 2015.

Evans v. Stephens, 407 F.3d 1272 (11th Cir. 2005).

Fagan, Jeffrey. "Crime and Neighborhood Change." In *Understanding Crime Trends*, edited by Arthur S. Goldberger and Richard Rosenfeld, 81–126. Washington, DC: National Academy of Sciences, National Academies Press, 2008.

Fagan, Jeffrey, and Garth Davies. "Street Stops and Broken Windows: *Terry*, Race, and Disorder in New York City." *Fordham Urban Law Journal* 28 (2000): 457–504.

Fagan, Jeffrey, Garth Davies, and Jan Holland. "The Paradox of the Drug Elimination Program in New York City Public Housing." *Georgetown Journal of Poverty Law and Policy* 13 (2006): 415–60.

Fagan, Jeffrey, Amanda Geller, Garth Davies, and Valerie West. "Street Stops and Broken Windows Revisited: The Demography and Logic of Proactive Policing in a Safe and Changing City." In *Race, Ethnicity and Policing: New and Essential Readings*, edited by Steven K. Rice and Michael D. White, 309–48. New York: New York University Press, 2010.

Fagan, Jeffrey, Franklin E. Zimring, and June Kim. "Declining Homicide in New York: A Tale of Two Trends." *Journal of Criminal Law and Criminology* 88, no. 4 (1998): 1277–324.

Farrell, Amy, and Jack McDevitt. *Rhode Island Traffic Stop Statistics: 2004–2005, Final Report.* Boston: Northeastern University, 2006.

Fazio, Russell H., Joni R. Jackson, Bridget C. Dunton, and Carol J. Williams. "Variability in Automatic Activation as an Unobtrusive Measure of Racial Attitudes: A Bona Fide Pipeline?" *Journal of Personality and Social Psychology* 69 (1995): 1013–27.

Feld, Barry C. "Race, Politics, and Juvenile Justice: The Warren Court and the Conservative 'Backlash.'" *Minnesota Law Review* 87 (2003): 1447–577.

Ferdico, John N., Henry F. Fradella, and Christopher D. Totten. *Criminal Procedure for the Criminal Justice Professional.* 12th ed. Belmont, CA: Wadsworth/Cengage, 2016.

Ferguson, Andrew G. "Big Data and Predictive Reasonable Suspicion." *University of Pennsylvania Law Review* 163 (2015): 327–410.

Ferguson, Andrew G., and Damien Bernache. "The 'High-Crime Area' Question: Requiring Verifiable and Quantifiable Evidence for Fourth Amendment Reasonable Suspicion Analysis." *American University Law Review* 57 (2008): 1587–644.

Fermino, Jennifer. "Mayor Bloomberg on Stop-and-Frisk: It Can Be Argued 'We Disproportionately Stop Whites Too Much and Minorities Too Little.'" *New York Daily News*, June 28, 2013. http://www.nydailynews.com/new-york/mayor-bloomberg-stop-and-frisk-disproportionately-stop-whites-minorities-article-1.1385410.

Florence v. Burlington Board of Chosen Freeholders, 132 S. Ct. 1510 (2012).

Florida v. Bostick, 501 U.S. 429 (1991).

Florida v. Royer, 460 U.S. 491 (1983).

Floyd v. City of New York, 2015 U.S. Dist. LEXIS 34453 (S.D.N.Y. March 19, 2015).

Floyd v. City of New York, 302 F.R.D. 69 (S.D.N.Y. 2014).

Floyd v. City of New York, 770 F.3d 1051 (2d Cir. 2014).

Floyd v. City of New York, 959 F. Supp. 2d 540 (S.D.N.Y. 2013).

Floyd v. City of New York, 959 F. Supp. 2d 668 (S.D.N.Y. 2013), *stay granted, Ligon v. City of New York*, 538 Fed. Appx. 101 (2d Cir. 2013), *vacated by, in part*, 743 F.3d 362 (2d Cir. 2014).

Floyd v. City of New York, Complaint and Demand for Jury Trial, 08-cv-01034-SAS (S.D.N.Y. January 31, 2008). http://ccrjustice.org/files/Floyd_Complaint_08.01.31.pdf.

Floyd v. City of New York, Opposition of Sergeants Benevolent Association to Motion of City of New York for a Limited Remand to the District Court for the Purpose of Exploring a Resolution, No. 13–3088 (2d Cir. February 7, 2014). http://ccrjustice.org/files/SBA%20Opp%20to%20City%27s%20Motion%20to%20Remand.%202%207%20 2014.pdf.

Floyd v. City of New York, Report of Jeffrey Fagan, Ph.D., 08-cv-01034-SAS (S.D.N.Y. October 15, 2010). https://ccrjustice.org/files/Expert_Report_JeffreyFagan.pdf.

Floyd v. City of New York, Second Supplemental Report of Jeffrey Fagan, Ph.D., 08-cv-01034-SAS (S.D.N.Y. November 29, 2012). http://www.ccrjustice.org/files/FaganSecondSupplementalReport.pdf.

Fox, James A., and Marianne W. Zawitz. *Homicide Trends in the United States*. Washington, DC: Bureau of Justice Statistics, 2007. http://www.bjs.gov/content/pub/pdf/htius.pdf.

Fradella, Henry F. "From Insanity to Beyond Diminished Capacity: Mental Illness and Criminal Excuse in the Post-*Clark* Era." *University of Florida Journal of Law and Public Policy* 18 (2007): 7–92.

Fradella, Henry F., Weston J. Morrow, Ryan G. Fischer, and Connie Ireland. "Quantifying *Katz*: Empirically Measuring Reasonable Expectations of Privacy in the Fourth Amendment Context." *American Journal of Criminal Law* 38, no. 3 (2011): 289–373.

Fraenkel, Osmond K. "Concerning Searches and Seizures." *Harvard Law Review* 34 (1921): 361–66.

Fratello, Jennifer, Andres F. Rengifo, Jennifer Trone, and Brenda Velazquez. *Coming of Age with Stop and Frisk: Experiences, Self-Perceptions, and Public Safety Implications*. Washington, DC: Vera Institute of Justice, 2013. http://www.vera.org/sites/default/files/resources/downloads/stop-and-frisk_technical-report.pdf.

Fridell, Lorie, Bob Lunney, Drew Diamond, and Bruce Kubu with Michael Scott and Colleen Laing. *Racially Biased Policing: A Principled Response*. Washington, DC: Police Executive Research Forum, 2001.

Fryer, R. G., Jr., P. S. Heaton, S. D. Levitt, K. M. Murphy. "Measuring Crack Cocaine and Its Impact." *Economic Inquiry* 51, no. 3 (2013): 1651–81.

Fyfe, James J. "Administrative Interventions on Police Shooting Discretion: An Empirical Examination." *Journal of Criminal Justice* 7, no. 4 (1979): 309–24.

———. "Police/Citizen Violence Reduction Project." *FBI Law Enforcement Bulletin* 58 (1989): 18–25.

———. "Police Use of Deadly Force: Research and Reform." *Justice Quarterly* 5, no. 2 (1988): 165–205.

———. "The Split-Second Syndrome and Other Determinants of Police Violence." In *Violent Transactions*, edited by Anne T. Campbell and John J. Gibbs, 207–25. Oxford: Basil Blackwell, 1986.

———. "Training to Reduce Police-Civilian Violence." In *And Justice for All: Understanding and Controlling Police Abuse of Force*, edited by William A. Geller and Hans Toch, 165–79. Washington, DC: Police Executive Research Forum, 1995.

Fyfe, James J., and Robert J Kane. *Bad Cops: A Study of Career-Ending Misconduct among New York City Police Officers; Final Report.* Grant no. 96-IJ-CX-0053. Washington, DC: National Institute of Justice, 2006.

Gain, Charles. *Discharge of Firearms Policy: Effecting Justice through Administrative Regulation—A Position Paper.* Oakland, CA: Oakland Police Department, 1971.

Geller, Amanda, and Jeffrey Fagan. "Pot as Pretext: Marijuana, Race, and the New Disorder in New York City Street Policing." *Journal of Empirical Legal Studies* 7, no. 4 (2010): 591–633.

Geller, William A., and Michael S. Scott. *Deadly Force: What We Know.* Washington, DC: Police Executive Research Forum, 1992.

Gelman, Andrew, Jeffrey Fagan, and Alex Kiss. "An Analysis of the New York City Police Department's 'Stop and Frisk' Policy in the Context of Claims of Racial Bias." *Journal of the American Statistical Association* 102, no. 479 (2007): 813–23.

Gisske v. Sanders, 9 Cal. App. 13 (1908).

Glendale Police Department. *SB1070 Instructor Points.* Glendale, AZ: Glendale Police Department, 2010.

Go-Bart Importing Co. v. United States, 282 U.S. 344 (1931).

Goel, Sharad, Justin M. Rao, and Ravi Shroff. "Precinct or Prejudice? Understanding Racial Disparities in New York City's Stop-and-Frisk Policy." *Social Science Research Network*, March 2, 2015. http://ssrn.com/abstract=2572718.

Golden, Megan, and Cari Almo. *Reducing Gun Violence: An Overview of New York City's Strategies.* New York: Vera Institute of Justice, 2004. http://vera.org/sites/default/files/resources/downloads/Reducing_gun_violence.pdf.

Goldman v. United States, 316 U.S. 129 (1942).

Goldstein, Herman. "Improving Policing: A Problem-Oriented Approach." *Crime and Delinquency* 25, no. 2 (1979): 235–58.

———. *Problem-Oriented Policing.* New York: McGraw-Hill, 1990.

Goodman-Delahunty, Jane. "Four Ingredients: New Recipes for Procedural Justice in Australian Policing." *Policing: A Journal of Policy and Practice* 4 (2010): 403–10.

Graham, Fred P. *The Due Process Revolution: The Warren Court's Impact on Criminal Law.* New York: Hayden, 1970.

Graham v. Connor, 490 U.S. 386 (1989).

Grant, J. Douglas, and Joan Grant. "Officer Selection and the Prevention of Abuse of Force." In *And Justice for All: Understanding and Controlling Police Abuse of Force*, edited by William A. Geller and Hans Toch, 150–64. Washington, DC: Police Executive Research Forum, 1995.

Greenberg, David F., Ronald C. Kessler, and Colin Loftin. "Social Inequality and Crime Control." *Journal of Criminal Law and Criminology* 76 (1985): 684–704.

Greene, Judith A. "Zero Tolerance: A Case Study of Police Policies and Practices in New York City." *Crime and Delinquency* 45 (1999): 171–87.

Green-Mazerolle, Lorraine, Justin Ready, William Terrill, and Elin Waring. "Problem-Oriented Policing in Public Housing: The Jersey City Evaluation." *Justice Quarterly* 17 (1999): 129–55.

Greenwald, Anthony G., and Mahzarin R. Banaji. "Implicit Social Cognition: Attitudes, Self-Esteem, and Stereotypes." *Psychological Review* 102 (1995): 4–17.

Grogger, Jeff, and Michael Willis. "The Emergence of Crack Cocaine and the Rise in Urban Crime Rates." *Review of Economics and Statistics* 82 (November 2000): 519–29.

Haberfeld, Maria R. *Critical Issues in Training.* Upper Saddle River, NJ: Prentice-Hall, 2002.

Hale, Matthew. *The History of the Pleas of the Crown.* 1st American ed., vol. 2. Philadelphia: Robert H. Small, 1847. First published 1736.

Hammer, Michael, and James Champy. *Reengineering the Corporation.* New York: HarperCollins, 1993.

Harcourt, Bernard E. *Illusion of Order: The False Promise of Broken Windows Policing.* Cambridge: Harvard University Press, 2001.

Harcourt, Bernard E., and Jens Ludwig. "Broken Windows: New Evidence from New York City and a Five-City Social Experiment." *University of Chicago Law Review* 73 (2006): 271–320.

Harris, Christopher J. "The Onset of Police Misconduct." *Policing: An International Journal of Police Strategies and Management* 37, no. 2 (2014): 285–304.

——. *Pathways of Police Misconduct: Problem Behavior Patterns and Trajectories from Two Cohorts.* Durham, NC: Carolina Academic Press, 2010.

Harris, David A. "Across the Hudson: Taking the Stop and Frisk Debate beyond New York City." *NYU Journal of Legislation and Public Policy* 16, no. 1 (2014): 853–82.

——. "Factors for Reasonable Suspicion: When Black and Poor Means Stopped and Frisked." *Indiana Law Journal* 69 (1994): 659–87.

——. "Frisking Every Suspect: The Withering of *Terry.*" *University of California Davis Law Review* 28 (1994): 1–52.

——. *Profiles in Injustice: Why Racial Policing Cannot Work.* New York: New Press, 2002.

Harvard Law Review Association. "Criminal Law: New York Authorizes Police to 'Stop-and-Frisk' on Reasonable Suspicion." *Harvard Law Review* 78, no. 2 (1964): 473–77.

Hawkins, William, and John Curwood. *Pleas of the Crown.* 8th ed. Vol. 2. London: C. Roworth, Bell-Yard, & Temple Bar, 1824. First published 1716.

Hechtman, Michael. "Bratton Raps Kelly and Bloomberg on Stop and Frisk." *New York Post,* March 31, 2014.

Here & Now. "Bill Bratton: You Can't Police without Stop-and-Frisk." *Here & Now with Robin Young and Jeremy Hobson*, February 25, 2014. http://hereandnow.wbur. org/2014/02/25/bill-bratton-nypd.

Hiibel v. Sixth Judicial Dist. Ct. of Nev., Humboldt County, 542 U.S. 177 (2004).

Hinds, Lyn. "Youth, Police Legitimacy and Informal Contact." *Journal of Police and Criminal Psychology* 24 (2009): 10–21.

Hinds, Lyn, and Kristina Murphy. "Public Satisfaction with Police: Using Procedural Justice to Improve Police Legitimacy." *Australian and New Zealand Journal of Criminology* 40 (2007): 27–42.

Hirschman, Charles, and Elizabeth Mogford. "Immigration and the American Industrial Revolution from 1880 to 1920." *Social Science Research* 38, no. 4 (2009): 897–920.

Hobsbawm, Eric J. *Industry and Empire, 1875–1914*. New York: Penguin, 1983.

Hoover v. Walsh, 682 F.3d 481 (6th Cir. 2012).

Hudson, David. "Building Trust between Communities and Local Police." *White House Blog*, December 1, 2014.

Hunt, Jennifer. "Police Accounts of Normal Force." *Journal of Contemporary Ethnography* 13, no. 4 (1985): 315–41.

Hynynen, Suvi. *Community Perceptions of Brownsville*. New York: Center for Court Innovation, 2011. http://www.courtinnovation.org/sites/default/files/documents/ Brownsville%20Op%20Data%20FINAL.pdf.

Illinois v. Gates, 462 U.S. 213 (1983).

Illinois v. Wardlow, 528 U.S. 119 (2000).

In re Will County Grand Jury, 604 N.E.2d 929 (Ill. 1992).

In re Winship, 397 U.S. 358 (1970).

I.N.S. v. Delgado, 466 U.S. 210 (1984).

International Association of Chiefs of Police. *Building Integrity and Reducing Drug Corruption in Police Departments*. Arlington, VA: International Association of Chiefs of Police, 1989.

Jablonski, Ray. "Cleveland Councilman Zack Reed Proposes Instituting Version of 'Stop and Frisk' Policy in Cleveland Police." Cleveland.com, July 23, 2014. http://www. cleveland.com/metro/index.ssf/2014/07/cleveland_councilman_zack_reed_6.html.

Joanes, Ana. "Does the New York City Police Department Deserve Credit for the Decline in New York City's Homicide Rates? A Cross-City Comparison of Policing Strategies and Homicide Rates." *Columbia Journal of Law and Social Problems* 33 (2000): 265–311.

Johnson, Bruce, Andrew Golub, and Eloise Dunlap. "The Rise and Decline of Hard Drugs, Drug Markets, and Violence in Inner-City New York." In *The Crime Drop in America*, edited by Alfred Blumstein and Joel Wallman, 164–206. New York: Cambridge University Press, 2006.

Johnson, Bruce D., Andrew Golub, and James McCabe. "The International Implications of Quality-of-Life Policing as Practiced in New York City." *Police Practice and Research* 11 (2010): 17–29.

Johnson v. United States, 333 U.S. 10 (1948).

Jones-Brown, Delores D., and Henry F. Fradella. "From *Simpson* to *Zimmerman*: Examining the Effects of Race, Class, and Gender in the Failed Prosecution of Two Highly-Publicized, Racially-Divisive Cases." In *Deadly Injustice: Trayvon Martin, Race, and the Criminal Justice System*, edited by Devon Johnson, Patricia Warren, and Amy Farrell, 215–44. New York: New York University Press, 2016.

Jones-Brown, Delores D., and Brian A. Maule. "Racially Biased Policing: A Review of the Judicial and Legislative Literature." In *Race, Ethnicity, and Policing: New and Essential Readings*, edited by Stephen K. Rice and Michael D. White, 140–76. New York: New York University Press, 2010.

Jones-Brown, Delores D., Brett G. Stoudt, Brian Johnson, and Kevin Moran. *Stop, Question and Frisk Policing Practices in New York City: A Primer*. Revised ed. New York: Center on Race, Crime, and Justice, 2013. http://www.atlanticphilanthropies. org/sites/default/files/uploads/SQF_Primer_July_2013.pdf.

Jost, John T., Laurie A. Rudman, Irene V. Blair, Dana R. Carney, Nilanjana Dasgupta, Jack Glaser, and Curtis D. Hardin. "The Existence of Implicit Bias Is Beyond Reasonable Doubt: A Refutation of Ideological and Methodological Objections and Executive Summary of Ten Studies That No Manager Should Ignore." *Research in Organizational Behavior* 29 (2009): 39–69.

Kalhan, Anil. "Stop and Frisk, Judicial Independence, and the Ironies of Improper Appearances." *Georgetown Journal of Legal Ethics* 27 (2014): 1043–127.

Kamisar, Yale. "Equal Justice in the Gatehouses and Mansions of American Criminal Procedure." In *A Criminal Justice in Our Time*, edited by A. E. Dick Howard, 1–95. Charlottesville: University Press of Virginia, 1965.

Kane, Robert J. "The Ecology of Police Misconduct." *Criminology* 40, no. 4 (2002): 867–96.

Kane, Robert J., and Michael D. White. "Bad Cops: A Study of Career-Ending Misconduct among New York City Police Officers." *Criminology and Public Policy* 8, no. 4 (2009): 737–69.

——. *Jammed Up: Bad Cops, Police Misconduct, and the New York City Police Department*. New York: New York University Press, 2012.

Kappeler, Victor E., Richard D. Sluder, and Geoffrey P. Alpert. *Forces of Deviance: Understanding the Dark Side of Policing*. Prospect Heights, IL: Waveland, 1998.

Katz, Lewis R. "*Terry v. Ohio* at Thirty-Five: A Revisionist View." *Mississippi Law Journal* 74 (2004): 423–86.

Katz v. United States, 389 U.S. 347 (1967).

Kelling, George L., and William J. Bratton. "Declining Crime Rates: Insiders' Views of the New York City Story." *Journal of Criminal Law and Criminology* 88 (1998): 1217–32.

Kelling, George L., and Catherine M. Coles. *Fixing Broken Windows: Restoring Order and Reducing Crime in Our Communities*. New York: Touchstone, 1996.

Kelling, George L., and Mark H. Moore. "The Evolving Strategy of Policing." *Perspectives on Policing*, no. 4. Washington, DC: U.S. Department of Justice, Office of Justice Programs, National Institute of Justice, 1988.

———. "From Political Reform to Community: The Evolving Strategy of Police." In *Community Policing: Rhetoric or Reality*, edited by Jack Greene and Stephen D. Mastrofski, 1–26. New York: Praeger, 1988.

Kelling, George L., and William H. Sousa. *Do Police Matter? An Analysis of the Impact of New York City's Police Reforms*. Civic Report, no. 22, December 2001. Center for Civic Innovation, Manhattan Institute, New York. http://www.manhattan-institute.org/pdf/cr_22.pdf.

Kelly, Raymond W. "New York Police Commissioner Ray Kelly Calls Stop-and-Frisk Decision 'Disturbing and Offensive.'" *New York Daily News*, August 12, 2013. http://www.nydailynews.com/news/politics/new-york-police-commissioner-ray-kelly-comments-stop-and-frisk-decision-article-1.1424689.

Kennedy, David. *Juvenile Gun Violence and Gun Markets in Boston*. Washington, DC: National Institute of Justice, 1997.

———. "Old Wine in New Bottles: Policing and the Lessons of Pulling Levers." In *Police Innovation: Contrasting Perspectives*, edited by David Weisburd and Anthony A. Braga, 155–70. New York: Cambridge University Press, 2006.

Kentucky v. King, 131 S. Ct. 1849 (2011).

Kerner Commission. *Final Report of the National Advisory Commission on Civil Disorders*. New York: Bantam, 1968.

Klinger, David. "Can Police Training Affect the Use of Force on the Streets? The Metro-Dade Violence Reduction Field Experiment." In *Holding Police Accountable*, edited by Candace McCoy, 95–107. Washington, DC: Urban Institute Press, 2010.

Klockars, Carl B., Sanja Kutnjak Ivkovich, William E. Harver, and Maria R. Haberfeld. *The Measurement of Police Integrity*. Washington, DC: U.S. Department of Justice, Department of Justice Programs, National Institute of Justice, 2000.

Knight, Heather. "Ed Lee Drops Stop-Frisk Plan amid Uproar." *San Francisco Gate*, August 7, 2012. http://www.sfgate.com/bayarea/article/Ed-Lee-drops-stop-frisk-plan-amid-uproar-3768219.php.

Kocieniewski, David. "Success of Elite Police Unit Exacts a Toll on the Streets." *New York Times*, February 15, 1999. http://www.nytimes.com/1999/02/15/nyregion/success-of-elite-police-unit-exacts-a-toll-on-the-streets.html.

Kuh, Richard H. "Reflection on New York's 'Stop-and-Frisk' Law and Its Claimed Unconstitutionality." *Journal of Criminal Law, Criminology, and Police Science* 56 (1965): 32–38.

Kusmer, Kenneth L., and Joe W. Trotter. *African American Urban History since World War II*. Chicago: University of Chicago Press, 2009.

Kyllo v. United States, 533 U.S. 27 (2001).

LaFave, Wayne. "Detention for Investigation by the Police: An Analysis of Current Practices." *Washington University Law Quarterly* 1962, no. 3, 331–99.

Lane, Kristin A., Jerry Kang, and Mahzarin R. Banaji. "Implicit Social Cognition and Law." *Annual Review of Law and Social Science* 3 (2007): 427–51.

Lane, Roger. "Urban Police and Crime in Nineteenth-Century America." In *Crime and Justice: Annual Review of Research*, vol. 2, edited by Norval Morris and Michael Tonry, 1–43. Chicago: University of Chicago Press, 1980.

Lardner, James, and Thomas Repetto. *NYPD: A City and Its Police*. New York: Henry Holt, 2000.

Lasson, Nelson B. *The History and Development of the Fourth Amendment to the United States Constitution*. Baltimore: Johns Hopkins Press, 1937.

Lauritsen, Janet L., and Karen Heimer. "Violent Victimization among Males and Economic Conditions: The Vulnerability of Race and Ethnic Minorities." *Criminology and Public Policy* 9, no. 4 (2010): 665–92.

Lauritsen, Janet L., and Robin J. Schaum. *Crime and Victimization in the Three Largest Metropolitan Areas, 1980–98*. Washington, DC: Bureau of Justice Statistics, U.S. Department of Justice, 2005.

La Vigne, Nancy G., Pamela Lachman, Shebani Rao, and Andrea Matthews. *Stop and Frisk: Balancing Crime Control with Community Relations*. Washington, DC: Office of Community Oriented Policing Services, 2014.

Lawrence v. Hedger, 3 Taunt. 14, 128 Eng. Rep. 6 (C.P. 1810).

Lee, Cynthia. "Making Race Salient: Trayvon Martin and Implicit Bias in a Not Yet Post-Racial Society." *North Carolina Law Review* 91 (2013): 1555–612.

———. "Reasonableness with Teeth: The Future of Fourth Amendment Reasonableness Analysis." *Mississippi Law Journal* 81, no. 5 (2012): 1–50.

Lee, Debora. "Councilman Zack Reed's Stop and Frisk Plan Called 'Unconstitutional.'" NewsNet5.com (Cleveland), July 30, 2014. http://www.newsnet5.com/news/local-news/cleveland-metro/reeds-stop-and-frisk-plan-called-unconstitutional.

LeMay, Michael C. *Transforming America: Perspectives on U.S. Immigration*. Vol. 1. Santa Barbara, CA: Praeger/ABC-CLIO, 2013.

Lerner, Craig S. "Reasonable Suspicion and Mere Hunches." *Vanderbilt Law Review* 59 (2006): 407–73.

Leventhal, Gerald S. "What Should Be Done with Equity Theory?" In *Social Exchange: Advances in Theory and Research*, edited by Kenneth J. Gergen, Martin S. Greenberg, and Richard H. Willis, 27–55. New York: Plenum, 1980.

Ligon v. City of New York, 538 Fed. Appx. 101 (2d Cir. 2013).

Ligon v. City of New York, 736 F.3d 118 (2d Cir. 2013).

Ligon v. City of New York, 736 F.3d 166, *reconsider denied*, 736 F.3d 231 (2d. Cir. 2013).

Ligon v. City of New York, 743 F.3d 362 (2d Cir. 2014).

Lind, E. Allan. "The Psychology of Courtroom Procedure." In *The Psychology of the Courtroom*, edited by Norbert L. Kerr and Robert M. Bray, 13–38. New York: Academic Press, 1982.

Lind, E. Allan, and Tom R. Tyler. *The Social Psychology of Procedural Justice*. New York: Plenum, 1988.

Liska, Allen E., Joseph J. Lawrence, and Michael Benson. "Perspectives on the Legal Order." *American Journal of Sociology* 87 (1981): 412–26.

Livingston, Debra. "Police Discretion and the Quality of Life in Public Places: Courts, Communities, and the New Policing." *Columbia Law Review* 97 (1997): 551–672.

Loury, Glenn C. *The Anatomy of Racial Inequality*. Cambridge: Harvard University Press, 2002.

MacDonald, John, Jeffrey Fagan, and Amanda Geller. "The Effects of Local Police Surges on Crime and Arrests in New York City." Columbia Public Law Research Paper no. 14–468, 2015. http://papers.ssrn.com/sol3/papers.cfm?abstract_id=2614058.

Maclin, Tracey. "The Central Meaning of the Fourth Amendment." *William and Mary Law Review* 35 (1993): 197–249.

———. "*Terry v. Ohio*'s Fourth Amendment Legacy: Black Men and Police Discretion." *St. John's Law Review* 72, no. 3 (1998): 1271–321.

Mapp v. Ohio, 367 U.S. 643 (1961).

Maryland v. Buie, 494 U.S. 325 (1990).

Maryland v. King, 133 S. Ct. 1958 (2013).

Mastrofski, Stephen D. "Community Policing: A Skeptical View." In *Police Innovation: Contrasting Perspectives*, edited by David Weisburd and Anthony A. Braga, 44–73. New York: Cambridge University Press, 2006.

Mazerolle, Lorraine, Emma Antrobus, Sarah Bennett, and Tom R. Tyler. "Shaping Citizen Perceptions of Police Legitimacy: A Randomized Field Trial of Procedural Justice." *Criminology* 51, no. 1 (2013): 33–63.

Mazerolle, Lorraine, Sarah Bennett, Jacqueline Davis, Elise Sargeant, and Matthew Manning. *Legitimacy in Policing*. Campbell Systematic Review. Oslo, Norway: Campbell Collaboration, 2012.

McAffee, Thomas B. "Setting Us Up for Disaster: The Supreme Court's Decision in *Terry v. Ohio*." *Nevada Law Journal* 12 (2012): 609–25.

McConnell, Allen R., and Jill M. Leibold. "Relations among the Implicit Association Test, Discriminatory Behavior, and Explicit Measures of Racial Attitudes." *Journal of Experimental Social Psychology* 37 (2001): 435–42.

McDonald, Phyllis. *Managing Police Operations*. Belmont, CA: Wadsworth, 2002.

McDowall, David, and Colin Loftin. "Do U.S. City Crime Rates Follow a National Trend? The Influence of Nationwide Conditions on Local Crime Patterns." *Journal of Quantitative Criminology* 25, no. 3 (2009): 307–24.

McEwan, Craig A., and Richard J. Maiman. "Mediation in Small Claims Court: Achieving Compliance through Consent." *Law and Society Review* 18 (1984): 11–50.

Meares, Tracey L. "Praying for Community Policing." *California Law Review* 90, no. 5 (2002): 1593–634.

———. "Programming Errors: Understanding the Constitutionality of Stop-and-Frisk as a Program, Not an Incident." *University of Chicago Law Review* 82 (2015): 159–79.

Merriam, Sharan B., and Rosemary S. Caffarella. *Learning in Adulthood*. 2d ed. San Francisco: Jossey-Bass, 1999.

Messner, Steven F., Sandro Galea, Kenneth J. Tardiff, Melissa Tracy, Angela Bucciarelli, Tinka Piper, Victoria Frye, and David Vlahov. "Policing, Drugs, and the Homicide Decline in New York City in the 1990s." *Criminology* 45, no. 2 (2007): 385–414.

Metropolitan Police Act of 1839, 2 & 3 Vict., c. 47, § 66.

Michigan Daily. "Dismiss Stop and Frisk." September 11, 2013. http://www.michigan-daily.com/opinion/09daily-no-stop-and-frisk-detroit12.

Michigan Department of State Police v. Sitz, 496 U.S. 444 (1990).

Michigan v. Chesternut, 486 U.S. 567 (1988).

Michigan v. Long, 463 U.S. 1032 (1983).

Miller, Wilbur R. *Cops and Bobbies: Police Authority in London and New York City, 1830–1870*. Chicago: University of Chicago Press, 1977.

Minnesota v. Dickerson, 508 U.S. 366 (1993).

Miranda v. Arizona, 384 U.S. 436 (1966).

Missouri v. McNeely, 133 S. Ct. 1552 (2013).

Mollen Commission. *Anatomy of Failure, a Path for Success: The Report of the Commission to Investigate Allegations of Police Corruption and the Anti-Corruption Procedures of the New York City Police Department*. New York: City of New York, 1994.

Monkkonen, Eric H. "History of Urban Police." In *Crime and Justice: Annual Review of Research*, vol. 15, edited by Norval Morris and Michael Tonry, 547–80. Chicago: University of Chicago Press, 1992.

———. *Police in Urban America, 1860–1920*. London: Cambridge University Press, 1981.

Morrow, Weston J. "Examining the Potential for Racial/Ethnic Disparities in Use of Force during NYPD Stop-and-Frisk Activities." Ph.D. diss., Arizona State University, 2015.

Muir, William K., Jr. *Police: Streetcorner Politicians*. Chicago: University of Chicago Press, 1977.

Murphy, Pierce. *Ombudsman's Special Report: Police Review and Recommendations; Interactions between the Boise Police Department and the Homeless*. Boise, ID: City of Boise Community Ombudsman, 2006.

Nagin, Daniel, and Greg Pogarsky. "Integrating Celerity, Impulsivity, and Extralegal Sanction Threats into a Model of General Deterrence: Theory and Evidence." *Criminology* 39, no. 4 (2001): 865–92.

Nalla, Mahesh K., Michael J. Lynch, and Michael J. Leiber. "Determinants of Police Growth in Phoenix, 1950–1988." *Justice Quarterly* 14, no. 1 (1997): 115–43.

National Advisory Commission on Civil Disorder. *Report of the National Advisory Commission on Civil Disorder*. New York: Bantam, 1968.

National Center on Police and Community Relations. *A National Survey of Police and Community Relations*. Washington, DC: U.S. Government Printing Office, 1967.

National Initiative for Building Community Trust and Justice. Website. http://trustand-justice.org/.

Navarette v. California, 134 S. Ct. 1683 (2014).

Neely, Richard. "The Warren Court and the Welcome Stranger Rule." In *The Warren Court: A Retrospective*, edited by Bernard Schwartz, 184–91. New York: Oxford University Press, 1996.

Neubauer, David W., and Henry F. Fradella. *America's Courts and the Criminal Justice System*. 11th ed. Belmont, CA: Wadsworth/Cengage Learning, 2014.

New Jersey v. T.L.O., 469 U.S. 325 (1985).

New York City Department of Health and Mental Hygiene. *Firearm Deaths and Injuries in New York City*. New York: New York City Department of Health and Mental Hygiene, 2013.

New York City Police Department (NYPD). *Getting Guns off the Streets of New York*. New York: New York City Police Department, 1994.

———. *Reclaiming the Public Spaces of New York*. New York: New York City Police Department, 1994.

New York Civil Liberties Union (NYCLU). "Stop-and-Frisk Data." N.d. http://www.nyclu.org/content/stop-and-frisk-data.

Nislow, James. "Are Americans Ready to Buy into Racial Profiling?" *Law Enforcement News*, October 15, 2001.

Nosek, Brian A. "Implicit-Explicit Relations." *Current Directions in Psychological Science* 16 (2007): 65–69.

Nosek, Brian A., Mahzarin Banaji, and Anthony G. Greenwald. "Harvesting Implicit Group Attitudes and Beliefs from a Demonstration Web Site." *Group Dynamics: Theory, Research, and Practice* 6, no. 1 (2002): 101–15.

NYPD Inspector General. "About NYPD Inspector General." 2014. http://www.nyc.gov/html/oignypd/pages/about/about.shtml.

Ofer, Udi, and Ari Rosmarin. *Stop and Frisk: A First Look*. Newark, NJ: American Civil Liberties Union of New Jersey, 2014.

Ohio v. Robinette, 519 U.S. 33 (1996).

Oliver v. United States, 466 U.S. 170 (1984).

Olmstead v. United States, 277 U.S. 438 (1928).

Ornelas v. United States, 517 U.S. 690 (1996).

Owen, Stephen S., Henry F. Fradella, Tod W. Burke, and Jerry Joplin. *Foundations of Criminal Justice*. 2nd ed. New York: Oxford University Press, 2015.

Palmiotto, Michael J. "An Overview of Police Training through the Decades: Current Issues and Problems." In *Police and Training Issues*, edited by Michael J. Palmiotto, 1–24. Upper Saddle River, NJ: Prentice-Hall, 2003.

Parker, Karen F. *Unequal Crime Decline: Theorizing Race, Urban Inequality and Criminal Violence*. New York: New York University Press, 2008.

Paybarah, Azi. "Bill Bratton: There Will Always Be Stop-and-Frisk." *Capital New York*, June 14, 2013. http://www.capitalnewyork.com/article/politics/2013/06/8530960/bill-bratton-there-will-always-be-stop-and-frisk.

Payne, B. Keith. "Prejudice and Perception: The Role of Automatic and Controlled Processes in Misperceiving a Weapon." *Journal of Personality and Social Psychology* 81 (2001): 181–92.

Payne, B. Keith, and C. Daryl Cameron. "Divided Minds, Divided Morals: How Implicit Social Cognition Underpins and Undermines Our Sense of Social Justice." In *Handbook of Implicit Social Cognition: Measurement, Theory, and Applications*, edited by Bertram Gawronski and B. Keith Payne, 445–62. New York: Guilford, 2010.

Payton v. New York, 445 U.S. 573 (1980).

PBS. "New Yorkers Weigh Safety and Harassment in 'Stop and Frisk' Police Policy." *PBS Newshour*, April 13, 2013. http://www.pbs.org/newshour/bb/nation-july-dec13-stopfrisk_08–13/.

Pennsylvania v. Mimms, 434 U.S. 106 (1977).

People v. Henneman, 10 N.E.2d 649 (Ill. 1937).

People v. Mills, 450 N.E.2d 935 (Ill. Ct. App. 1983).

People v. Rivera, 201 N.E.2d 32 (N.Y. 1964).

People v. Simon, 290 P.2d 531 (Cal. 1955).

People v. Superior Court of Yolo County, 478 P.2d 449 (Cal. 1970).

Persico, Nicola, and Petra Todd. "The Hit Rates for Racial Bias in Motor Vehicle Searches." *Justice Quarterly* 25 (2008): 37–53.

Peruche, Michelle, and E. Ashby Plant. "The Correlates of Law Enforcement Officers' Automatic and Controlled Race-Based Responses to Criminal Suspects." *Basic and Applied Social Psychology* 28 (2006): 193–99.

Peters v. New York, 392 U.S. 40 (1968).

Plant, E. Ashby, and B. Michelle Peruche. "The Consequences of Race for Police Officers' Responses to Criminal Suspects." *Psychological Science* 16, no. 3 (2005): 180–83.

Plessy v. Ferguson, 163 U.S. 537 (1896), *overruled by Brown v. Board of Education*, 347 U.S. 483 (1954).

Plumhoff v. Rickard, 134 S. Ct. 2012 (2014).

Pratt, Travis C., Francis T. Cullen, Kristie R. Blevins, Leah E. Daigle, and Tamara D. Madensen. "The Empirical Status of Deterrence Theory: A Meta-Analysis." In *Taking Stock: The Status of Criminological Theory*, vol. 15, edited by Francis T. Cullen, John P. Wright, and Kristie R. Blevins, 367–95. New Brunswick, NJ: Transaction, 2006.

President's Commission on Law Enforcement and Administration of Justice. *Task Force Report: The Police*. Washington, DC: U.S. Government Printing Office, 1967.

President's Task Force on 21st Century Policing. *Final Report of the President's Task Force on 21st Century Policing*. Washington, DC, Office of Community Oriented Policing Services, 2015.

Queen v. Tooley, 2 Ld. Raym. 1296, 92 Eng. Rep. 349 (K.B. 1709).

Quillian, Lincoln, and Devah Pager. "Black Neighbors, Higher Crime? The Role of Racial Stereotypes in Evaluations of Neighborhood Crime." *American Journal of Sociology* 107, no. 3 (2001): 717–67.

Ratcliffe, Jerry H., Elizabeth R. Groff, Cory P. Haberman, Evan T. Sorg, and Nola Joyce. *Philadelphia, Pennsylvania Smart Policing Initiative: Testing the Impacts of Differential Police Strategies on Violent Crime Hotspots*. Washington, DC: Bureau of Justice Assistance, 2013.

Ratcliffe, Jerry H., Travis Taniguchi, Elizabeth R. Groff, and Jennifer D. Wood. "The Philadelphia Foot Patrol Experiment: A Randomized Controlled Trial of Police Patrol Effectiveness in Violent Crime Hotspots." *Criminology* 49, no. 3 (2011): 795–831.

Rau, Alia Beard. "Arizona Immigration Bill: Police Chiefs Criticize Measure." *Arizona Republic*, April 21, 2010. http://www.azcentral.com/news/election/azelections/articles/2010/04/21/20100421arizona-immigration-bill-police-chiefs-criticize.html.

Rayman, Graham. "New NYPD Tapes Introduced in Stop and Frisk Trial." *Village Voice*, March 22, 2013. http://www.villagevoice.com/news/new-nypd-tapes-introduced-in-stop-and-frisk-trial-6721026.

———. "The NYPD Tapes: Inside Bed-Stuy's 81st Precinct." *Village Voice*, May 4, 2010. http://www.villagevoice.com/2010-05-04/news/the-nypd-tapes-inside-bed-stuy-s-81st-precinct/.

Reisig, Michael D., and Camille Lloyd. "Procedural Justice, Police Legitimacy, and Helping the Police Fight Crime: Results from a Survey of Jamaican Adolescents." *Police Quarterly* 12 (2009): 42–62.

Reitzel, John D., Nicole Leeper Piquero, and Alex R. Piquero. "Problem-Oriented Policing." In *Critical Issues in Policing*, 5th ed., edited by Roger G. Dunham and Geoffrey P. Alpert, 419–31. Long Grove, IL: Waveland, 2005.

Rengifo, Andres F., and Lee Ann Slocum. "Community Responses to 'Stop-and-Frisk' in New York City: Conceptualizing Local Conditions and Correlates." *Criminal Justice Policy Review*, 2014. doi:10.1177/0887403414560013.

Rice, Stephen K., and Michael D. White, eds. *Race, Ethnicity, and Policing: New and Essential Readings*. New York: New York University Press, 2010.

Richardson, L. Song, and Phillip A. Goff. "Self-Defense and the Suspicion Heuristic." *Iowa Law Review* 98 (2012): 293–336.

Ridgeway, Gregory Kirk. *Analysis of Racial Disparities in the New York Police Department's Stop, Question, and Frisk Practices*. Santa Monica, CA: RAND, 2007. http://www.rand.org/pubs/technical_reports/TR534.html.

———. *Cincinnati Police Department Traffic Stops: Applying RAND's Framework to Analyze Racial Disparities*. Santa Monica, CA: RAND, 2009.

Rios, Victor M. *Punished: Policing the Lives of Black and Latino Boys*. New York: New York University Press, 2011.

Rise v. Oregon, 59 F.3d 1556 (9th Cir. 1995).

Rivera, Ray, Al Baker, and Janet Roberts. "A Few Blocks, 4 Years, 52,000 Police Stops." *New York Times*, July 11, 2010. http://www.nytimes.com/2010/07/12/nyregion/12frisk.html?_r=1&emc=eta1.

Rochin v. California, 342 U.S. 165 (1952).

Ronayne, John A. "The Right to Investigate and New York's 'Stop and Frisk' Law." *Fordham Law Review* 33 (1964): 211–38.

Rosen, William. *The Most Powerful Idea in the World: A Story of Steam, Industry, and Invention*. New York: Random House, 2010.

Rosenfeld, Richard, and Robert Fornango. "The Impact of Police Stops on Precinct Robbery and Burglary Rates in New York City, 2003–2010." *Justice Quarterly* 31 (2014): 96–122.

Rosenfeld, Richard, Robert Fornango, and Eric Baumer. "Did Ceasefire, Compstat, and Exile Reduce Homicide?" *Criminology and Public Policy* 4, no. 3 (2005): 419–49.

Rosenfeld, Richard, Robert Fornango, and Andres F. Rengifo. "The Impact of Order-Maintenance Policing on New York City Homicide and Robbery Rates, 1998–2001." *Criminology* 45 (2007): 355–84.

Rosenthal, Lawrence. "Pragmatism, Originalism, Race, and the Case against *Terry v. Ohio*." *Texas Tech Law Review* 43 (2010): 299–356.

Roth, Jeffrey A., Jan Roehl, and Calvin C. Johnson. "Trends in Community Policing." In *Community Policing: Can It Work?*, edited by Wesley G. Skogan, 3–29. Belmont, CA: Wadsworth, 2004.

Rudovsky, David. "Law Enforcement by Stereotypes and Serendipity: Racial Profiling and Stops and Searches without Cause." *University of Pennsylvania Journal of Constitutional Law* 3 (2011): 296–366.

Russo, Melissa, Jonathan Dienst, and Andrew Siff. "De Blasio Picks Bill Bratton as Next NYPD Commissioner, 'New Day' Promised." NBCNewYork.com, December 6, 2013. http://www.nbcnewyork.com/news/local/Bill-Bratton-New-NYPD-Police-Commissioner-de-Blasio-232838251.html.

Sampson, Robert J., and Stephen W. Raudenbush. "Systematic Social Observation of Public Spaces: A New Look at Disorder in Urban Neighborhoods." *American Journal of Sociology* 105, no. 3 (1999): 603–51.

Schmerber v. California, 384 U.S. 757 (1966).

Schneckloth v. Bustamonte, 412 U.S. 218 (1973).

Schneiderman, Eric T. *A Report on Arrests Arising from the New York City Police Department's Stop-and-Frisk Practices*. Albany: Office of the New York State Attorney General, 2013.

Scott v. Harris, 550 U.S. 372 (2007).

Segal, Josh. "'All of the Mysticism of Police Expertise': Legalizing Stop-and-Frisk in New York, 1961–1968." *Harvard Civil Rights-Civil Liberties Law Review* 47 (2012): 573–616.

Sherman, Lawrence W. "Repeat Calls for Service: Policing the 'Hot Spots.'" In *Police and Policing: Contemporary Issues*, edited by Dennis Jay Kenney, 150–65. New York: Praeger, 1989.

Sherman, Lawrence W., Patrick R. Gartin, and Michael E. Buerger. "Hot Spots of Predatory Crime: Routine Activities and the Criminology of Place." *Criminology* 27 (1989): 27–56.

Sherman, Lawrence W., and Dennis P. Rogan. "Effects of Gun Seizures on Gun Violence: 'Hot Spots' Patrol in Kansas City." *Justice Quarterly* 12 (1995): 673–93.

Sherman, Lawrence W., Janell D. Schmidt, and Dennis P. Rogan. *Policing Domestic Violence: Experiments and Dilemmas*. New York: Free Press, 1992.

Sherman, Lawrence W., and David Weisburd. "General Deterrent Effects of Police Patrol in Crime Hot Spots: A Randomized Controlled Trial." *Justice Quarterly* 12 (1995): 625–48.

Shjarback, John A., and Michael D. White. "Departmental Professionalism and Its Impact on Indicators of Violence in Police-Citizen Encounters." *Police Quarterly* 19 (2016): 32–62.

Sibron v. New York, 392 U.S. 40 (1968).

Silverman, Eli B. *NYPD Battles Crime: Innovative Strategies in Policing*. Boston: Northeastern University Press, 1999.

Silverman v. United States, 365 U.S. 505 (1961).

60 Minutes. "Counterinsurgency Cops: Military Tactics Fight Street Crime." CBS, August 4, 2013.

Skogan, Wesley. "The Promise of Community Policing." In *Police Innovation: Contrasting Perspectives*, edited by David Weisburd and Anthony A. Braga, 27–43. New York: Cambridge University Press, 2006.

Skogan, Wesley, and Kathleen Frydl. *Fairness and Effectiveness in Policing: The Evidence*. Washington, DC: Committee to Review Research on Police Policy and Practices, National Academies Press, 2004.

Skogan, Wesley G., and Susan M. Hartnett. *Community Policing, Chicago Style*. New York: Oxford University Press, 1997.

Skolnick, Jerome H. *Justice without Trial: Law Enforcement in a Democratic Society*. New York: Wiley, 1966.

Skolnick, Jerome H., and James J. Fyfe. *Above the Law: Police and the Excessive Use of Force*. New York: Free Press, 1993.

Smart Policing Initiative. Website. http://www.smartpolicinginitiative.com/.

Smith, Dennis C., and William J. Bratton. "Performance Management in New York City: Compstat and the Revolution in Police Management." In *Quicker, Better, Cheaper: Managing Performance in American Government*, edited by Dall W. Forsythe, 453–82. Albany, NY: Rockefeller Institute Press, 2001.

Smith, Dennis Charles, and Robert Purtell. "Does Stop and Frisk Stop Crime?" Paper presented at the annual research conference of the Association of Public Policy and Management, Los Angeles, CA, November 6–8, 2008.

——. "An Empirical Assessment of NYPD's 'Operation Impact': A Targeted Zone Crime-Reduction Strategy." June 27, 2007. Robert F. Wagner Graduate School of Public Service, New York. http://wagner.nyu.edu/files/faculty/publications/impact-zoning.doc.

Smith, William R., Donald Tomaskovic-Devey, Matthew Zingraff, H. Marcinda Mason, Patricia Y. Warren, Cynthia Pfaff Wright et al. *The North Carolina Highway Traffic Study: Final Report to the National Institute of Justice*. Washington, DC: U.S. Department of Justice, 2003.

Smith v. Maryland, 442 U.S. 735 (1979).

Solis, Carmen, Edwardo L. Portillos, and Rod K. Brunson. "Latino Youths' Experiences with and Perceptions of Involuntary Police Encounters." *Annals of the American Academy of Political and Social Science* 623, no. 1 (2009): 39–51.

Spence v. State, 525 So. 2d 442 (Fla. Dist. Ct. App. 1988).

Spitzer, Elliot. *The New York City Police Department's "Stop and Frisk" Practices*. Albany: Office of the New York State Attorney General, 1999.

Stafford, Mark C., and Mark Warr. "A Reconceptualization of General and Specific Deterrence." *Journal of Research in Crime and Delinquency* 30, no. 2 (1993): 123–35.

State v. Carty, 790 A.2d 903 (N.J. 2002).

State v. Lund, 573 A.2d 1376 (N.J. 1990).

State v. Schlosser, 774 P.2d 1132 (Utah 1989).

Stoudt, Brett G., Michelle Fine, and Madeline Fox. "Growing Up Policed in the Age of Aggressive Policing Policies." *New York Law School Law Review* 56 (2011): 1331–70.

Strecher, Victor G. "Revising the Histories and Futures of Policing." *Police Forum* 1, no. 1 (1991): 1–9.

Sullivan, Christopher, and Kerry Ulmer. "An Examination of the Constitutional Issues Related to New York City Police Department Policing Tactics and Policies." In *The New York City Police Department: The Impact of Its Policies and Practices*, edited by John A. Eterno, 21–46. Boca Raton, FL: CRC Press, 2014.

Sullivan, E. Thomas, and Toni M. Massaro. *The Arc of Due Process in American Constitutional Law*. New York: Oxford University Press, 2013.

Sundby, Scott E. "A Return to Fourth Amendment Basics: Undoing the Mischief of *Camara* and *Terry*." *Minnesota Law Review* 72 (1988): 383–448.

Sunshine, Jason, and Tom R. Tyler. "The Role of Procedural Justice and Legitimacy in Shaping Public Support for Policing." *Law and Society Review* 37 (2003): 513–48.

Taylor, Kate. "Stop-and-Frisk Policy 'Saves Lives,' Mayor Tells Black Congregation." *New York Times*, June 11, 2012.

Taylor, Telford. *Two Studies in Constitutional Interpretation: Search, Seizure and Surveillance and Fair Trial and Free Press*. Columbus: Ohio State University Press, 1969.

Tennessee v. Garner, 471 U.S. 1 (1985).

Terkel, Amanda. "Ray Kelly on Stop and Frisk: 'No Question' Violent Crime Will Rise if Program Is Stopped." *Huffington Post*, August 18, 2013. http://www.huffingtonpost.com/2013/08/18/ray-kelly-stop-and-frisk_n_3776035.html.

Terry v. Ohio, 392 U.S. 1 (1968).

Thompson, Anthony C. "Stopping the Usual Suspects: Race and the Fourth Amendment." *New York University Law Review* 74 (1999): 956–1013.

Tonry, Michael. *Punishing Race: A Continuing American Dilemma*. New York: Oxford University Press, 2011.

Tucson Sentinel. "Declaration of Jack Harris on SB 1070." July 6, 2010. http://www.tucsonsentinel.com/documents/doc/070610_harris_1070_doc/.

Tyler, Tom R. "Legitimacy and Legitimation." *Annual Review of Psychology* 57 (2006): 375–400.

———. *Why People Obey the Law*. New Haven: Yale University Press, 1990.

Tyler, Tom R., and Jeffrey Fagan. "Legitimacy and Cooperation: Why Do People Help the Police Fight Crime in Their Communities?" *Ohio State Journal of Criminal Law* 6 (2008): 231–75.

Tyler, Tom R., and Yuen J. Huo. *Trust in the Law: Encouraging Public Cooperation with the Police and Courts*. New York: Russell Sage, 2002.

Tyler, Tom R., Kenneth A. Rasinski, and Nancy Spodick. "Influence of Voice on Satisfaction with Leaders: Exploring the Meaning of Process Control." *Journal of Personality and Social Psychology* 48 (1985): 72–81.

Uchida, Craig D., and Marc L. Swatt. "Operation LASER and the Effectiveness of Hotspot Patrol: A Panel Analysis." *Police Quarterly* 16, no. 3 (2013): 287–304.

Uchida, Craig D., Marc L. Swatt, David Gamero, Jeanine Lopez, Erika Salazar, Elliot King, Rhona Maxey, Nathan Ong, Douglas Wagner, and Michael D. White. *Los Angeles, California Smart Policing Initiative: Reducing Gun-Related Violence through Operation LASER*. Washington, DC: Bureau of Justice Assistance, U.S. Department of Justice, 2012. http://www.smartpolicinginitiative.com/sites/all/files/spotlights/LA%20Site%20Spotlight%20FINAL%20Oct%202012.pdf.

United States v. Arnold, 523 F.3d 941 (9th Cir. 2008).

United States v. Arvizu, 534 U.S. 266 (2002).

United States v. Cortez, 449 U.S. 411 (1981).

United States v. Cruz, 909 F.2d 422 (11th Cir. 1989).

United States v. Drayton, 536 U.S. 194 (2002).

United States v. Dunn, 480 U.S. 294 (1987).

United States v. Dunning, 666 F.3d 1158 (8th Cir. 2012).

United States v. Fisher, 364 F.3d 970 (8th Cir. 2004).

United States v. Hensley, 469 U.S. 221 (1985).

United States v. Jacobsen, 466 U.S. 109 (1984).

United States v. Jones, 132 S. Ct. 945 (2012).

United States v. Jordan, 232 F.3d 447 (5th Cir. 2000).

United States v. Mendenhall, 446 U.S. 544 (1980).

United States v. Miller, 425 U.S. 435 (1976).

United States v. Sokolow, 490 U.S. 1 (1989).

United States v. Sprinkle, 106 F.3d 613 (4th Cir. 1997).

United States v. White, 401 U.S. 745 (1971).

USA Today. "NYPD Confirms CIA Advisory Role on 'Trade Craft Issues.'" August 16, 2011. http://www.usatoday.com/news/washington/story/2011-08-26/NYPD-confirms-CIA-advisory-role-on-trade-craft-issues/50143402/1.

U.S. Department of Justice. "Conduct of Law Enforcement Agencies." N.d. http://www.justice.gov/crt/about/spl/police.php.

Van Maanen, John. "The Asshole." In *Policing: A View from the Street*, edited by Peter K. Manning and John Van Maanen, 221–38. New York: Random House, 1978.

Victor v. Nebraska, 511 U.S. 1 (1994).

Volk, Kristin. "Cleveland Councilmen Reed and Johnson Propose 'Stop, Question and Frisk' to Curb City's Gun Violence." NewsNet5.com (Cleveland), July 29, 2014. http://www.newsnet5.com/news/local-news/cleveland-metro/cleveland-councilmen-reed-and-johnson-propose-stop-question-and-frisk-to-curb-citys-gun-violence.

Waldeck, Sarah E. "Cops, Community Policing, and the Social Norms Approach to Crime Control: Should One Make Us More Comfortable with the Others?" *Georgia Law Review* 34, no. 3 (1999): 1253–310.

Walker, Hunter. "Ray Kelly Defends NYPD on Stop and Frisk and Muslim Surveillance at Heated Council Hearing." *Observer*, March 25, 2012. http://observer.com/2012/03/ray-kelly-defends-nypd/.

Walker, Samuel. *The New World of Police Accountability*. Thousand Oaks, CA: Sage, 2005.

———. *Popular Justice: A History of American Criminal Justice*. New York: Oxford University Press, 1980.

———. *Taming the System: The Control of Discretion in Criminal Justice, 1950–1990*. New York: Oxford University Press, 1992.

Walker, Samuel, and Carl A. Archbold. *The New World of Police Accountability*. 2d ed. Thousand Oaks, CA: Sage, 2014.

Walker, Samuel, and Charles M. Katz. *The Police in America: An Introduction*. 8th ed. Boston: McGraw-Hill, 2013.

Ward, David. "Population Growth, Migration, and Urbanization, 1860–1920." In *North America: The Historical Geography of a Changing Continent*, 2nd ed., edited by Thomas F. McIlwraith and Edward K. Muller, 299–319. Lanham, MD: Rowman and Littlefield, 2001.

Ward, Robert V. "Consenting to a Search and Seizure in Poor and Minority Neighborhoods: No Place for a 'Reasonable Person.'" *Howard Law Journal* 36 (1993): 239–58.

Warner, Sam B. "The Uniform Arrest Act." *Virginia Law Review* 28, no. 3 (1942): 315–47.

Warren, Patricia Y., and Donald Tomaskovic-Devey. "Racial Profiling and Searches: Did the Politics of Racial Profiling Change Police Behavior?" *Criminology and Public Policy* 8, no. 2 (2009): 343–69.

Weightman, Gavin. *The Industrial Revolutionaries: The Making of the Modern World, 1776–1914*. New York: Grove, 2007.

Weisburd, David, and Anthony A. Braga, eds. *Police Innovation: Contrasting Perspectives*. New York: Cambridge University Press, 2006.

Weisburd, David, and John E. Eck. "What Can Police Do to Reduce Crime, Disorder, and Fear?" *Annals of the American Academy of Political and Social Science* 593 (2004): 42–65.

Weisburd, David, and Rosann Greenspan, with Edwin E. Hamilton, Hubert Williams, and Kellie A. Bryant. *Police Attitudes toward Abuse of Authority: Findings from a National Study*. Washington, DC: U.S. Department of Justice, Office of Justice Programs, National Institute of Justice, 2000.

Weisburd, David, Cody W. Telep, Joshua C. Hinkle, and John E. Eck. "Is Problem-Oriented Policing Effective in Reducing Crime and Disorder? Findings from a Campbell Systematic Review." *Criminology and Public Policy* 9, no. 1 (2010): 139–72.

Weisburd, David, Cody W. Telep, and Brian A. Lawton. "Could Innovations in Policing Have Contributed to the New York City Crime Drop Even in a Period of Declining Police Strength? The Case of Stop, Question and Frisk as a Hot Spots Policing Strategy." *Justice Quarterly* 31, no. 1 (2014): 129–53.

Welsh, Kelly. "Black Criminal Stereotypes and Racial Profiling." *Journal of Contemporary Criminal Justice* 23, no. 3 (2007): 276–88.

White, Michael D. "Controlling Police Decisions to Use Deadly Force: Reexamining the Importance of Administrative Policy." *Crime and Delinquency* 47, no. 1 (2001): 131–51.

———. *Current Issues and Controversies in Policing*. Boston: Allyn and Bacon/Pearson, 2007.

———. "Jim Longstreet, Mike Marshall, and the Lost Art of Policing Skid Row." *Criminology and Public Policy* 9, no. 4 (2010): 883–96.

———. "The New York City Police Department, Its Crime-Control Strategies and Organizational Changes, 1970–2009." *Justice Quarterly* 31, no. 1 (2014): 74–95.

———. *Police Officer Body-Worn Cameras: Assessing the Evidence*. Washington, DC: U.S. Department of Justice, Office of Justice Programs Diagnostic Center and COPS Office, 2014.

———. "Preventing Racially Biased Policing through Internal and External Controls: The Comprehensive Accountability Package." In *Race, Ethnicity, and Policing: New and Essential Readings*, edited by Stephen K. Rice and Michael D. White, 468–88. New York: New York University Press, 2010.

White, Michael D., James J. Fyfe, Suzanne P. Campbell, and John S. Goldkamp. "The Police Role in Preventing Homicide: Considering the Impact of Problem-Oriented Policing on the Prevalence of Murder." *Journal of Research in Crime and Delinquency* 40 (2003): 194–225.

White, Michael D., and Robert J. Kane. "Pathways to Career-Ending Police Misconduct: An Examination of Patterns, Timing and Organizational Responses to Officer Malfeasance in the NYPD." *Criminal Justice and Behavior* 40, no. 11 (2013): 1301–25.

White, Michael D., and Charles M. Katz. "Policing Convenience Store Crime: Lessons from the Glendale, Arizona Smart Policing Initiative." *Police Quarterly* 16, no. 3 (2013): 305–22.

Whren v. United States, 517 U.S. 806 (1996).

Wilkinson, Deanna L., Chauncey C. Beaty, and Regina M. Lurry. "Youth Violence—Crime or Self-Help? Marginalized Urban Males' Perspectives on the Limited Efficacy of the Criminal Justice System to Stop Youth Violence." *Annals of the American Academy of Political and Social Science* 623, no. 1 (2009): 25–38.

Williams, Glanville L. "Police Detention and Arrest Privileges under Foreign Law—England." *Journal of Criminal Law, Criminology, and Police Science* 51, no. 4 (1960): 413–18.

Williams, Hubert, and Patrick V. Murphy. "The Evolving Strategy of Police: A Minority View." *Perspectives on Policing*, no. 13. Washington, DC: U.S. Department of Justice, Office of Justice Programs, National Institute of Justice, 1990.

Willis, James J., Stephen D. Mastrofski, and David Weisburd. "Making Sense of COMPSTAT: A Theory-Based Analysis of Organizational Change in Three Police Departments." *Law and Society Review* 41, no. 1 (2007): 147–88.

Wilson, James Q., and George L. Kelling. "Broken Windows: The Police and Neighborhood Safety." *Atlantic Monthly* 249 (1982): 29–38.

Wilson, Timothy D., Samuel Lindsey, and Tonya Y. Schooler. "A Model of Dual Attitudes." *Psychological Review* 107 (2000): 101–26.

Winston v. Lee, 470 U.S. 753 (1985).

Wintemute, Garen J. "Guns and Gun Violence." In *The Crime Drop in America*, edited by Alfred Blumstein and Joel Wallman, 45–96. New York: Cambridge University Press, 2006.

Wong Sun v. United States, 371 U.S. 471 (1963).

Ybarra v. Illinois, 444 U.S. 85 (1979).

Xie, Min. "Area Differences and Time Trends in Crime Reporting: Comparing New York with Other Metropolitan Areas." *Justice Quarterly* 31, no. 1 (2014): 43–73.

Zimring, Franklin. *The City That Became Safe: New York's Lessons for Urban Crime and Its Control.* Oxford, UK: Oxford University Press, 2012.

———. *The Great American Crime Decline.* New York: Oxford University Press, 2007.

INDEX

ABOUT THE AUTHORS

Michael D. White is Professor in the School of Criminology and Criminal Justice at Arizona State University and is Associate Director of ASU's Center for Violence Prevention and Community Safety. Dr. White's primary research interests involve the police, including use of force, technology, and misconduct. He is the co-author of *Jammed Up: Bad Cops, Police Misconduct, and the New York City Police Department.*

Henry F. Fradella is Professor in and Associate Director of the School of Criminology and Criminal Justice at Arizona State University. He researches the evolution and impact of substantive, procedural, and evidentiary criminal law and the dynamics of legal decision making. He is the co-author of *Criminal Procedure for the Criminal Justice Professional* and *America's Courts and the Criminal Justice System.*